Fundamentals of
Manufacturing Processes

Fundamentals of
Manufacturing Processes

G K Lal
S K Choudhury

Alpha Science International Ltd.
Harrow, U.K.

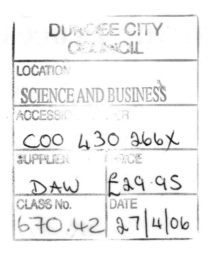
G K Lal
S K Choudhury
Department of Mechanical Engineering
Indian Institute of Technology Kanpur
Kanpur, India

Alpha Science International Ltd.
Hygeia Building, 66 College Road
Harrow, Middlesex HA1 1BE, U.K.

ISBN 1-84265-274-5

Printed in India.

Preface

Manufacturing basically is the art and science of transforming materials into value added products. This transformation involves a series of interrelated activities and operations such as product design and development, material selection, process planning, inventory control and quality assurance. Manufacturing, therefore, has become a system where a number of sub-systems interact in a dynamic manner. The manufacturing sub-system is the heart of this system where material is converted from one form to another using a set of processes and operations. A product design may be of high quality, but if it has to become a reality, it must be produced at a competitive price and in a reasonable time in order to survive in the market. Persons associated with design, development and production should, therefore, be fully acquainted with the capabilities and limitations of various manufacturing processes.

This book is an attempt to emphasize the fundamentals involved in various manufacturing processes used in fabrication-type manufacturing. For this purpose, the processes have been classified as constant mass operations (casting, forming and heat treatment), material removal operations (machining and grinding) and material addition operation (welding and brazing). These are covered in Chapters 2 to 11. Since the book is written for the beginners, only the primary manufacturing processes are considered. Also, the book is written in textbook style (with numerical examples and review questions at the end of each chapter) to suit the requirements of core-level engineering students. Materials presented in this book have been extracted from a large number of books (listed under bibliography) and presented in such a manner that the entire material could be covered in a semester course of forty lectures. Several line diagrams have been taken from the listed books and redrawn after suitable modifications to meet the requirements of a book of this level. The introductory chapter presents the historical developments in manufacturing, while the last chapter indicates modern manufacturing and future trends.

Several colleagues and associates who had long association with us in teaching the core level, introductory course on manufacturing at IIT Kanpur have helped in the development of this manuscript. The assistance of Dr. N. V. Reddy, in this regard, is gratefully acknowledged. The manuscript of this book has been painstakingly typed and composed by Mrs. Sandhya Agnihotri. Financial assistance for the development of this manuscript has been provided by the Ministry of Human Resources Development, Government of India through its Quality Improvement Programme at IIT Kanpur. Our heartfelt thanks are also due to Dr. (Mrs.) Karuna Lal and Mrs. Ludmila Choudhury and our children for their encouragement and loving support.

G. K. Lal

S. K. Choudhury

Indian Institute of Technology Kanpur

Contents

Chapter 1

Introduction

1.1 Historical Perspective

Manufacturing has been a human activity for a very long time. In fact it dates back to the production of stone articles by, the primitive man, using his muscle power and skill in the Prehistoric times. The word manufacturing itself is derived from Latin which means making of articles by hand (manus-hand; factus-made). Manufacturing remained in the hands of artisans and their apprentices for centuries and all the early developments in manufacturing techniques were brought about by these individuals to meet their needs and requirements. The historical developments of manufacturing processes are summarised in Table 1.1.

The art of foundry, the process of making castings in moulds, dates back to the dawn of civilisation. Excavations of Mohenjodaro and Harappa provide abundant examples of metal work and jewellery during 'Indus Valley Civilisation' (5000 BC). The craftsmen of Greek and Roman civilisations also practised casting technique during early historic times. The first metal that was melted by man appears to be copper. Although no definite period has been assigned to it, but it perhaps overlaps with the Stone Age. Bronze replaced copper around 2500 BC, while iron was discovered around 1000 BC. Copper, bronze and later 'iron age' transformed the ancient civilisation in Indus Valley, China, Egypt, Mesopotamia and Babylon.

Machining tool has been in existence for a very long time. It is not known, when, where and which invention brought the concept of machine tools but it is believed that lathe-the turning machine-has been derived from the potter's wheel (Fig. 1.1) that existed before 2500 BC. Excavations have unearthed wooden bowls with groove marks to prove that turning was practiced as early as 1700 BC and

Table 1.1 Historical development of manufacturing processes.

Year	Material	Casting	Forming	Machining	Welding
4000 BC	Gold Silver Copper	Clay mould	Cold forging	Stone tools	
2500 BC	Bronze	Lost wax process	Sheet metal forming	Drilling	Brazing
1000 BC	Iron		Hot forging	Iron saw	Forge welding
0 AD	Brass			Wood turning, Stone grinding	
1000 AD			Wire drawing		
1400 AD		Sand casting	Water hammer	Pole lathe	
1600 AD		Permanent mould	Lead rolling	Wheel lathe	
1800 AD	Carbon steel		Steel rolling Deep drawing Lead extrusion	Turning Boring Screw cutting	

Year	Materials	Casting	Extrusion	Machines / Processes	Welding
1900 AD	HSS Aluminium oxide		Tube extrusion	Electric drive Gear cutting Hobbing Automats	Gas welding Arc welding
1920 AD	Tungsten carbides	Die casting		Special purpose machines	Coated electrodes
1940 AD	Plastics		Hot extrusion (Steel)		
1950 AD			Cold extrusion (Steel)	Electro-discharge machining, Electro-chemical machining Ultrasonic machining	Gas metal and gas tungsten arc welding
1980 AD				Industrial robots Computer-aided manufacturing Flexible manufacturing system.	

Fig. 1.1 Potter's wheel.

the art was perfected before the end of 6th century BC.

The concept of tool and tool angles was perceived from the time the primitive man started thinking in terms of hand-held tools with tree branch as a lever (Fig. 1.2). Stone tools were later replaced by metallic tools and a novel stone grinding technique (Fig. 1.3) was developed to sharpen tools.

Fig. 1.2 Hand-held tool with tree branch as a lever.

The idea of rotating a stone wheel on a spindle and realising that sharp edges can be produced through use of rotating wheel brought in the concept of grinding. Figure 1.3 shows an assistant rotating the wheel using a crank while the grinder sitting above the axis of the wheel, leans forward, holds the workpiece (sword) in his extended arms and grinds it by providing to and fro motion. Wheels mounted on a spindle with a crank started appearing around 850 AD.

Fig. 1.3 Stone wheel grinding.

The earliest known machine tool-lathe-consisted of a cord wound around the spindle with its two free ends being pulled by a helper to

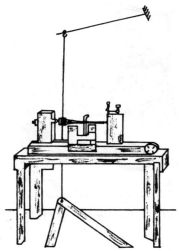

Fig. 1.4 Lathe, 1400 AD (After Steeds, 1969).

provide alternating motion to the wooden workpiece while the operator applied the hand-held cutting tool to the workpiece periphery only when it was rotating in the cutting direction. Later unidirectional motion was attempted by winding an endless cord around the spindle and passing it over a flywheel which was rotated by hand.

The first lathe that worked without an assistant had one end of the cord attached to a treadle which the operator worked with his foot while the other end was tied to a flat piece of wood overhead acting as a spring. The tool was still held in hand. Improvement brought a tool fixed on the machine. A sketch of one such lathe used around 1400 AD is shown in Fig. 1.4.

The wooden plank attached overhead was called *lath* and it is believed that the name lathe used for turning machines was derived from this word.

Drilling, in early days, was carried out by winding a cord on the drill and attaching its two ends on to a wooden rod. By providing to and fro motion to the rod, alternating motion was provided to the tool for drilling. This technique is still used in some places by the carpenters for drilling holes in wood.

The art of forge welding (joining two metallic pieces by heating and hammering) was practiced even around 2500 BC but it got perfected only around 1000 BC. The use of filler materials for joining purposes was also known and practiced before 2500 BC.

Hot forging was extensively practiced around 1000 BC, but it took a long time to develop the technique of drawing wires. A wire

Fig. 1.5 Wire drawing setup (1000 AD).

drawing set-up in use around 1000 AD is shown in Fig. 1.5.

Development of hot forging, forge welding and grinding became imperative after the discovery of iron and its increasing use for weapons. The concept of grinding (850 AD) itself contained unidirectional motion, but it took many years (1450 AD) to apply this to lathe and drilling machines.

Many distinguishing features of modern machine tools were anticipated in design and later implemented on small scale by clock makers. In fact clock makers were pioneers of many advanced manufacturing techniques during the period 1400 to 1700 AD. The need for improved manufacturing techniques was necessitated by the demand for more accurate clocks which in turn required precisely manufactured gears, arbours and screw threads. While the principle of screw thread was known during the time of Archimedes, the manufacturing technique required marking and cutting the threads by hand.

The first screw cutting lathe was made by a German clock maker in 1480 AD. The machine had provisions for sliding the tool post for both longitudinal as well as transverse feeds, and it cut threads of the same pitch as that of the spindle. Leonardo da Vinci, the great Renaissance intellectual and designer, designed a lathe around 1500 AD which had arrangements for change of gear wheels so that screw threads of different pitches could be produced. In fact Leonardo da Vinci designed a range of machines, many of them with novel features.

After a long wait, Ramsden was able to produce an accurate screw cutting lathe around 1780 AD. He constructed a series of such lathes in which screws produced on one lathe were used on successive lathes. Using this iterative process he finally succeeded in producing a high quality screw cutting lathe.

During the second half of 18th century, Britain was discovering new places on earth and needed an accurate marine chronometer. In order to produce a chronometer, which would meet the required specifications, machines and instruments of greater accuracy were developed. A good example is the accurate heat measuring instrument which enabled Joseph Black to formulate the theory of latent heat based on which James Watt designed his steam engine.

During the later half of 17th century, the use of timber for ship building, iron smelting, and fuel had increased manifold and led to timber famine towards the end of the century. Exploitation of alternate sources of energy became a necessity and timber was gradually replaced by coal. Smelting of iron from coal was begun around 1711 AD but surface coal did not provide satisfactory results. Deeper mining became a necessity but was hindered because of non-availability of higher capacity pumps for quick removal of underground water.

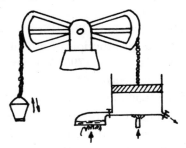

Fig. 1.6 Newcomen's engine.

Newcomen's engines (Fig. 1.6) were installed in coal mines but they were huge in size and also very inefficient. James Watt, while repairing one of Newcomen's engines, realised its fundamental shortcomings and came up with his design of a steam engine, in 1762 AD, which worked with high pressure steam rather than atmospheric air. In 1769 AD he took the patent but failed to develop a full size engine. His main problem was the need for an accurate piston and cylinder assembly.

John Wilkinson (1728-1808 AD) was the greatest iron maker of his time. He had developed a variety of water-powered boring machines (Fig. 1.7) for producing iron guns and cannons. Wilkinson was perhaps the only cylinder maker who could meet the challenge posed by Watt's engine design. The new cylinder that he designed, in 1775 AD, made Watt's attempt successful. Wilkinson was, however, not satisfied with the accuracy he achieved and used the first steam engine Watt made to power his boring machine to achieve better ac-

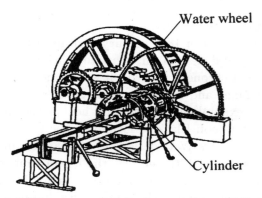

Fig. 1.7 Water-powered boring machine (After Rolt, 1965).

curacy. Watt's engines were soon powering Wilkinson's mills (Fig. 1.8).

By the end of 18th century, steam engines made power available in large amount and at many locations. This led to growth in production and mechanization. The 'First Industrial Revolution' had thus started with the production of steam engines. The Soho Foundry (London) established, in 1796 AD, with these engines was considered to be 'The Engineering Workshop' of the time. By 1820 AD steam power driven machine tools were ready for sale.

Need for higher strength material was now greatly felt and it was somewhat met by the introduction of carbon steels. Although it was known for quite sometime that the strength difference in steel was due to carbon content but it took many years, in 1831 AD, before Liebig could perfect the technique of determining the amount of carbon in steel in 1831 AD. *Steel age* had come and it was possible to produce sufficiently rigid and precision machines.

Henry Maudslay (1771-1831 AD) brought several new concepts in machine tool design. He introduced the tool slide and rest with tool head in 1794 AD. It was equipped with lead screw and had provision for taper turning-the features available in modern machine tools. He also produced a series of screw cutting machines which were almost a prototype of modern lathe. He designed and made the first micrometer, in 1805 AD, and used it for comparing the precision of instruments. Maudslay himself was not only an inventive genius, but he also gave a number of great disciples like Clement, Fox, Roberts, Nasmyth, Whitworth and others who developed and introduced planing, shaping, drilling, punching, slotting and milling machines between 1825 to 1865 AD.

The need for stronger marine vessels led to the introduction of

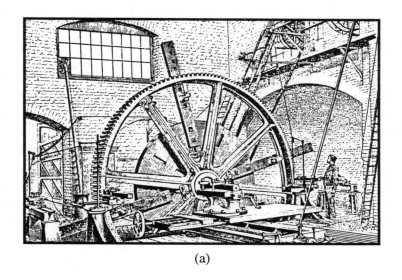

(a)

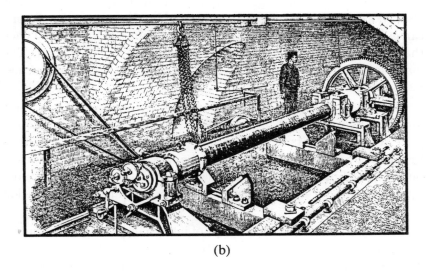

(b)

Fig. 1.8 Steam engine driven (a) boring machine and (b) lathe at Wilkinson's Soho Foundry. (After Steeds, 1969).

rolling mills that produced flats for making the 'Iron Ship' which crossed the Atlantic in 1838 AD. Development of locomotive engine by Stevenson brought in public railways and the need for rail rolling process (1875 AD), and to meet the needs of multi-storied buildings, the rolling of structured sections was introduced.

By mid 19th century Britain became the leading country in science and technology. Their engineers got world-wide fame and there was literally no competitor. In fact the European railways was built almost exclusively by British engineers. Britain's Joseph Whitworth (1803-87 AD) designed and built machine tools of such high quality that subsequent British engineers depended heavily on his inventions.

The war of independence in America is surprisingly relevant to the development of manufacturing. Around 1720 AD, Britain fearing threat for their successful export market in America, prohibited the production of pig iron there. However, when pressure built-up against this, they permitted the production but forbade erection of rolling mills and steel furnaces. Even after granting political independence to America, Britain tried to keep herself technologically dependent on them by prohibiting export of tools, machines and engines. Even the people engaged in iron and machine works were not allowed emigration to America. Infuriated by this, the young American engineers started building their own machines at such rapid pace that Britain ultimately came down to seek mutual co-operation. The main developments of machines took place in the textile and armament industries.

True industrial revolution started when the concept of mass production was introduced in 1748 AD to lower the cost of production price so that benefits of engineering could reach the common man. Proliferation of machines now started and a large number of special purpose machines, automatic and semi-automatic machines were designed and produced. The trend was to move towards mechanisation or hard automation.

Whitney introduced the concept of interchangeability in manufacturing towards the end of 18th century in America. Interchangeability was earlier tried in several armament factories in France during early 18th century but was not very successfully. Interchangeability demanded greater accuracy and reduced tolerance on the components produced to ensure proper matching and assembly. This demand for higher accuracy led to the development and use of high speed steel tools and SiC and Al_2O_3 grinding wheels around 1900 AD. Introduction of electric motor and gear drive, also around 1900 AD, improved the quality of manufactured products. Machines could now be individually driven and electric circuits were designed to provide necessary control.

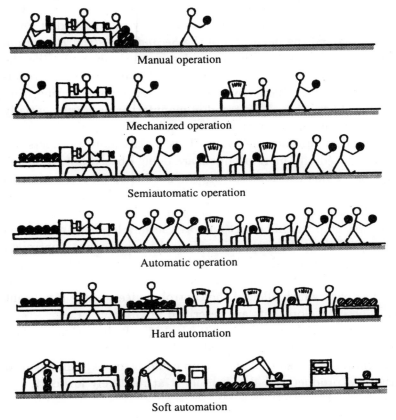

Fig. 1.9 Stages of automation (After Ghosh, 1997).

Significant improvements were achieved in the art of joining metals at the beginning of 20th century. The electric arc welding and oxy-accetylene gas welding techniques were developed around this time and little later coated electrodes were introduced.

Use of metallic moulds and patterns came in the scene in the form of die casting processes so that dimensional accuracy and production rate could be enhanced and subsequent finishing could be minimised.

Demand for lighter yet durable materials led to the development of whole lot of polymer products and their processing techniques such as injection moulding and extrusion between 1925 and 1950 AD. Similarly, introduction of hard, temperature resistant materials and their processing led to a large number of unconventional machining techniques such as electro-discharge machining, electro-chemical machining, ultrasonic machining and laser beam machining in 1960s.

Advent of computers in the second half of 20th century brought in entirely new approach to manufacturing. Components along with solid-state electronics permitted fabrication of devices of great versatility that could perform the assigned task very rapidly and at lower cost. This marked the beginning of the *Second Industrial Revolution* and the attempt was to enhance and sometimes even replace the mental efforts. The trend now was to move towards *flexible automation* to permit quick change-over of automated manufacturing from one product to another. This trend in manufacturing was essentially due to change in consumer preferences and stiff competition characterised by short product life cycle. This means more products are being introduced and more products are being phased out, resulting in lower order quantities of the output products. The era of *mass production* or *hard automation* was, therefore, going away and the age of *batch production* or *flexible automation* had started.

The first step in this direction was the development of numerically controlled machine tools in which the process was controlled by numbers, letters and symbols coded on a tape. Subsequently, microprocessor-based systems were introduced with sensors providing the feedback which allowed the control device to take intelligent action. These developments are described in Chapter 11.

The stages of automation depicted in Fig. 1.9 show that the factories will now consist of automated work cells linked with a flexible computerised system so that the set-up could be quickly modified to take the new product and also produce it at relatively low cost.

1.2   Manufacturing System

Manufacturing as a term for making of goods or articles reveals nothing about the complexity of the problem. In fact manufacturing involves a series of related activities and operations such as product design and development, material selection, process planning, inventory control, quality assurance and marketing. Manufacturing, therefore, is no longer a simple operation that could be handled by an artisan or his disciple. It has now become a system where a number of sub-systems interact in a dynamic manner.

The creation of goods and services is accomplished through productive systems and the term *Production system* in general refers to any system that produces useful products or services. Production, on the other hand, can be considered as a process of transformation of a set of input elements whereby the utility of goods or services is increased (Fig. 1.10). For example, the input could be parts and the

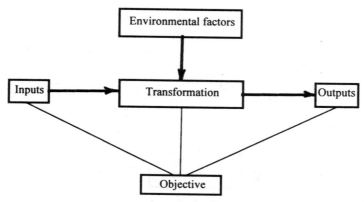

Fig. 1.10 Production system.

assembled product serves as output.

Similarly, in the service sector, say a hospital system, the input could be incoming patients and treated patients as outputs. Since our interest is confined to manufacturing, we will consider only those production systems which deal with manufacturing where transformation· is obtained using one of the engineering methods. Such a production system has been called *Manufacturing production system* or simply *Manufacturing system.*

A manufacturing system is depicted as an input-output system in Fig. 1.11. Here the input elements undergo technological transformation to yield a set of output elements. The technological transformation must be optimised with reference to an objective function which could be cost, productivity or profit.

The implementation of technological transformation involves a large number of elements in a closed loop. Consider a typical manufacturing system as shown in Fig. 1.12. Here the major organisational elements or sub-systems of an industrial enterprise are depicted. The input to the system is a managerial decision making function that specifies the requirements. Based on these requirements the product is developed and the design for manufacturing is carried out. The next step is process planning where the sequence of individual manufacturing processes and operations needed to produce the part are indicated. The manufacturing sub-system now executes the operations to obtain the specified end product. The major feedback to the system is in terms of marketing analysis that provides the demand data and indicates what to produce, when to produce, how long to produce and how many to produce. The feedback from customer/consumer helps in the improvement of product design and quality.

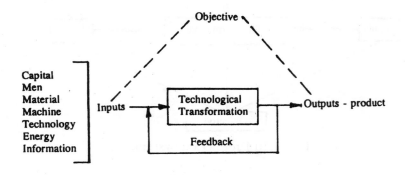

Fig. 1.11 Manufacturing as an input-output system.

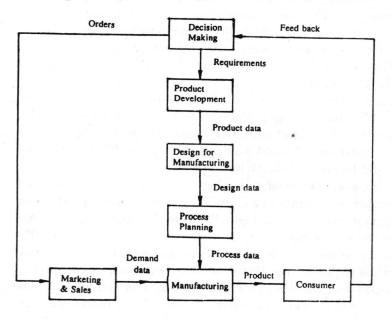

Fig. 1.12 A typical manufacturing system.

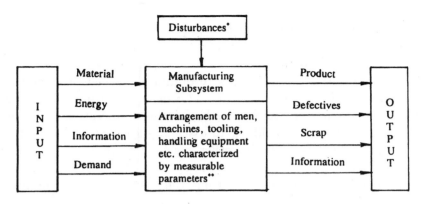

* Controlled by manipulating the controllable inputs

* Measurable parameters could be production rate,
production cost, % defective, inventory level etc.

Fig. 1.13 Manufacturing sub-system.

Manufacturing is the heart of the system where material is converted from one form to another and value is added. The manufacturing sub-system is a collection of processes and operations that are used to obtain the desired product in the required quantity. In other words, the arrangement of men, machine, toolings and handling equipment in the sub-system is so controlled that the desired product quality, production rate, production cost and inventory level are maintained.

Figure 1.13 gives a general picture of manufacturing sub-system. The inputs (material, energy, information and demand) are provided to the complex arrangements of machines, toolings, handling equipment and men where the material is processed and the value added product comes out. Since all inputs cannot be fully controlled by the system, the effect of any disturbance in the system must be countered by making appropriate adjustments in the inputs or in the system itself. For example, material availability or procurement, and demand pattern may get influenced by disturbances both outside and inside the system.

1.3   Manufacturing Processes

The main activity in the manufacturing sub-system is to convert the unfinished product into a finished product. This can be achieved using three principal types of manufacturing:

- Process-type manufacturing

- Fabrication-type manufacturing
- Assembly-type manufacturing

Process-type manufacturing involves continuous flow of materials through a series of process steps to obtain a finished product like chemicals. *Fabrication-type manufacturing* involves manufacturing of individual parts or components by a series of operations, such as rolling, machining and welding. In *assembly-type manufacturing* the parts or components are put together to get a complete product, such as a machine.

In fabrication-type manufacturing, the basic manufacturing processes that are used are:

- Casting
- Forming
- Machining
- Grinding and finishing
- Unconventional Machining
- Joining
- Heat treatment

In *casting* molten metal is poured into a mould cavity of desired shape and the metal on solidification takes the shape of the cavity. Common casting processes are sand casting, investment casting, die casting and continuous casting.

Forming operations are carried-out to modify the shape and size of the material. Metal forming can be done both hot (above recrystallization temperature) or cold (below recrystallization temperature).

Machining involves removing of excess material from selected areas to get the desired shape. Material removal is activated through interaction of tool and workpiece. When the cutting tool is replaced by a bonded abrasive wheel, the process is known as *grinding*. These processes are used for obtaining better surface finish and tolerance.

There are a large variety of *joining* processes which include welding, soldering and brazing, mechanical fastening and adhesive bonding. These processes are commonly used in assembling of the product.

Heat treatment operations are carried-out to alter the mechanical or metallurgical properties of metal through heating and cooling. The common heat treating operations are hardening, tempering, normalizing and annealing.

In general, a number of processes (P) may be employed for converting a raw material into a final product. Each of these processes may employ one or more machines (M). Associated with each machine there may be one or more job positions or stations (S) at each of which at least one operation (O) is carried-out. The combination of these machines, stations and operations provide the final product which is finally assembled, tested and packaged (Fig. 1.14).

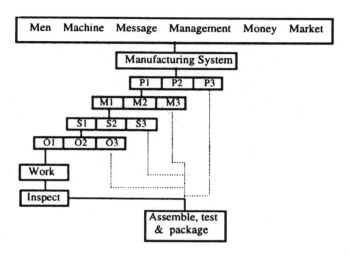

Fig. 1.14 Manufacturing set-up.

Casting and hot forming are invariably the primary processes to which the raw material is first subjected to. For example, the rods or bars that are available as standard sections are initially obtained by hot forming (rolling) and through subsequent cold forming other sizes and shapes are obtained. They can also be machined to give a different configuration. Similarly, cast components can be machined to get the desired shape and size. Welding and other joining processes, heat treatment, finishing and assembly are usually done at the final stage. The general picture is illustrated in Fig. 1.15.

These fabrication-type manufacturing processes can be classified into three broad categories: (i) Constant mass operation, (ii) Material removal operations and (iii) Material addition operations. The processes that fall under each category are indicated in Table 1.2. The understanding of these manufacturing processes is essential for design, development and production. A product design may be functionally of a high quality but if it has to become a reality it must be produced at a competitive price and in a reasonable time to achieve customer satisfaction. In order to satisfy this basic requirement of quality and service life at affordable price, persons associated with design, development and production must be fully acquainted with the manufacturing processes. As mechanical engineers our main interest is in the fabrication-type manufacturing processes, the fundamentals

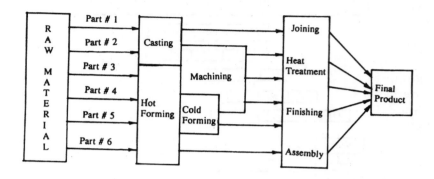

Fig. 1.15 Manufacturing operations.

Table 1.2 Classification of manufacturing processes

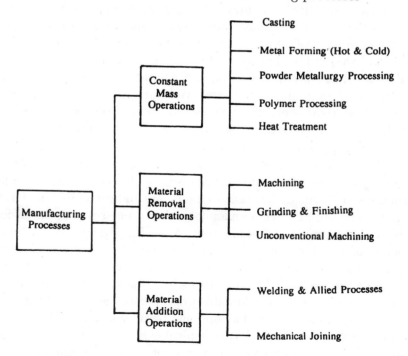

of these processes are discussed in the subsequent chapters.

1.4 Manufacturing Materials

Materials for manufacturing, commonly known as *engineering materials*, can be broadly classified into four categories: (i) metals, (ii) ceramics, (iii) polymers, and (iv) composites.

Metals used in manufacturing can be broadly divided into two groups: (i) ferrous metals and (ii) non-ferrous metals. Ferrous metals are based on iron and the group includes cast iron and steel. Pure iron is rarely used as engineering material and it is usually used as alloys. *Alloys* are composed of two or more elements, atleast one of which is a metallic element. Ferrous alloys are the most commonly used manufacturing materials and are always used as Fe-C alloys. Depending upon the carbon content, ferrous alloys are classified as cast iron when carbon is more than 2.11%, or steel when it is 2.11% or less.

1.4.1 Cast Irons

Cast iron usually has 2 to 4% of carbon (C), 0.5 to 3% of silicon (Si), 0.4 to 1% of manganese (Mn) and a few other elements to improve its casting properties. Depending upon the morphology of carbon (form in which carbon is present), several types of cast iron are obtained. These include gray cast iron, white cast iron, ductile cast iron, malleable cast iron and several types of alloy cast irons.

Gray cast iron, by far, is the most commonly used cast iron. In it carbon is present in the form of graphite flakes distributed throughout. When fractured, the exposed surface of metal has gray appearance and a graphite smudge is obtained on fingers, when rubbed across the surface. This dispersion of graphite flakes provides good internal lubricating properties, hence excellent machinability and excellent vibration damping characteristics. Gray cast iron is brittle and has poor tensile strength (ability to withstand tensile forces) and poor ductility (ability to plastically deform). It has, however, high compressive strength (ability to withstand compressive forces), good wear resistance and good corrosion resistance. Gray cast iron is commonly used for machine bodies, engine blocks and pump and motor housings.

In *white cast iron*, produced by rapid cooling of molten gray cast iron, carbon remains chemically combined in the form of iron carbide (cementite). When fractured, its surface has a shining white appearance. It is hard, brittle and has excellent wear resistance. These properties make it most suitable for applications requiring high wear resistance, for example, railway brake shoes, grinding balls and crushing rollers.

Malleable cast iron is obtained by heat treating white cast iron to decompose iron carbide into iron and graphite. Graphite in malleable cast iron appears as clusters or agglomeration of many small graphite flakes. This structure promotes, ductility and toughness (ability to absorb shock). Because of these properties, they are used for making small tools, pipe fittings, automobile parts and farm implements.

In *ductile cast iron*, graphite is present in spheroid forms rather than in flakes. This is obtained by adding a small amount of magnesium (Mg) or cesium to the molten gray cast iron before pouring. The added material is known as nodulizing agent and the product is often called *nodular cast iron*. Ductile cast iron has good ducility, high strength, toughness, wear resistance and excellent casting qualities. These make it a popular material for small and intricate castings.

Cast irons are often alloyed with various elements to achieve special properties. These *alloy cast irons* include heat-treatable types that can be hardened, heat-resistant types that retain their hardness at elevated temperatures (hot hardness) and corrosion-resistance types.

1.4.2   Steels

Steel is a ferrous alloy containing 0.02 to 2.11% of carbon and other alloying elements such as manganese, chromium, nickel and molybdenum. In fact, a large variety of steels are now available commercially— each has its own composition. These steels can, however, be broadly classified as plain carbon steels, alloy steels, stainless steels and tool steels.

Plain carbon steels have carbon as the principal alloying element with small amount of other elements (0.4% Mn, 0.05% S, 0.04% P). The tensile strength of plain carbon steel increases with increase in carbon content but its ductility decreases. Depending upon the carbon content, they are classified as low-carbon steels, medium-carbon steels and high-carbon steels.

Low carbon steels contain less that 0.2% C and are by far the most commonly used engineering material. These steels, popularly known a *mild steels*, are extensively used for making plates, sheets, tubes, machine components and nuts and bolts which require high strength.

Medium carbon steels have carbon content in the range of 0.2 to 0.5% and are used where higher strength is required. Applications include manufacturing of engine parts such as connecting rod and crank-shaft and machine components.

High carbon steels have carbon content in excess of 0.5%. These steels are used where still higher strength is required and are extensively used for making tools, blades and springs.

Alloy steels contain additional alloying elements to improve the mechanical properties of plain carbon steels. The alloying elements that are commonly added are manganese (to improve strength and hardness), chromium (to improve strength, wear resistance and hot hardness), molybdenum (to improve heat resistance and toughness), copper (to improve strength and corrosion resistance), nickel (to improve strength and toughness) and silicon (to improve strength and toughness). The alloying elements are invariably added in combination but the total amount is usually less than 5% by weight. A large variety of alloy steels are now available, each has its own combination of elements.

The differentiation between plain carbon steels and alloy steels is somewhat arbitrary since both contain alloying elements. Alloy of iron and carbon containing more than 1.65% of manganese, or 0.6% of silicon, or 0.6% of copper are designated as alloy steels. They are also called an alloy steel when specified amount of other alloying elements are added to give a desired property. Alloy steels, because of better strength to weight ratio, are used in transportation, mining and agricultural equipment, their structural sections are used in building and other structures, and in plate form they are used in bridges, buildings and ships.

Stainless steels are highly alloyed steels designed to provide high corrosion resistance along with high strength and ductility. The principal alloying element in stainless steel is chromium which is usually above 12%. Other alloying elements often present in stainless steels are nickel, molybdenum, titanium, silicon and manganese. Typical applications of these steels are for kitchen, surgical, chemical and food processing equipment and in machining when high corrosion resistance is required.

Tool steels are another highly alloyed steels designed for use as tools and dies in machining and forming processes. They are designed to provide high strength and toughness, and wear resistance at both room and elevated tempeatures. Tool steels are basically high-carbon steels in which wear resistance and toughness are balanced through use of alloying elements such as tungsten (1.5 to 20%), chromium (0.2

to 15%), molybdenum (0.8 to 15%), cobalt (0.75 to 12%), vanadium (0.15 to 3%), silicon (0.5 to 2%) and manganese (0.2 to 1.6%). By controlling the composition of alloying elements, a variety of tool steels, such as high-speed steels, mould steels, hot-work tool steels and cold-work tool steels are obtained.

1.4.3   Non-ferrous Metals

Non-ferrous metals include all metal elements and alloys that are not based on iron. They cover a wide range of materials, including the most commonly used metals such as aluminium, copper and magnesium to high-strength, high-temperature alloys of tungsten, tantalum and molybdenum. Non-ferrous metals and alloys have important engineering applications primarily because of their resistance to corrosion, high strength-to-weight ratio, and high electrical and thermal conductivity. Typical applications of non-ferrous metals and their alloys are given below.

Aluminium and *aluminium alloys* are extensively used for aircraft, bus, car, and marine craft bodies, cooking utensils, cans, foils, electric wire, structure material and furniture. The main considerations for their selection are high strength-to-weight ratio, resistance to corrosion and high thermal and electrical conductivity.

Copper and *copper alloys* are extensively used in electrical and electronic components, electric wires, heat exchangers, cooking utensils, decorative objects and plumbings. These applications are primarily because they are the best conductors of heat and electricity and have good corrosion resistance.

Brass (typically 65% copper and 35% zinc) and *bronze* (typically 90% copper and 10% tin) are two most common alloys of copper. Brass has high electrical and thermal conductivity along with adequate strength and ductility. Bronze are characterized by their good strength, toughness, wear resistance and corrosion resistance.

Magnesium and *magnesium alloys* are typically used for aircraft and missile components, material handling equipment, printing and textile machinery, sporting goods, and general light weight components. Magnesium is the lightest engineering metal that has a specific gravity of about 1.75, compared to 2.7 for aluminium and 7.8 for iron. In pure form magnesium is weak for any engineering application and is always alloyed with various elements to impart specific properties such has high strength-to-weight ratio.

Nickel is a silver-white metal which is mainly used in electroplating for appearance and for improving corrosion resistance. It is also used extensively in stainless steels and nickel-based alloys. *Nickel al-*

loys are noted for high strength and corrosion resistance at elevated temperatures. A variety of nickel-based alloys have been developed which have a range of strength at different temperatures. *Monel*, a nickel-copper based alloy, is used extensively in chemical and food processing industries because of excellent corrosion resistance characteristics. *Super alloys* based on nickel are used extensively for high temperature applications, such as for jet engine, gas turbine and rocket components, and in nuclear power plants.

Zinc is a low melting point metal and its main use is in galvanizing (providing corrosion protection through zinc coating) on iron and steel. The other important use of zinc is in the production of brass. *Zinc alloys* are primarily used for die casting of components for automobile and appliance industries.

Titanium, although expensive, has high strength-to-weight ratio and is corrosion resistant even at elevated temperatures. *Titanium alloys* with alloying elements such as aluminium, vanadium, molybdenum and manganese have strength comparable to those of alloy steels and can be used at temperatures upto 550°C. Because of high strength-to-weight ratio, corrosion resistance, and retention of strength at elevated temperature, titanium alloys are attractive materials for aerospace applications (aircraft, jet engine and missile components), marine, racing car and chemical and petrochemical equipment components.

1.4.4 Ceramics

Ceramic materials are compounds of both metallic and non-metallic elements and are generally available in the form of oxides, carbides and nitrides. The large number of possible compositions of elements, enable availability of a wide variety of ceramics are now available. Ceramics, in general, are brittle, have high strength and hardness at elevated temperature, and low thermal and electrical conductivity. Clay, alumina, quartz, silicon carbide, tungsten carbide, silicon nitride and cubic boron nitride are typical examples of ceramics.

Many ceramic products are made from clay. These include bricks, tiles, sewer pipes, china and porcelain. *Alumina* is often used as refractory ceramic in the form of bricks in furnaces and crucibles. Alumina along with silicon carbide are used in grinding wheels and sand paper. Silicon carbide and tungsten carbide are two commonly used carbides. *Silicon carbide* is extensively used for making resistance heating elements, while *tungsten carbide* is a popular cutting tool material. The nitride ceramics are hard and brittle, and melt at high temperature. *Silicon nitride* has applications in gas turbines and rocket engines, while *cubic boron nitride* is extensively used for making grinding wheels and cutting tools because of their extreme hardness.

Glass is an inorganic, non-metallic compound and is a ceramic as a glassy state solid material. Most of the commercial glasses have silica (SiO_2), most commonly found as quartz in silica sand and sand stone, as their principal ingredient. Additional ingredients are added to alter the optical properties, thermal stability and chemical resistance.

Glasses have low thermal conductivity, high electrical resistivity and dielectric strength. Because of these properties, the use of glass ranges from window glass, bottles, light bulb glass, laboratory glassware and cookware to special glasses used for fibre optics communication, lenses for eye glasses and optician instruments such as cameras and microscopes, insulating fibre-glass wool and fibre-glass reinforced plastic.

1.4.5   Polymers

Polymers are compounds consisting of long-chain molecules with each molecule made up of repeating units connected together. Most polymers are carbon based and are therefore considered organic materials. Polymers are generally characterized by low density, strength and thermal and electrical conductivity, and good chemical resistance. Most polymers, however, can be used only in the low temperature range (below 350°C).

From engineering point of view, these polymers can be classified as: (i) thermoplastics, (ii) thermosets and (iii) elastomers. *Thermoplastics* are solid materials at room temperature, but they become viscous liquids when heated to a few hundred degrees. This allows them to be shaped into products. The heating and cooling cycle of these materials can be repeated as often as desired without any degradation of the polymer. Common examples of this type of polymer are nylon, acrylics, cellulosics, polyethylenses and polyvinylchloride. Commercially, thermoplastics are the most important polymer and constitute almost 70% of polymers produced. These materials can be moulded, extruded and rolled into sheets.

Thermosets soften when heated, but harden on cooling into an infusible solid. The curing reaction in this type of polymers is therefore irreversible. On reheating thermosets often burn-up and char rather soften. Typical examples of this category of polymers are epoxies, phonolics and certain polyesters. Common products made from this type of polymers include knobs and handles of pots and pans, and light switches.

Elastomers or *rubbers* are those polymers which undergo large elastic deformation when subjected to mechanical stresses but return to their original shape and size when the stresses are removed. These elastomers can be natural rubber or synthetic polymers. A variety of additives can be blended with synthetic polymers to impart specific properties. Applications of elastomers include protection against corrosion and abrasion, absorption of vibration and shock, electrical insulation and non-skid surfaces. Products include tires, footwear, gaskets, seals and flooring.

1.4.6 Composite Materials

Composite materials are heterogeneous solids consisting of two or more different materials that are metallurgically or mechanically bonded together. The combination of these materials produces properties of composite materials that are not only different from those of its constituents but are often far superior. These materials generally possess a unique combination of properties such as strength, weight, stiffness, corrosion resistance, hardness and conductivity. For example, a composite can be designed to have high strength but very light in weight to give them high strength-to-weight ratio.

Composite materials can be broadly classified into three categories:

- Laminar or layer composites
- Particulate composites
- Fibre-reinforced composites

This classification is based on the relative distribution of materials in the composites. In *laminar* or *layer composites* two or more layers of materials are bonded together to form an integral piece. Material layers (often of different materials) are usually thick enough that such composite can be easily identified. The common examples of this type of composites are plywood, galvanized sheets, glazed tiles, coated tools, insulated wires, safety glass and bimetallic strip.

Particulate composites are obtained when discrete particles of one material is surrounded by a matrix of another material. Concrete (cement, sand and gravel) and asphalt mixed with gravel are common examples of particulate composites used in construction. Grinding wheels consisting of abrasive particles (aluminium oxide and silicon carbide) bonded in a matrix of glass or polymeric material is another common example. Cemented carbides consisting of particles of tungsten carbide dispersed in a metal matrix (cobalt) is a particulate composite extensively used as a cutting tool. In particulate composites, because of uniform distribution of particulates in the matrix, the properties are isotropic, that is, the properties are uniform in all direction.

Fibre-reinforced composites consist of thin fibres of one material embedded in a matrix of another material. Fibres are filaments of reinforcement and can be either long continuous fibres or chopped sections of continuous fibers (discontinuous fibres). Fibres can be arranged in a variety of orientation. They can be placed in the direction of loading to impart directional properties, or could be randomly oriented. Fibres are considered to be the principal constituent since they carry most of the load. Fibres are used as reinforcing material because the filament form of most material is significantly stronger than the bulk material. Glass is the most widely used fiber in polymers, while silicon carbide and aluminium oxide are the main fibre materials for ceramics. Other important fibre materials are carbon, polymers and boron.

The properties of fibre-reinforced composites depend upon the properties of fibre material, volume fraction of fibre, orientation of fibres, properties of matrix and degree of bonding between fibre and matrix. Polymeric matrix materials are used for low temperature application (below 300°C), while metal matrix materials are used for high temperature applications. Steel-reinforced concrete used in construction, nylon-reinforced tires for automobile and glass-fibre-reinforced plastic for car bodies, furnitures, boron-reinforced aluminium composites for aircraft and rockets components are some of the common application of this type of composites.

1.5 Selection of Materials

An ever-increasing variety of materials, each having its own characteristics, advantages and limitations, has made the choice of the best material for a product rather difficult. A particular material, however, is selected on the basis of following considerations:

- Properties of material
- Cost of material
- Availability of material and reliability of supply
- Service life of material
- Appearance (colour and surface texture) of the material

Properties of materials that are generally considered include the mechanical properties (strength, ductility, toughness, hardness and strength-to-weight ratio), the physical properties (density, specific heat, thermal expansion, conductivity and melting point), and the chemical properties (oxidation, corrosion, flammability and toxicity). In addition, their manufacturing properties, which indicate whether they can be cast, formed, machined and welded with ease, are important.

Cost of material is obviously very important from economic considerations. Availability of material in the desired shape, size and quantity is important, otherwise substitutes may have to be used. Reliability of supply will dictate the availability of material as and when required.

Service life indicates the dimensional stability of the product. Wear and corrosion shorten the useful life of a product. Appearance is important from the point of appeal to the consumer.

1.6   Selection of Manufacturing Processes

The best process for manufacturing a product is often difficult to identify. This is primarily because most products can be manufactured by more than one process. The selection of a manufacturing process is, however, based on the following considerations:

- Manufacturing cost
- Production volume and production rate
- Characterstics and properties of workpiece material
- Limitations on shape and size
- Surface finish and tolerance requirements
- Functional requirements of the product.

The cost of manufacturing is obviously the main consideration in the selection of process. For successfully marketing a product, its manufacturing cost must be competitive with similar products. For higher production volume, machines with higher degree of automation are used. Such machines give higher production rate and give lower cost per unit.

Characteristics and properties of materials greatly influence their manufacturing characteristics, that is, suitability of the material to respond to a particular type of operation (machining, forming, casting and welding). Each manufacturing process is capable of providing a certain quality of finish (surface finish) and dimensional accuracy (tolerance). Every process gives a range of tolerance and surface finish. Closer tolerance and better surface finish increases the cost of manufacturing because further processing becomes necessary.

Functional requirements for achieving the expected service life often dictate the hardness, wear resistance, refractiveness and stiffness of the product and put a limit on the choice of material and the manufacturing process.

Review Questions

1.1 What basic innovations brought about the first industrial revolution? What role did the invention of steam engine play?

1.2 How war of independence in USA was related to developments in manufacturing?

1.3 What led to the development of flexible automation?

1.4 What role did computer play in bringing about the second industrial revolution?

1.5 Describe a manufacturing system indicating its major elements or sub-systems.

1.6 What are cast irons? Indicate the one that is most commonly used and why?

1.7 What are steels? Broadly classify them and indicate their most common applications.

1.8 What are ceramic materials and what are their typical characteristics?

1.9 What are thermoplastics and thermosets? What is the basic difference in their properties?

1.10 What are composite materials? Classify them giving typical examples.

1.11 What are basic considerations in selecting a particular material for manufacturing?

1.12 On what considerations the best manufacturing process is selected for manufacturing a product?

Chapter 2

Casting Processes

2.1 Introduction

Casting is one of the most popular means of formation of the desired shape. It is perhaps the oldest method of manufacturing and invariably the first step in the sequence of manufacturing a product. In this process the raw material is melted, heated to the desired temperature, and poured into the mould cavity where it takes the desired shape. After the molten metal solidifies in the mould cavity the product is taken out to get the casting.

The final product or the casting can have any configuration the designer desires and can be made from any metal that can be melted. The size and weight of cast parts can vary widely, from a few millimeters and a fraction of a gram to several meters and several tons. For example, the cast bronze statue of the Sun Buddha in Japan is more than 20 meters high and weighs around 500 tons, while a cast zipper tooth is only a few millimeters long and weighs barely a few grams. Products having very complex shapes, hollow sections, complicated internal cavities and irregular curved surfaces made from metals that are difficult to machine can be easily produced by the casting process. In fact just about any shape or configuration can be obtained by this process.

Many casting processes are available today and the choice of a process for producing a particular part depends upon several factors, such as production cost, production rate, size, shape, surface finish and physico-mechanical properties. The casting processes differ from each other basically in the type of material used for preparation of the mould and the method of pouring the molten material. The mould material is generally sand or metal and the pouring method may use gravity, vacuum, low or high pressure.

2.2   Basic Features

The basic features common to various casting processes can be summarized as:

- Pattern and mould
- Melting and pouring
- Solidification and cooling
- Removal, cleaning, finishing and inspection

2.2.1   Pattern and Mould

A *pattern*, usually made of either wood or metal, is a replica of the final product and is used for preparing the mould cavity. The mould cavity, which contains the molten metal, is essentially a negative of the final product. The mould material should, therefore, possess a refractory character and must withstand the pouring temperature. When the mould is used for a single casting, it is made of sand. Such moulds are called *expendable moulds* since they are destroyed while taking out the casting. When the mould is used repeatedly, it is made of metal or graphite and is called a *permanent mould*. A pattern is used for making a cavity in an expendable mould, whereas, a permanent mould is an assembly of two or more metal blocks with appropriate inner cavities. The permanent moulds are obviously more expensive and are used for large scale production, whereas expendable or single-use moulds are used for production of smaller quantities. For making holes or hollow cavities inside a casting, cores made of either sand or metal are used.

2.2.2   Melting and Pouring

Several types of furnaces are available for melting metals and their selection depends on the type of metal, the maximum temperature required and the rate and the mode of molten metal delivery. Melting furnaces which are commonly used are induction furnace (maximum temperature 1750°C), side-blow converter (1700°C) and cupola (1650°C). These are shown in Figures 2.1 and 2.2.

An appropriate technique must be deviced to pour the molten metal into the mould cavity. Before pouring, provision must be made for the escape of all air or gases from the mould while the molten metal is entering the mould. The gating system which serves to deliver the poured metal to all sections of the mould cavity must be designed to minimize turbulent flow and erosion of mould cavity.

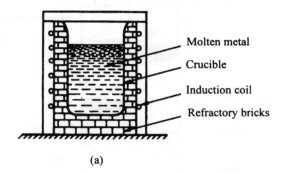

(a)

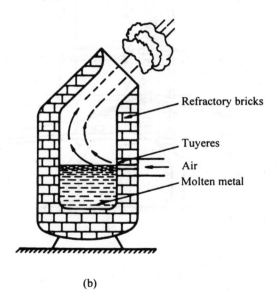

(b)

Fig. 2.1 (a) Induction furnace and (b) side-blow converter.

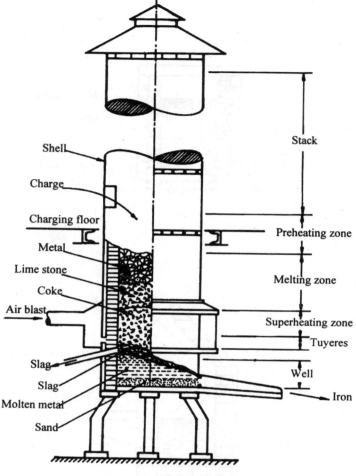

Fig. 2.2 Cupola.

Two other factors that are important are the pouring temperature and the pouring rate.

2.2.3 Solidification and Cooling

The solidification and cooling processes should be carefully controlled, since the desired properties of the casting largely depend on the solidification time and the rate of cooling. Shrinkage of casting during cooling of solidified metal should not be restrained by the mould material, otherwise internal stresses developed may cause crack formation in the casting. Proper care should also be taken in the design of casting so that solidification shrinkage can occur without producing defects.

Table 2.1 Classification of casting processes.

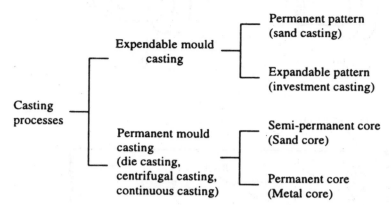

2.2.4 Removal, Cleaning, Finishing and Inspection

In permanent mould casting processes, the metal blocks are separated to remove the casting after it has cooled down completely, whereas in case of expendable casting, the sand mould is usually broken to remove the casting. After the casting is removed from the mould it is thoroughly cleaned and the excess metal, usually along the mould parting line and the place where the molten metal was poured, is removed using a portable grinder. The castings are then tested for defects. While visual inspection may reveal surface defects, other inspection techniques, such as pressure test, magnetic particle inspection, radiographic test and ultrasonic inspection are used to detect internal defects.

2.3 Classification of Casting Processes

Casting processes can be classified on the basis of the type of mould and pattern used in the process as shown in Table 2.1.

The basic features of some of the widely used casting processes are discussed in the subsequent sections. The next section deals with expandable mould casting (sand casting).

2.4 Expendable-mould, Permanent-pattern Casting (Sand Casting)

Castings begin with molten material, and any metal or non- metal which can be melted can be used for casting. Here metal casting is discussed since casting processes are of primary importance in the production of metal products. Metals most frequently used for

(a)   (b)

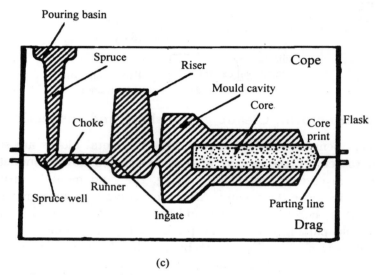

(c)

Fig. 2.3 Sand casting: (a) final casting, (b) pattern and (c) two-part sand mould.

casting are cast iron, steel, bronze, brass, aluminium and certain zinc alloys. Cast iron is the most commonly used metal for casting since it posseses sufficient fluidity at pouring temperature, has low shrinkage and substantial strength and is relatively much cheaper.

Compared to other casting processes, sand casting is the most popular one and is widely used in practice. The process uses an expendable single-use sand mould and a permanent pattern, usually wooden, for casting. It is a low cost process with little limitations on size and shape.

2.4.1 Preparation of Sand Mould

A typical two-part sand mould is shown in Fig. 2.3. The final casting required is shown in Fig. 2.3(a). The process of casting starts with the construction of a pattern which is an approximate duplicate of the final product, as shown in Fig. 2.3(b). For hollow castings, a

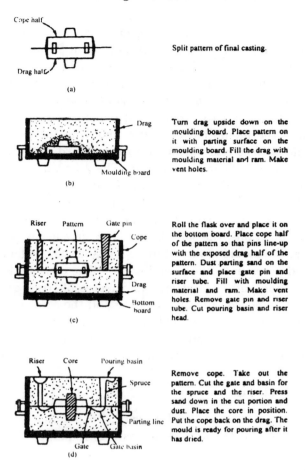

Split pattern of final casting.

(a)

Turn drag upside down on the moulding board. Place pattern on it with parting surface on the moulding board. Fill the drag with moulding material and ram. Make vent holes.

(b)

Roll the flask over and place it on the bottom board. Place cope half of the pattern so that pins line-up with the exposed drag half of the pattern. Dust parting sand on the surface and place gate pin and riser tube. Fill with moulding material and ram. Make vent holes. Remove gate pin and riser tube. Cut pouring basin and riser head.

(c)

Remove cope. Take out the pattern. Cut the gate and basin for the spruce and the riser. Press sand down in the cut portion and dust. Place the core in position. Put the cope back on the drag. The mould is ready for pouring after it has dried.

(d)

Fig. 2.4 Preparation of sand mould.

core is required and to support the core inside the mould cavity *core prints* are provided. The pattern is now placed in a *flask* which is a box containing the moulding aggregate in Fig. 2.3(c). The upper half of the flask is called *cope* and its lower half is known as *drag*. The moulding material, baked green sand mixed with clay for improved mouldability, is then packed around the pattern and rammed properly. Hand packing and ramming of sand is used in small foundries when only a few castings of a certain design are to be made. In other cases, moulding machines are used to perform the job.

For split patterns, the drag is turned upside down on the moulding board and then the pattern is placed on it with the parting surface down on the board. Other pieces for gating and rising systems (pouring basin, Sprue, runner and riser) are also placed along with the pattern, after which the moulding material is packed around them-first with facing sand up to a depth of about 25 mm and then with backing sand. The moulding material should be properly rammed so that it gets into all pockets and sharp corners. Uniform hard ramming of the moulding material is necessary to obtain a smooth casting surface, and to avoid metal penetration into the sand and swelling of the mould cavity. After removing the excess sand from the mould surface and placing a bottom board, the drag is inverted and the moulding board is removed. The drag surface is then dusted with fine silica sand to prevent the sand in the cope from sticking to the sand in the drag. The cope is now placed on top of the drag and after placing the cope pattern, the gating system and the riser in proper positions, the sand is packed as in the case of drag. After ramming, the mould is vented by a thin vent wire to facilitate escape of air and gases from the mould cavity. The cope is then separated from the drag and the patterns and pieces of, riser and the gating system are removed. Finally, the drag and the cope are put together to provide a replica of the final product in the form of cavities in the drag and the cope. The mould is now ready for pouring. The various steps in the preparation of the mould are summarized in Fig. 2.4.

2.4.2 Patterns

A variety of patterns are used in casting, depending upon the casting configuration and the number of castings required. The basic types of patterns are:

- Single-piece pattern
- Split pattern
- Follow-board pattern
- Cope and drag pattern
- Match-plate pattern
- Loose-piece pattern
- Sweep pattern
- Skeleton pattern

Single-piece patterns are the simplest and least expensive of all types of patterns and are used when only a limited number of castings are required.

Split patterns permit moulding of more complex shapes in moderate quantity. These patterns are split into two parts along the parting line with the upper half forming cavity in the cope and the lower half in the drag.

Follow-board patterns are used for structurally weak patterns which are likely to break during ramming. Here the bottom board is modified to follow the contour of the weaker section. Once the drag is rammed the follow board is removed, the drag is inverted and the cope part is rammed.

Cope and drag patterns are essentially split patterns with two halves of the pattern mounted separately on two match plates. The cope and drag moulds can therefore be prepared separately and assembled to form the complete mould. This type of pattern is usually preferred for heavy castings.

Match-plate patterns are obtained by attaching two halves of the split pattern on opposite sides of the match plate. After preparing the cope and drag cavities, the match plate is removed to get the complete pattern. This type of pattern is good for small castings since several patterns can be mounted on the match plate.

Loose-piece patterns are used when withdrawal of pattern after moulding is not possible. Loose pieces are therefore used for moulding the obstructing parts of the contour. These loose pieces are attached to the remainder of the mould by pins, and the design of the pattern is such that the entire pattern, except the loose pieces, can be withdrawn first from the mould and the loose pieces, then recovered through the cavity created by the main pattern. Such patterns are not only expensive but they also slow down the moulding process.

Sweep patterns are forms used to sweep the desired shape of the mould cavity. For example, a large axisymmetrical mould cavity can be generated by rotating an appropriate section about an axis. This eliminates the need for a large three-dimensional pattern.

Skeleton patterns are made of wooden strips outlining the desired shape of casting. The moulder fills this skeleton with sand and hand-finishes the mould to get the final pattern. This type of pattern useful for large castings having simple geometrical shapes.

Figure 2.5 shows typical examples of various types of patterns.

2.4.3 Allowances

The patterns indicated above are always made somewhat larger than the final casting since certain allowances must be made in the pattern. These are shrinkage, draft, finish, distortion and shake allowances.

Shrinkage allowance is provided to compensate for the shrinkage or contraction when the temperature of solidifying casting drops from freezing to room temperature. In fact the shrinkage in casting takes place when (a) the temperature of liquid metal drops from pouring to freezing temperature, (b) the metal changes from liquid to solid state, and (c) the solid-phase temperature drops from freezing to

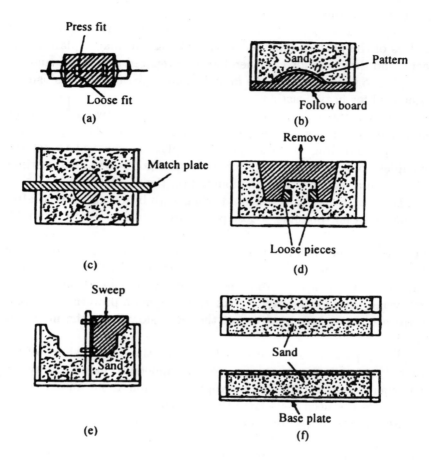

Fig. 2.5 Types of patterns: (a) split pattern, (b) follow-board pattern, (c) match-plate pattern, (d) loose-piece pattern, (e) sweep pattern and (f) skeleton pattern.

(a)   (b)
Fig. 2.6 Draft allowance.

room temperature. The shrinkage allowance essentially compensates for stage (c). The shrinkage during stages (a) and (b) are compensated by the risers, as discussed later. Typical shrinkage allowances for common casting metals are given in Table 2.2.

Table 2.2 Shrinkage allowances for common casting materials.

Material	Shrinkage Allowance (mm/mm)
Aluminum	0.013
Brass	0.016
Bronze	0.013
Cast iron	0.011
Cast steel	0.021
Copper	0.016

Draft allowance is the taper provided to the vertical faces of the pattern to facilitate in drawing the pattern out of the mould without causing any damage to the mould (Fig. 2.6). Draft is always added to the exterior dimensions of the pattern and is typically in the range of 0.01 to 0.025 mm/mm. The value chosen depends upon the pattern material (wood, metal or plastic) and the size of casting. Inner faces are generally provided higher draft (upto 0.06 mm/mm).

Finish or *machining allowance* is the extra material added to the casting which is removed during machining and finishing operations. The surface finish and the dimensional accuracy achievable by casting is obviously not very good and it is improved by subsequent finishing. The amount of extra material or machining allowance depends upon the casting material, size of casting and finish required. Typical values are given in Table 2.3.

Distortion allowance is provided on weaker sections of castings to prevent distortion during casting. Long and thin sections, V and U sections and other irregular-shaped castings get distorted when a section of the casting shrinks while the other section is restricted. For example, the closed end of a U-section will converge slightly on cooling, while the open ends (lego) will be held by the sand in a fixed position. One way to prevent it is to provide extra material in the sections which are likely to distort.

Table 2.3 Machining allowances for common casting materials.

Material	Machining Allowance (mm)
Aluminium	1.5 to 3.0
Brass	1.5 to 3.0
Bronze	1.5 to 3.0
Cast iron	2.5 to 6.0
Cast steel	3.0 to 9.0
Copper	1.5 to 3.0

Shake allowance is a negative allowance provided to compensate for the enlargement of the vertical faces due to rapping of pattern to facilitate its removal from the mould. This allowance is generally provided in large castings. The allowance can, however, be reduced if increased draft is provided for easy removal of pattern.

2.4.4 Moulding Materials

Major parts of moulding material in sand casting are

(i) 70 - 85% silica sand (SiO_2)

(ii) 10-12% bonding material (clay and cereal).

(iii) 3-6% water

Silica sand, bonding material and water are mixed together so that the following requirements are met:

(a) *Refractoriness* to withstand high temperature of molten metal. This is provided by the silica sand.

(b) *Cohesiveness* to retain the moulded shape. Cohesiveness or strength is obtained by bonding the sand particles with clay and water.

(c) *Permeability* to permit gases to escape through the moulding material. This depends upon the size and shape of sand particles, type of bonding material, compaction pressure and moisture content.

(d) *Collapsibility* for easy removal of casting and to permit the metal to shrink. This can be increased by adding cereals or other organic materials which burn out when exposed to molten metal.

The performance of a mould depends upon the following factors:
• Permeability
• Green strength
• Dry strength

Permeability is a measure of porosity from the openings between the grains and is expressed as the rate of air flow through a standard specimen under specified pressure conditions. For large size sand grains the permeability number is high, i.e, the gases, air and steam from the mould can escape more easily when the molten metal is poured, but large grains result in coarse casting surface. Therefore, to increase the permeability as well as to achieve smoother casting surface, the surface of the mould cavity, made of coarse sand, is covered with a thin layer of fine-grain facing sand. Sand grains may be angular or round in shape. Sharp angular grains cannot pack together as closely as round grains, resulting in higher permeability.

Various types of clay are used to bind the sand particles for increased mouldability. The clay content is considered optimum when it completely coats the sand particles without filling the spaces between the grains. Therefore, the type as well as the amount of binder will have a substantial effect on permeability.

Moisture content also has a significant effect on permeability. When the moisture content is low, fine clay particles block the spaces between the grains, thus decreasing the permeability. Again, an excess of moisture may fill the voids and decrease the permeability.

Figures 2.7 (a) to (d) show the effects of grain shape, size and moisture content on permeability and green strength of mould. *Green strength* is the property of green moulding sand (moulding sand that contains moisture) to hold the mould shape. It usually refers to the stress required to rupture a standard specimen under compressive loading. *Permeability*, on the other hand, refers to the porosity from the openings between the sand particles. Permeability is usually defined in terms of permeability number which represents the rate of a flow through a standard specimen under a standard pressure.

Sand particles can be broadly classified as round or angular. Angular grains do not pack as closely as round grains and therefore give higher permeability (Fig. 2.7a) but lower green strength (Fig. 2.7b). Similarly, finer grains give higher green strength (Fig. 2.7c).

Moisture content has the same effect on green strength as on permeability. Green strength initially increases with the addition of moisture and reaches a maximum value, and as the moisture content increases further it weakens the mould and the green strength

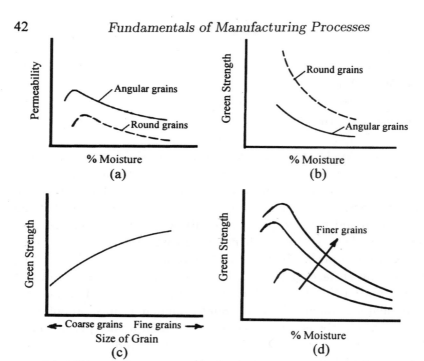

Fig. 2.7 Effect of grain shape, size and moisture content on permeability and green strength (After Doyle et al, 1969).

decreases (Fig. 2.7d).

Dry strength is the strength of the dry moulding sand. When the molten metal is poured the mould sand quickly gets dried. The ability of this dried sand to retain the mould cavity depends on its dry strength. Dry strength, in general, varies the same way as the green strength with grain size, shape and moisture content.

2.4.5 Melting and Pouring

Casting begins with pouring of molten metal in the mould cavity. The quality of casting is often influenced by the melting process used. The melting technique should not only provide the molten metal at the required temperature, but should also provide the material of good quality and in the required quantity. Cupola is extensively used for melting cast iron, primarily because of lower initial cost and cost of melting. A number of other furnaces such as induction furnace and side-blow converter are available for melting foundry alloys, but their choice essentially depends upon the type of alloy being melted, maximum temperature required and rate and mode of delivery.

Molten metal often reacts with oxygen and the metal oxides (slag) produced may get into the mould during pouring, and produce an

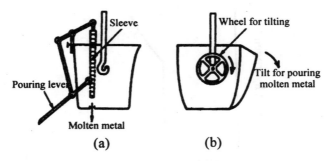

Fig. 2.8 Pouring vessels.

inferior casting. This can be controlled by covering the molten metal with fluxes or by carrying out melting and pouring in vacuum. Alternately, ladles which pour the molten metal from beneath the surface (Fig. 2.8) can be used.

The two main considerations during pouring are:
(i) the pouring temperature, and
(ii) the pouring time or the pouring rate.

The fluidity of the molten metal, which affects its ability to flow and fill the mould cavity, depends on the casting material and the mould configuration. In general, the lower is the viscosity, the higher is the fluidity. Therefore, at higher pouring temperatures, the fluidity will increase since the viscosity decreases. If the pouring is carried out at a temperature higher than that required, increased fluidity may cause the molten metal to even get into the small voids between the sand particles and cause surface defects. At low pouring temperatures, the fluidity of molten metal may not be sufficient to fill the entire mould cavity.

The other problem that is associated with the pouring temperature is the amount of trapped gases in the liquid metal. Figure 2.9 shows the solubility of gas in a metal as a function of temperature. It is clear that the amount of dissolved gas decreases drastically when the material undergoes freezing. In the liquid state also, the solubility of gas increases significantly with an increase in temperature. Therefore, in order to minimize the defects in casting due to trapped gases, the pouring temperature or the extent of superheat should be kept low. In ferrous metals, the removal of gases like hydrogen and nitrogen is often accomplished by passing carbon monoxide gas through the molten metal. For non-ferrous metals, chlorine, helium or argon gases are invariably used.

The fluidity considerations and minimization of gas solubility are two conflicting requirements. The optimum pouring temperature is,

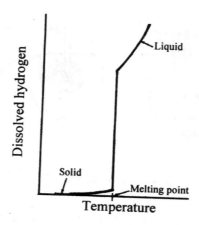

Fig. 2.9 Solubility of gas as a function of temperature.

however, decided on the basis of fluidity requirements. The temperature should be such that the molten metal fills all sections of the mould before beginning to freeze and at the same time there should be no penetration into the voids between the sand particles in the mould.

The pouring rate, in general, depends upon the casting material and the casting configuration. For example, the pouring rate chosen for cast iron may not be relevant for steel since their cooling rates are different. Similarly, some non-ferrous metals which loose heat slowly may require low pouring rate. The size of casting, particularly its volume and surface area, also have significant effect on the cooling rate and must be considered while deciding the pouring rate.

If the rate of pouring of liquid metal is low, then the time taken to fill the mould cavity may be sufficiently long and the molten metal may begin to solidify before the mould is completely filled. This would result in visible casting defects due to insufficient metal. One could avoid it by using higher pouring temperature, but gas solubility and fluidity may cause problems. Alternatively, higher pouring rate may be used, but this may cause erosion of mould surface and turbulence. The optimum pouring rate is, therefore, a compromise taken to ensure that the entire mould cavity is filled before the start of solidification, without causing erosion of mould surfaces and undue turbulence.

On the basis of experience and experiments, some empirical relationships have been suggested for estimating the pouring time T_p. The relationship for cast iron and steel castings are given below.

Cast iron castings:

$$T_p = K(1.4 + \frac{t}{14.6})W^{0.5} \quad \text{(for } W \leq 450 \text{ kg)} \qquad (2.1)$$

$$T_p = K(1.2 + \frac{t}{16.6})W^{0.33} \quad \text{(for } W > 450 \text{ kg)} \qquad (2.2)$$

Steel castings:

$$T_p = (2.4 - 0.4 \log W)W^{0.5} \qquad (2.3)$$

Here T_p is the pouring time (s), W is the mass of casting (Kg), t is the average thickness of casting (mm) and K is the fluidity factor which depends on the iron composition and pouring temperature.

2.4.6 The Gating System

The gating system serves to deliver the molten metal to all sections of the mould cavity through a combination of channels. It is designed to:

(i) Minimize turbulent flow so that absorption of gases, oxidation of metal and erosion of mould surfaces are minimized,

(ii) Regulate the entry of molten metal into the mould cavity,

(iii) Ensure complete filling of mould cavity, and

(iv) Promote a temperature gradient within the casting so that all sections irrespective of size and shape could solidify properly.

The basic elements of the gating system are:

- Pouring basin
- Sprue
- Sprue well
- Choke
- Runner
- Ingates
- Blind
- Riser

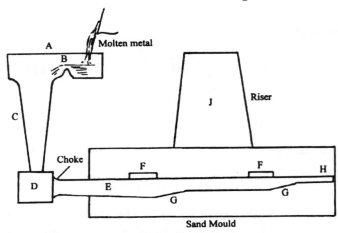

Fig. 2.10 The gating system.

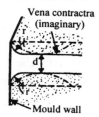

Fig. 2.11 Choke.

The molten metal from the ladle is poured into the *pouring basin* (A) from where it moves into the Sprue and through the runner to other areas. The basin maintains a constant pouring head through weir (B) and holds back slag and dirt which float on the surface of the molten metal.

The *Sprue* is the vertical channel (C) through which metal is brought down to enter the runners. It is usually tapered downwards as shown in Fig. 2.10 to prevent aspiration of gases through the Sprue. As the molten metal comes down, it gains velocity and requires a smaller cross-section to maintain a constant flow rate. Therefore, to prevent vortex formation and sucking of gases the cross-section of Sprue is reduced gradually from the top to the bottom. The ideal shape will perhaps be parabolic, but tapered shape is generally used because it is easier and economical to produce.

At the bottom of the Sprue is a reservoir for molten metal called the *Sprue well* (D). It serves to dissipate the kinetic energy of the falling stream of molten metal. The molten metal then changes direction and flows into the runner (E) through the choke. The *choke* (Fig. 2.11) is provided to avoid creation of vacuum when the molten metal enters the runner. Because of sudden change in the flow direction, the liquid metal stream tends to contract around sharp corner due to momentum effect. The constricted region is called *vena contracta* where vacuum tends to get created. In order to avoid this, the choke is provided with a shape which conforms to the shape of vena contracta. Alternately, sharp change in flow direction may be avoided by providing a corner radius which approximately fits the vena contracta.

Runner (E) is the horizontal channel which takes the molten metal from the Sprue well and distributes it to the ingates (F) around the mould cavity. A runner is generally located in the parting plane and has a trapezoidal cross-section. When the molten metal is to enter the mould cavity through multiple ingates, the cross-section of the runner is reduced at each runner break-up (G) to allow equal distribution of molten metal through all the ingates (Fig. 2.10). The main purpose of ingates is to feed the molten metal into the mould cavity at a rate which is consistent with the solidification rate. Ingates have smaller cross-sectional area if the casting solidifies slowly and larger cross-sectional area for faster solidification rate.

The first molten metal to enter the mould is relatively cooler and is most likely to contain dirt, slag and sand particles. The *blind* (H) is provided essentially to trap this relatively cold material and foreign particles.

Risers (J) are reservoirs designed and located to feed molten metal to the solidifying casting to compensate for solidification shrinkage. In order to perform this function, the risers are designed to solidify after the casting. Further, the volume of riser should be sufficient to compensate for solidification shrinkage. A large volume riser has longer solidification time, but it increases the cost. The riser should, therefore, be designed for minimum possible volume while maintaining a solidification time longer than that of the casting. The flow of liquid metal from the riser to the solidifying casting occurs only during the early part of the solidification process. This means that the volume of riser should be much more than the shrinkage volume. A value of three times the shrinkage volume is generally considered to be adequate. Volumetric shrinkage values of some of the common foundry materials are given in Table 2.4.

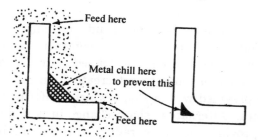

Fig. 2.12 Chill.

Table 2.4 Solidification shrinkage of common foundry metals.

Material	Shrinkage%
Aluminum	6.6
Brass	4.5
Copper	4.9
Gray cast iron	1.9 to negative
Medium carbon steel	2.5 - 3.0
White cast iron	4.0 - 5.5

To increase the cooling rate of casting, *chills* are often used. These are essentially heat sinks in the form of chill blocks or thin fins made of high thermal-conductivity materials (Fig. 2.12). Similarly, to decrease the cooling rate of the riser, some exothermal compounds are applied on the outside surface of the riser, or insulating sleeves are put around the riser.

The location of the riser is another important consideration to ensure that the liquid metal from the riser is supplied to the desired locations within the casting. To achieve this, a riser should be located in such a way that directional solidification is obtained. Since the heaviest section of the casting solidifies last, the riser should be located to feed this section. The heaviest section will now act as a riser for other sections which are not so heavy or thick (Fig. 2.13). For small castings, a single riser can feed the entire casting, but more

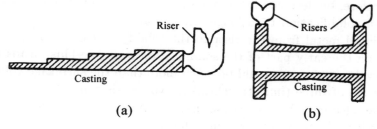

(a)   (b)

Fig. 2.13 Riser location.

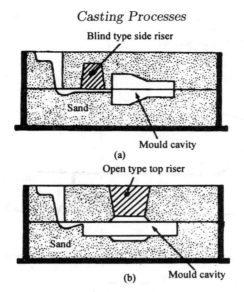

Fig. 2.14 Types of risers.

than one riser is required for large castings. The number of risers and their locations will depend upon the casting configuration.

Various types of risers are in use (Fig. 2.14). The *top riser* is located on top of the casting and has the advantage of additional pressure head and smaller feeding distance over the *side riser* which is placed adjacent to the casting. *Open risers* have top surface open to the atmosphere, while the *blind risers* are completely surrounded by the moulding sand. Blind risers are generally bigger in size because of additional surface area for heat conduction.

2.4.7 Cooling and Solidification

After the molten metal is filled in the mould cavity, it is allowed to solidify into the desired shape. The solidification process decides the structural features of cast material and controls the properties of casting. Also, several casting defects, such as porosity and shrinkage defects can be minimized through control of the solidification process. The basic understanding of the cooling and solidification process is, therefore, essential for producing sound castings.

Pure metals melt and freeze at a particular temperature called the *equillibrium melting* or *freezing temperature* above which they are completely liquid and below it completely solid. The liquid metal is poured into the mould cavity at a temperature much higher than the freezing temperature to allow sufficient time for the liquid metal to flow into all corners of the mould cavity before it begins to freeze. The difference between the pouring temperature and the freezing

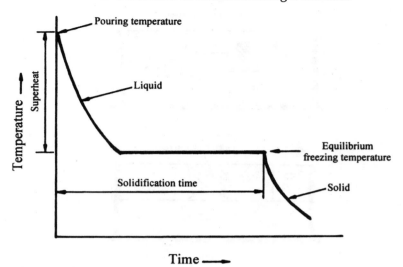

Fig. 2.15 A typical cooling curve for pure metal.

temperature is known as *superheat*. The superheated liquid cools rather quickly to its freezing point and the temperature then remains constant while the metal loses its heat of fusion. Further cooling occurs only after the metal is completely solid. A typical cooling curve depicting these phenomena is shown in Fig. 2.15.

Liquid metals solidify because the arrangements of atoms in a solid crystal are at lower free energy than those in the liquid state. At freezing temperature, both liquid and solid atoms interchange positions, the change in free energy is zero and equilibrium is obtained. Solidification of liquid metal will not start unless the free energy or temperature is lowered.

The change from liquid to solid phase does not occur all at once. The process of solidification starts with *nucleation*, the formation of stable solid particles within the liquid metal. Nuclei of solid phase, generally a few hundred atoms in size, start appearing at a temperature below the freezing temperature. When a pure metal is suddenly cooled, formation of solid crystals is sometimes inhibited and the cooling curve falls below the freezing point as shown in Fig. 2.16. Such cooling of liquid metals below the freezing temperature is called *supercooling* or *undercooling*. In pure metals when supercooling is around 20% of the freezing temperature, nucleation starts and the heat of fusion causes the temperature to return to the freezing level. Supercooled atoms are in highly agitated conditions and only those nuclei that have a critical size are stable. In fact two factors that govern nucleation are the free energy available from solidification pro-

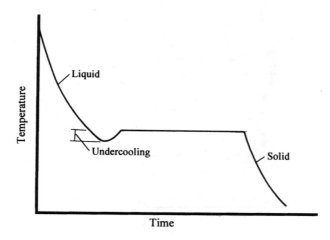

Fig. 2.16 Cooling curve depicting undercooling.

cess, and the energy required to form a liquid-solid interface. The
net effect of these two factors is that the total energy of a nucleus
reaches a maximum only at a particular particle size for a given supercooling and it is this critical size particle that must be created
for the nucleus to be stable. Increase in supercooling increases the
free energy available from liquid-solid transformation, thus decreasing the critical size required for stability but the thermal fluctuations
which tend to create stable nuclei decreases. These effects cause the
nucleation rate to first increase and then decrease with an increase in
supercooling, giving a maximum value. Presence of foreign particles
in the molten metal sufficiently alters the liquid-solid interface energy
to initiate nucleation, thereby reducing the supercooling requirement
for initiation of nucleation. Sometimes foreign particles (nucleating
agents) are added to the molten metal to increase nucleation.

Once a stable nucleus is formed, the second phase of solidification-
the *growth* of grains begins by acquiring atoms from the liquid. The
growth rate also depends upon the extent of supercooling. With
an increase in supercooling, it reaches a maximum value and then
drops off. In fact, the rate of growth and nucleation rate follow the
same general trend with supercooling. Growth of crystals occurs in
all directions but is faster along the crystallographically favourable
directions. The direction of growth also depends upon the cooling
direction and the rate at which heat is extracted. Growth ceases on
solidification of all the liquid metal.

When liquid metal is poured into the mould cavity, it gets su-

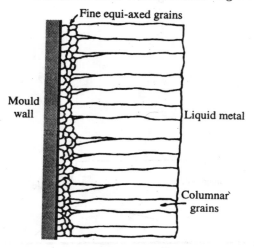

Fig. 2.17 Formation of thin shell of fine equiaxed grains at mould walls (After Heine, Loper & Rosenthal, 1976).

percooled at the mould walls and nucleation starts on these surfaces. Since the extraction of heat is greatest at the mould walls, small randomly-oriented crystals grow near the mould faces. Thus, nucleation is predominant during the early stages of solidification and as a consequence, a thin skin or shell of fine equiaxed grains are produced as shown in Fig. 2.17. During the formation of this thin skin, the latent heat of fusion is released and the remaining liquid metal soon loses most of the supercooling. Further nucleation, therefore, gets restricted and grain growth starts. The liquid metal now begins to freeze on to the thin skin and the thickness of the solidified metal grows progressively inwards towards the centre. The growth rate depends upon the rate of heat transfer from the casting. Only those grains which have favourable orientation will grow in the cooling direction and the net effect is a zone of long columnar grains with their axes perpendicular to the mould face as shown in Fig. 2.18(a). The grains that are less favourably oriented are blocked from further growth.

In a typical solid-solution alloy, the columnar grains do not extend upto the centre of casting but are interrupted by an inner zone of equiaxed grains as shown in Fig. 2.18(b). Thus, alloys generally produce a partially columnar and partially equiaxed grain structure. The inner zone of equiaxed grains can be extended throughout the casting (Fig. 2.18c) by the addition of a nucleating agent or catalyst (Fig. 2.18c). Typical nucleating agents that promote equiaxed grains in castings are sodium, magnesium and bismuth.

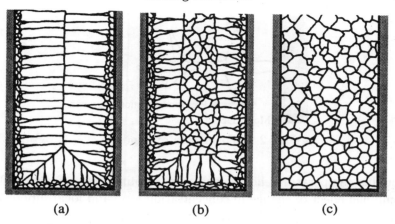

Fig. 2.18 Cast structure of metals: (a) pure metals, (b) alloys and (c) through addition of nucleating agents (After Heine, Loper & Rosenthal, 1976).

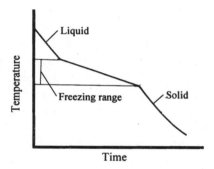

Fig. 2.19 Cooling curve for alloys.

In alloys, such as iron-carbon system, freezing or solidification occurs over a range of temperature (Fig. 2.19). The freezing range depends upon the alloy system and the composition of alloys. When such a metal is poured into the mould cavity and cooled to the freezing temperature, no fine line of demarcation exists between the solid and liquid metal. In this case, the 'start of freezing' is initiated at the mould surface and it progresses towards the centre of the casting. Here 'start of freezing' implies that grain formation while progressing towards the centre (cooling direction) does not solidify the metal completely but leaves behind islands of liquid metal in between the grains which freeze later after further cooling. In this type of solidification, the composition of solidifying metal differs from that of the liquid metal. The concentration level of alloying element in liquid is obviously higher and this affects the solidification process. Also an increase in liquidus concentration level tends to lower the

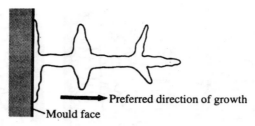

Fig. 2.20 Formation of dendrite.

liquidus temperature, hence local supercooling gets affected. The combined effect of change in concentration level and local supercooling causes the initial columnar grains to branch, and the branches in turn branch again. The result is the formation of a branched grain skeleton (Fig. 2.20) which resembles a tree and is known as *dendrite* (Greek *dendron*-tree like).

When the cooling rate and the resulting thermal gradient is such that it produces supercooling which promotes nucleation, a fine grain size is obtained. Most commercial alloys when poured into the mould cavity and allowed normal cooling produce columnar grains near the mould surfaces and equiaxed grains near the centre of casting as shown in Fig. 2.18b. The same alloy when treated with a nucleating agent produces relatively fine grained structure (Fig. 2.18c) since it reduces the amount of supercooling required for nucleation.

The dendrite network that is formed during solidification of alloys often makes the movement of liquid metal to compensate for solidification shrinkage difficult. Consequently, the risk of having voids within the casting (micro porosity) increases. This will adversely affect the strength and ductility of the cast material. A common way of reducing this risk is the use of *chills*, which are cold blocks of high thermal conductivity metals, placed adjacent to the mould cavity. They are essentially large heat sinks and are used to accelerate the cooling rate and promote directional solidification. Sometimes chills are placed within the mould cavity so that heat is quickly absorbed to increase the rate of solidification. Since internal chills ultimately become part of the casting, they must be made of the same alloy.

2.4.8   Solidification Time

Cooling curves are useful for depicting several important features of a casting. The pouring temperature decides the extent of superheat, which is the difference between the pouring and freezing temperatures as shown in Fig. 2.15. The superheat indicates the total time that is available for completely filling the mould cavity. The higher the superheat, the more is the time available to complete the pouring before the material begins to solidify. Higher superheat will be required for intricate castings so that fluidity of the liquid metal is sufficient to enter all corners of the casting before freezing starts. The superheat is generally decided on the basis of fluidity requirements.

Once the material cools down to the freezing tempearture, the solidification process for pure metals does not require a decrease in tempearture and a plateau in the cooling curve, called *thermal arrest*, is obtained. The *solidification time* is the total time required for the liquid metal to solidify that is, the time from the start of pouring to completion of solidification as indicated in the figure.

The solidification time t_s has been found to be directly proportional to volume V and inversely proportional to surface area A. Here volume governs the heat content while the surface area indicates the area through which heat is extracted. For a large variety of shapes and sizes, the relationship which has come to be known as *Chvorinov's rule* is of the form

$$t_s \propto (\frac{V}{A})^n$$

or

$$t_s = K(\frac{V}{A})^n \tag{2.4}$$

Here K is the mould constant which depends upon:

- The metal being cast,
- The moulding material,
- The average mould thickness, and
- The amount of superheat.

The value of K is generally estimated by casting a test specimen under the same conditions. The value of exponent n has been found to vary between 1.5 to 2, but this value is usually assumed to be 2.

2.4.9 Riser

As discussed earlier, the liquid metal once poured in the mould cavity shrinks during cooling. This shrinkage occurs in three stages:

(i) When the temperature of liquid metal drops from pouring to freezing temperature,

(ii) When the metal changes from liquid to solid state, and

(iii) When the temperature of the solid phase drops from freezing to room temperature.

The shrinkage for stage (iii) is compensated by providing shrinkage allowance on pattern, while the shrinkage during stages (i) and (ii) are compensated by providing risers. *Risers* are added reservoirs of molten metal designed to feed metal to the solidifying casting to compensate for solidification shrinkage. The volumetric shrinkage for common metals are given in Table 2.4. Additional feed metal must be provided by the riser in case of bulging of mould cavity due to excessive metal pressure or because of soft mould. Since the riser has to compensate for shrinkage and for bulging of the mould cavity, it must stay fluid till the entire casting is filled. In fact the riser must solidify last, otherwise the liquid metal will start flowing from casting to the riser. The riser should also promote directional solidification. In view of these, the variables that are considered to be important are:

- Shape of riser,
- Size of riser, and
- Location of risers.

Since the metal in the riser is subject to the same laws of solidification as the metal in the casting, Chvorinov's rule can be used to decide the shape of the riser. For long solidification time, the shape of the riser should be such that V/A is maximum, that is, the shape chosen should have a small surface area per unit volume. A sphere would therefore be an ideal shape for a riser. Spherical risers, however, cause considerable practical difficulties in pattern and mould making, and hence the next most effective shape- a cylinder- is generally chosen.

The size of a riser can be estimated using Chvorinov's rule by assuming the riser solidification time to be greater than the solidification time of casting. For design purposes, the riser is generally assumed to take 25% longer time to solidify than the casting. Thus,

$$(t_s)_{Riser} = 1.25(t_s)_{Casting} \tag{2.5}$$

or

$$(\frac{V}{A})^2_{Riser} = 1.25(\frac{V}{A})^2_{Casting} \tag{2.6}$$

since mould constant K is same in both cases.

For a cylindrical riser contained entirely within the mould (blind riser) as shown in Fig. 2.14(a),

$$V_{Riser} = \frac{\pi D^2 H}{4} \tag{2.7}$$

and

$$A_{Riser} = \pi DH + 2(\frac{\pi D^2}{4}) \qquad (2.8)$$

where D and H are diameter and height of the cylinder.
Now,

$$(\frac{V}{A})_{Riser} = \frac{\frac{\pi D^2 H}{4}}{\pi DH + \frac{\pi D^2}{2}} = \frac{\frac{D}{4}}{1 - \frac{D}{2H}} \qquad (2.9)$$

or

$$D = 4(\frac{V}{A})_{Riser}(1 - \frac{1}{2r}) \qquad (2.10)$$

where

$$r = \frac{H}{D} \qquad (2.11)$$

By specifying r, the volume of riser can be estimated using the above equations.

Similarly, for a cylindrical riser that sits on top of the casting with top open to the atmosphere (open riser) as shown in Fig. 2.14(b),

$$V_{Riser} = \frac{\pi D^3 r}{4} \qquad (2.12)$$

$$A_{Riser} = \pi D^2 r + \frac{\pi D^2}{4} \qquad (2.13)$$

$$(\frac{V}{A})_{Riser} = \frac{Dr}{4r + 1} \qquad (2.14)$$

and

$$D = (\frac{V}{A})_{Riser}(\frac{4r + 1}{1}) \qquad (2.15)$$

Again the riser volume can be estimated by specifying r.

The minimum riser volume required to compensate for shrinkage is usually taken as three times the shrinkage volume of casting since the liquid metal flows from the riser only during the early part of solidification. Therefore, it must be ensured that the volume of riser estimated using Chvorinov's rule is more than three times the shrinkage volume of casting.

Risers are located in such a way that it permits directional solidification. If the design of casting produces solidification which sweeps from one end to the other, the riser may be located at the end of the mould cavity freezing last (Fig. 2.13a). This way the solidification will move towards the riser and it can continuously feed molten metal to the mould cavity and compensate for shrinkage. When such solidification is not possible, the casting is sub-divided into several sections with each section solidifying towards their respective risers.

In castings requiring multiple risers, each portion of the casting may be treated as individual simple casting. Risers must be located closest to the heaviest sections of the casting and its cross-section should be larger to ensure that it solidifies last (Fig. 2.13b). Since heavy sections of a casting freeze last, they act as risers for thinner sections while the risers feed the heavy sections.

The risers are generally located a short distance away from the casting since they are ultimately separated from the final casting. The connecting channel between the casting and the riser should therefore be large enough to ensure that this link does not freeze before the casting.

2.4.10   Cleaning and Finishing

After the casting has solidified, it is removed from the mould and cleaning and finishing operations are performed before it is sent for quality assurance and inspection. The following steps are involved in cleaning and finishing operations:

(i) The casting is taken out of the mould by shaking and the moulding sand is recycled often with suitable additions.

(ii) The remaining sand, some of which may be embedded in the casting, is removed by means of *shot blasting*. In this process, the casting surface is continuously impacted by small round particles of steel, bronze, copper or glass. Steel balls are generally used for harder castings, while balls made of bronze, copper or glass are used for softer non-ferrous materials.

(iii) The excess material in the form of Sprue, runners and gates alongwith the flashes formed due to the flow of molten metal into the gaps between two mould halves are removed. In brittle material castings they are broken manually, while in the case of ductile materials they are removed by sawing or grinding.

(iv) The entire casting surface is then cleaned by either shot blasting or chemical pickling.

(v) Sometimes the finished castings are subjected to various heat treatments to reduce residual stresses or to improve its mechanical properties.

2.4.11   Casting Defects

Defects in castings may occur due to one or more of the following reasons:

(i) Fault in design of casting and pattern

(ii) Fault in design of mould and core

(iii) Fault in design of gating system and riser

(iv) Improper choice of moulding sand

(v) Improper metal composition

(vi) Inadequate melting temperature and rate of pouring

Common casting defects are classified in Table 2.5 and are shown in Fig. 2.21

Surface Defects

The surface defects are usually due to poor design and quality of sand moulds leading to insufficient strength. Poor ramming is often the main cause.

Blow is a relatively large cavity produced by gases which displace the molten metal from convex casting surfaces. *Scar* is a shallow blow generally occurring on flat casting surfaces. A scar covered with a thin layer of metal is called *blister*. These defects are essentially due to inadequate permeability or improper venting. Sometimes excessive gas forming constituents in the moulding sand also cause these defects.

Drop is an irregularly-shaped projection on the cope surface caused by dropping of sand. A *scab* results when an upheaved sand gets separated from the mould surface and the molten metal flows between the displaced sand and the mould. *Penetration* occurs when the molten metal flows between the sand particles in the mould. Fusion of sand particles on the casting surface in these cases produces a rough surface often with a glossy appearance. These defects are generally due to inadequate strength of sand mould but can also occur when the fluidity of metal is excessively high.

Buckle is a vee-shaped depression on the surface of a flat casting caused by expansion of a thin layer of sand at the mould face. A proper amount of volatile additivies in moulding sand could eliminate this defect by providing room for expansion.

Internal Defects

The internal defects found in castings are mainly due to trapped gases and dirty metal. Gases get trapped due to hard ramming or improper venting. These defects also occur when excessive moisture or excessive gas forming materials are used for mould making.

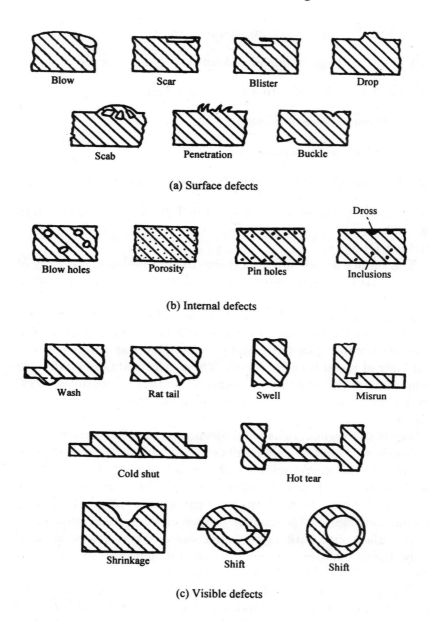

Fig. 2.21 Casting defects (After Ghosh & Mallik, 1985).

Table 2.5 Classification of casting defects.

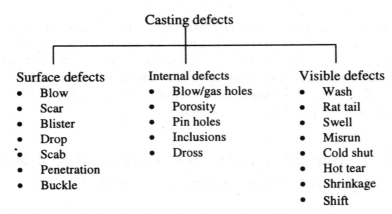

Surface defects	Internal defects	Visible defects
• Blow	• Blow/gas holes	• Wash
• Scar	• Porosity	• Rat tail
• Blister	• Pin holes	• Swell
• Drop	• Inclusions	• Misrun
• Scab	• Dross	• Cold shut
• Penetration		• Hot tear
• Buckle		• Shrinkage
		• Shift

Blow holes, *porosity* and *pin holes* are essentially entrapped gas bubbles in the casting. Blow holes are large spherical-shaped gas bubbles, while porosity indicates a large number of uniformly distributed tiny holes. Pin holes are tiny blow holes appearing just below the casting surface.

Inclusion and *dross* are due to dirty metal coming into the mould cavity. While inclusion refers to non-metallic particles in the metal matrix, lighter impurities that appear on the casting surface are called dross.

Visible Defects

A large number of casting defects can be seen with the naked eyes. Such visible defects are either due to the mould or the molten metal. Insufficient mould strength, improper mould setting, insufficient metal, low pouring temperature and bad design of casting are some of the common causes leading to visible casting defects.

Wash is the low projection near the gate caused by erosion of sand by the flowing metal. *Rat tail* is a long, shallow, angular depression caused by expansion of sand. *Swell* is the deformation of vertical mould surface due to hydrostatic pressure caused by moisture in the sand.

Misrun and *cold shut* are caused by insufficient superheat provided to the liquid metal. When this causes the metal to freeze before reaching the farthest point, the defect is called misrun. Cold shut, on the other hand, occurs when liquid metal fed from two sides fails to fuse at the centre.

Hot tear is the crack in the casting caused by high residual stresses. *Shrinkage* is essentially solidification contraction and occurs when an improper riser is used.

Misalignment between two halves of the mould or incorrect core location gives the casting defect called *Shift*.

A review of these common defects will indicate that the remedy for one casting defect may be the cause for another. For example, a higher pouring temperature may be required to eliminate misrun or cold shut, but this may cause rat tail or swell due to expansion of sand. Therefore, it is important to select optimum values for input parameters so that defects could be minimized.

2.5   Expendable-pattern & Expendable-mould Casting (Investment Casting)

These processes use expendable moulds and single-use patterns. The pattern is made of a material which is melted out or burned up during casting to create the mould cavity. The pattern, therefore, can be left in the mould and one does not have to worry about parting line, draft and core which are so important in sand casting. Because of these, there are hardly any shape restrictions, and intricate and complex castings can be easily produced. Casting, as before, is removed after breaking the mould.

A typical example in this category of casting is *investment casting*, earlier known as the *lost-wax process* and has existed since ancient times. Two investment casting procedures—the *investment shell casting* and the *investment flask casting* are commonly used. The sequence of operations in a typical shell investment casting is given below:

1. Fabrication of a master pattern: Master pattern is made using easily-worked materials like metal, wood or plastic.

2. Fabrication of a master die: A die can be cast out of low-melting-point metal using the master pattern. Steel or wooden dies are often machined directly eliminating the first step.

3. Preparation of wax patterns: Wax patterns are made by pouring molten wax into the die. After the wax has solidified, it is taken out of the die. Sometimes plastic and frozen mercury are also used in place of wax for making patterns.

4. Assembly of wax patterns: Depending upon the size of the casting several wax patterns are assembled together in the form of a tree or a cluster with a central sprue and runners.

5. Coating of cluster: The cluster is now coated with a thin layer of refractory material. This step is performed by dipping the whole cluster into a thin slurry of very finely ground refractory material mixed with hydrolyzed ethyl silicate, alcohol and a gelling agent.

6. Producing a final layer of refractory material: In this step the coated cluster is dipped repeatedly in the relatively coarsely ground refractory material to achieve the desired thickness of coating.

7. Hardening of coating: Usually the coated cluster is left for drying up and hardening for a few hours.

8. Melting of wax patterns: For this purpose the mould is placed in an oven upside down and the wax is allowed to flow out of the mould which is collected for reuse.

9. Preheating the mould: This is performed by firing the mould at 700-1000°C to impart strength to the mould and ensure the flow of molten metal to all intricate and thin sections.

10. Filling the hot mould: Molten metal is filled in the mould by gravity, vacuum pressure or force.

11. Breaking of the mould: The casting is obtained by breaking the mould.

12. Cleaning of casting: Sprue and runners are now removed and the casting is cleaned and finished.

Figure 2.22 shows these sequences schematically.

The investment flask casting differs from investment shell casting in steps 5, 6, and 7. Here, after assembling the wax pattern around the Sprue, a metal flask is placed around the cluster of patterns and is completely filled with the refractory slurry. After the mould material is set, the wax pattern is melted out of mould to get the cavities for casting.

The investment casting technique is generally used for castings weighing less than 5 kg with maximum dimension less than 300 mm. The thickness is usually restricted to 15 mm. The commonly used metals in investment casting are aluminium, copper, nickel, carbon and alloy steels, stainless steel and tool steel.

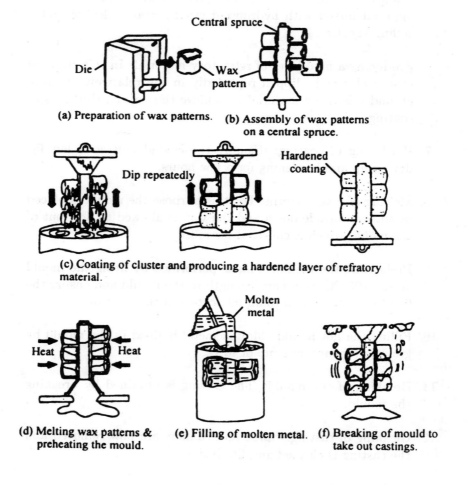

Central spruce

Die

Wax
pattern

(a) Preparation of wax patterns.

(b) Assembly of wax patterns
on a central spruce.

Dip repeatedly

Hardened
coating

(c) Coating of cluster and producing a hardened layer of refratory
material.

Heat   Heat

Molten
metal

(d) Melting wax patterns &
preheating the mould.

(e) Filling of molten metal.

(f) Breaking of mould to
take out castings.

Fig. 2.22 Investment shell moulding (After ASM Metals Handbook, 1988).

2.6 Permanent-mould Casting

While in expendable mould casting a separate mould is required for each casting, in permanent-mould casting processes a metallic mould is repeatedly used. The mould material used has sufficiently high melting temperature to withstand the pouring temperature and thermal stresses. Alloy steels are the most commonly used mould material but gray cast iron is also sometimes used. More recently some refractory metal alloys have found increasing application. Graphite mould have also been used for casting steel.

These processes are generally restricted to casting of lower-melting-point non-ferrous metals because of repeated use of metallic mould. Aluminium, copper and magnesium based alloys have found extensive use.

The mould is generally in two halves, hinged together for easy and accurate opening and closing of mould. Internal cavities are formed with the help of movable or fixed cores. Ejector pins are often provided for removing the solidified casting. Since mould material is not permeable, clearance along parting planes and ejector pins serve as vents. The mould is usually preheated at the beginning of a production run and then maintained at a fairly uniform temperature by controlling the cooling rate by means of fins or water circulation. To prevent the casting from sticking on to the mould walls, various types of refractory coatings are applied to the mould inner surfaces. This coating also prolongs the life of the mould by reducing erosion by the liquid metal. Also, the mould is opened and casting is removed immediately after solidification to prevent shrinking of casting on the mould surface on further cooling.

Besides giving better surface finish and higher dimensional accuracy, these processes provide stronger castings because of better cooling rate. Almost defect-free castings can also be obtained through selective heating and cooling of mould. Since the mould cost is generally high, high-volume production is necessary to be cost effective. Shape limitation is also imposed because the solidified casting has to be readily removable.

Common permanent-mould casting processes are: (a) Gravity-feed permanent-mould casting, (b) Low-pressure permanent-mould casting, (c) Die casting, (d) Centrifugal casting and (e) Continuous casting

2.6.1   Gravity-feed permanent-mould casting

In this process (Fig. 2.23) a permanent mould in two halves is used and the molten metal is poured into the cavity under the force of gravity. This process is performed manually as well as mechanically with the help of casting machines which support the stationary and movable mould halves on its table.

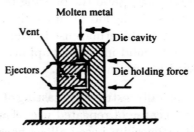

Fig. 2.23 Gravity-feed permanent-mould casting.

The process is widely used for casting aluminium alloys.

2.6.2   Low-pressure Permanent-mould Casting

In this process the mould is placed above the melting furnace and the molten metal is forced to flow into the mould cavity through a vertical tube by applying a low pressure of 50-100 kN/m^2 to the molten bath (Fig. 2.24). Since the molten metal enters the mould cavity under pressure, the mould or die halves should be held together with sufficient force to resist the pressure of the molten metal in the cavity. Since the molten metal does not get exposed to the atmosphere, the process is particularly suitable for casting rapidly oxidizing metals such as aluminium. By controlling the pressure and extracting the molten metal from the bottom of the pool, defects due to turbulance, trapped gases and dirty metal are minimized. Further, since the molten metal is continuously supplied to the mould cavity under pressure, and the pressure is maintained until the casting has solidified, shrinkage is compensated and no riser is required. A thin coating inside the mould cavity ensures good surface quality of the castings.

2.6.3   Die Casting

In die casting the molten metal is forced to flow into a permanent metallic mould under moderate to high pressures, and held under pressure during solidification. Molten metal under pressures upto 150 MPa forces the metal into the intricate details of the cavity and

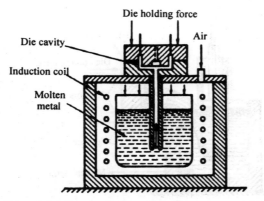

Fig. 2.24 Low-pressure Permanent-mould Casting.

also produces a smooth surface and excellent dimensional accuracy. The mould halves are, however, required to be held together by a sufficiently high die-holding force.

High pressure used in die casting often cause turbulance and air entrapment. In order to minimize these, larger ingates are used. Also, initial pressure is often kept low and is increased to a higher value after the mould is completely filled.

Moulds for die casting processes are usually made from hardened steels and they may contain two or more mould cavities. Multiple-cavity dies are used to cast several small pieces at a time with a common gating system for all the pieces as in the case of investment casting. Dies have a separate section for water-cooling and knock-out ejector pins. These make the die-casting dies and moulds quite expensive, but high production rate and high quality of castings requiring limited finishing justify the cost of the whole process. Basically non-ferrous metals and alloys are used for die-casting, but ferrous castings have also been produced recently.

There are two types of die-casting processes used in practice-the hot-chamber process, and the cold-chamber process.

In *hot-chamber process* the molten metal is pumped from the melting pot directly to the mould cavity at a pressure of around 40 MPa (Fig. 2.25). A mechanical plunger or air-injection system forces the molten metal into the mould cavity through the gooseneck which is partially submerged in the melting bath. This process is basically used for zinc-and tin-based alloys.

The *cold-chamber process* is used for higher-melting-point metals. Here the metal is melted in a separate furnace and a quantity, sufficient for one casting, is transferred to the die-casting machine cylinder, where the plunger feeds it into the mould cavity at pres-

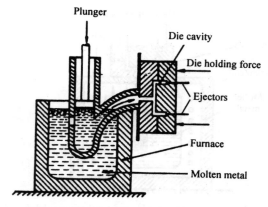

Fig. 2.25 Hot-chamber die casting.

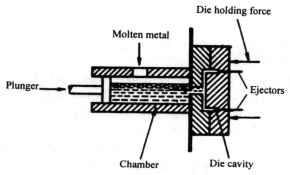

Fig. 2.26 Cold-chamber die casting.

sures upto 150 MPa (Fig. 2.26). This process is commonly used for zinc, magnesium, aluminium and brass alloys.

In all die-casting processes, a die lubricant is applied to the mould surfaces between each operation. Usually graphite or MoS_2 in an oily carrier is used.

2.6.4   Continuous Casting

This process is used to produce blooms, billets, slabs and tubes directly from molten metal. It involves pouring of molten metal into a metallic mould, which has facilities to rapidly cool the poured metal to the freezing level, and extracting the solid product in a continuous manner from the other end.

For this purpose the molten metal is first poured into a holding furnace from where it flows into the mould at a controlled rate. Water cooling jackets are provided to the mould for rapid cooling of the molten metal. The solidified product is then extracted from the other end of the mould at a controlled speed by gripping it between

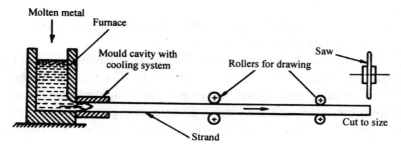

Fig. 2.27 Continuous casting operation.

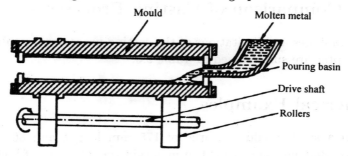

Fig. 2.28 Centrifugal casting process.

rolls. The metal can be further cooled by a direct spray of water. Continuous oscillation of the mould prevents sticking of casting on the mould surface. The process starts with a dummy rod placed into the mould upon which the first molten metal is poured. After solidification the first product is extracted along with the dummy bar which is then separated. The solid product is finally cut to the required size by either a torch or a circular saw. These are shown in Fig. 2.27, which depicts the most commonly used continuous casting operation.

Solid or hollow shapes of uniform cross-section like round, square, rectangular, hexagonal, fluted, scalloped and gear toothed can be conveniently produced by this process. Physical properties and surface finish obtained are also comparable to those obtained from other permanent mould processes. The materials commonly used for casting are copper, aluminium, steel and cast iron.

2.6.5 Centrifugal Casting

A typical centrifugal casting process is shown in Fig. 2.28. Here a permanent mould made of metal or ceramic is rotated at high speed (300 to 3000 rpm). The molten metal is then poured into the mould cavity and the centrifugal force causes the molten metal to conform to the cavity provided in the mould. The inner surface of the casting, however, remains cylindrical.

The process finds wide application in the manufacturing of pipes, bushings, cylinder lines, gears and flywheels. The process can be used for all castable metals and alloys but the commonly used ones are aluminium, steel and cast iron. The process gives castings of good surface finish, dimensional accuracy and external surface details.

2.7   Comparison of Casting Processes

The advantages and limitations of the casting processes described in this chapter are summarized in Table 2.6.

Numerical Examples

Q.1 In a sand mould, a Sprue of 175 mm height and 800 mm² top diameter is provided to maintain the flow rate of liquid at 1,000,000 mm³/s. What should be the diameter at the base of downSprue to prevent aspiration of molten metal? ($g=9815$ mm/s²).

Solution:

Flow Rate $Q = 1,000,000$ mm³/s

Velocity in downSprue

$$\begin{aligned} v &= \sqrt{2gh} \\ &= \sqrt{2 \times 9815 \times 175} \\ &= 1853.4 \ mm/s \end{aligned}$$

Area at the base of downSprue to maintain the flow rate,

$$\begin{aligned} A &= \frac{Q}{v} \\ &= \frac{1,000,000}{1853.4} = 539.5 \ \text{mm}^2 \end{aligned}$$

Q.2 Assuming uniform cooling in all directions, determine the dimensions of a 100 mm cube casting after it cools down to room temperature. The solidificaiton shrinkage for the cast metal is 5% and the solid contraction is 7.5%.

Solution:

Table 2.6 Comparison of casting processes.

Casting Processes	Advantages	Limitations
Sand casting	• Almost any metal can be cast. • No limit on size and shape. • Low equipment cost. • Economical for low-volume production.	• Coarse finish. • Dimensional accuracy not so good. • Finishing required. • Low production rate.
Investment casting	• Almost any metal can be cast. • Good surface finish. • Good dimensional accuracy. • Fairly high production rate. • Intricate shapes can be cast. • Low finishing cost.	• Limitation on part size. • Expensive pattern and mould. • High labour cost.
Permanent mould casting	• Good surface finish. • Goo dimensional accuracy. • High production rate.	• High mould cost. • Suitable for high volume production. • Suitable for casting of simple shapes. • Suitable for low-melting-point metals.

Die casting

- Excellent surface finish
- Excellent dimensional accuracy
- High production rate
- Complex shapes can be cast
- Little or no finishing cost

- Limitation on part size
- High cost of die
- Generally limited to casting of non-ferrous metals

Centrifugal casting

- High production rate
- Good dimensional accuracy and surface finish

- Expensive set-up
- Good for production of cylindrical parts only

Volume of casting $V = 100^3 = 1,000,000$ mm^3

$$\text{Volume after solidification shrinkage} \quad = \quad 10^6 \times (1 - 0.05)$$
$$= \quad 950,000 \text{ mm}^3$$

$$\text{Volume at room temperature} \quad = \quad 950,000 \times (1 - 0.075)$$
$$= \quad 878,750 \text{ mm}^3$$

$$\text{Dimensions of each side of the cube} \quad = \quad (878,750)^{1/3}$$
$$= \quad 95.8 \text{ mm}$$

Q.3 What will be the solidification time for a 1000 mm diameter and 30 mm thick casting of aluminium if the mould constant is 2.0 sec/mm^2?

Solution:

Chvorinov's rule gives solidification time,

$$t_s = K \left(\frac{V}{A}\right)^2$$

Here

$$K = 2 \text{ sec/mm}^2$$
$$V = \frac{\pi \times 1000^2 \times 30}{4} = 23,561,945 \text{ mm}^3$$
$$A = 2 \times \frac{\pi D^2}{4} = \frac{2 \times \pi \times 1000^2}{4} = 1,570,796 \text{ mm}^2$$

Therefore,

$$t_s = 2 \times \left(\frac{23,561,945}{1,570,796}\right)^2$$
$$= 450 \text{ sec or } 7.5 \text{ min}$$

Q.4 Which one of the following casting shapes would have least solidification time (a) a shpere of diameter $D = 25$ mm, (b) a cylinder with both diameter d and height $h = 25$ mm and (c) a cube with length of sides $l = 25$ mm.

Solution:

Solidification time

$$t_s = K \left(\frac{V}{A}\right)^2$$

Therefore,

$$(t_s)_{sphere} = K\left(\frac{\frac{\pi D^3}{6}}{\pi D^2}\right)^2 = \frac{KD^2}{36}$$

$$= \frac{K \times 25^2}{36}$$

$$= 17.36K$$

$$(t_s)_{cyl.} = K\left(\frac{\frac{\pi d^2 h}{4}}{\frac{2\pi d^2}{4} + \pi dh}\right)^2 = K\left(\frac{dh}{2d + 4h}\right)^2$$

$$= 17.36K$$

$$(t_s)_{cube} = K\left(\frac{l^3}{6l^2}\right)^2 = \frac{Kl^2}{36} = \left(\frac{25}{6}\right)^2 K = 17.36K$$

All three will have the same solidification time.

Q.5 For a cylindrical riser of a given volume, determine the diameter-to-length ratio which will maximize the solidfication time.

Solution:

$$\text{Volume of cylinder } V = \frac{\pi}{4}d^2h$$

$$\text{or } h = \frac{4V}{\pi d^2}$$

$$\text{Area of cylinder } A = \pi dh + 2 \times \frac{\pi d^2}{4}$$

$$\text{or } A = \pi d\frac{4V}{\pi d^2} + 2 \times \frac{\pi d^2}{4}$$

$$= \frac{4V}{d} + \frac{\pi d^2}{2}$$

Here d and h are cylinder diameter and height, respectively. Since solidification time

$$t_s \alpha \left(\frac{V}{A}\right)^2$$

maximum solidification time is obtained when A is minimum, that is,

$$\frac{\partial A}{\partial d} = 0$$

or

$$-\frac{4V}{d^2} + \pi d = 0$$

or
$$d^3 = \frac{4V}{\pi} = d^2h$$

or
$$d = h$$

using the above equations for V and A.

Hence
$$\frac{d}{h} = 1$$

for maximum solidification time.

Review Questions

2.1 What are the major limitations of sand casting?

2.2 What are the distinguishing features between pattern and casting?

2.3 What allowances are generally provided on patterns?

2.4 What is shrinkage allowance and what does it compensate?

2.5 List the commonly used patterns for sand casting?

2.6 What is the difference between a split pattern and a match-plate pattern?

2.7 What properties determine the quality of a sand mould?

2.8 Explain the effects of grain shape and size on permeability and green strength of sand mould?

2.9 Why should turbulent flow of liquid metal in mould cavity be avoided during pouring?

2.10 Describe the features of a gating system.

2.11 On what considerations the pouring temperature and pouring time are decided?

2.12 How does solidification of pure metals differ from solidification of alloys?

2.13 What are the three sources of contraction or shrinkage in metal casting?

2.14 What are chills and what is their function?

2.15 What is Chvorinov's rule in casting and in what way it is useful?

2.16 What are risers and what purpose do they serve?

2.17 On what considerations the location of risers is decided?

2.18 Describe the process of nucleation and grain growth in sand casting?

2.19 What are nucleating agents and why are they used in casting?

2.20 Why is it that in most cases solidification does not begin until the temperature of the liquid metal falls somewhat below the equilibrium melting temperature?

2.21 How is directional solidification achieved in metal casting?

2.22 What would be the most effective shape of a riser from (i) ideal point of view and (ii) practical point of view?

2.23 List the common causes of defects in sand casting.

2.24 Explain why hot tearing occurs in sand castings?

2.25 What defects are likely to occur in sand castings when higher pouring temperature is used?

2.26 How shrinkage cavities are formed in sand castings?

2.27 Distinguish between (i) cold shut and misrun, (ii) penetration and drop, and (iii) porosity and pinholes.

2.28 What is the difference between investment shell casting and investment flask casting?

2.29 What will happen if the mould material provides too much restraint to the solidifying and cooling metal in sand casting?

2.30 What are the main advantages of investment casting over other casting processes?

2.31 Why risers are not used in die casting?

2.32 How does air from mould cavity escape in die-casting process?

2.33 What is continuous casting and what advantages does it offer?

2.34 Why are ejector pins required in die casting?

2.35 How is pressure applied on cold-chamber die cast parts?

Chapter 3

Metal Forming

3.1 Introduction

When materials are subjected to external loads, they get deformed. The deformation may be elastic, plastic or fracture, depending upon the load and the properties of the material. Elastic deformation is said to have occurred when the material returns to its original shape on removal of load, and when it does not return to its original shape on removal of load but retains its new configuration, the material is said to have deformed plastically. Further deformation causes the material to fracture resulting in separation of a part of material from the body of material.

The most familiar example of elastic and plastic deformation, and fracture is a simple tensile test in which the specimen is gradually pulled and the corresponding increase in length is recorded. The result (Fig. 3.1) shows a linear range OA where the increase in length is proportional to the applied load. This portion of the curve is the elastic range since the specimen in this range returns to its

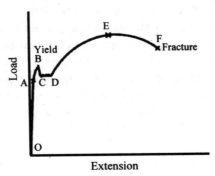

Fig. 3.1 Load-extension curve.

original length when the applied load is removed. Point A therefore represents the *proportionality limit*. Sometimes the material remains elastic little beyond the linear range, say upto point B. This point usually defines the *elastic limit*. Generally, there is little difference between points A and B. Beyond the elastic limit is the plastic range since removal of load leaves permanent extension in the specimen. The point which represents the initiation of plastic deformation is called the yield point. In mild steel (steel containing 0.3 to 0.6% carbon) yielding is usually accompanied by a sudden drop in load and increase in the length of the specimen at constant load depicted by region CD of the curve. Most metals and alloys, however, do not show this yielding behaviour and the transition from elastic to plastic deformation is usually gradual. The load-extension curve is not linear in the plastic range and this increased load-bearing ability of the material is due to strain-hardening or work-hardening.

Many metals after undergoing plastic deformation develop greater resistance to further plastic flow. This phenomenon of metal becoming stronger is known as *strain-hardening*. In the plastic zone, therefore, two opposing factors determine the load required for a given extension. While strain-hardening leads to an increase in load, the reduction in area decreases the load required. At some point E, the strain-hardening is no longer able to cope up with the reduction in area of cross-section of the specimen and a maxima in load occurs. This point defines the ultimate stress of the material. Beyond point E, localized deformation in the specimen decreases the cross-sectional area and further elongation occurs in the thinned portion only which ultimately leads to fracture of the specimen at point F. Point E is therefore an indicative of an instability condition and is called the *instability point*.

The load-extension diagram (Fig. 3.1) is essentially the nominal stress-strain curve of the material since *nominal stress* is defined as the load divided by the original cross-sectional area of specimen and *nominal/engineering strain* as the extension per unit original length. The cross-section of the specimen changes as the test proceeds, therefore, the actual stress to which the specimen is subjected should be based on the current area of cross-section rather than the original cross-sectional area. The *true stress* σ can be computed by dividing the current load P by the current area of cross-section A. Thus,

$$\sigma = \frac{P}{A} \qquad (3.1)$$

The corresponding *true strain e* is defined as a summation of incre-

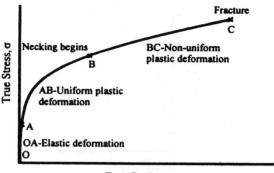

Fig. 3.2 True stress-true strain curve.

mental strains, that is

$$e = \int_{\ell_o}^{\ell} \frac{d\ell}{\ell} = \ln(\frac{\ell}{\ell_o})$$ (3.2)

where ℓ_o is the original length of the specimen and ℓ is the current length.

Use of true strain has two advantages. The true strain are additive in sequential processes that is,

$$\begin{aligned}
e &= e_1 + e_2 + e_3 \\
&= \ln\frac{\ell_1}{\ell_o} + \ln\frac{\ell_2}{\ell_1} + \ln\frac{\ell_3}{\ell_2} \\
&= \ln\frac{\ell_3}{\ell_o}
\end{aligned}$$ (3.3)

Secondly, the volume constancy condition, neglecting the small change in volume due to elastic deformation, can be simply written as

$$e_x + e_y + e_z = 0$$ (3.4)

where e_x, e_y, e_z are true strains in three mutually perpendicular directions.

The tensile test data when plotted as true stress-true strain curve (Fig. 3.2) shows that the material continues to strain-harden up to the point of fracture. Unlike mild steel, most metals do not have a well-defined yield point. For such metals (Fig. 3.3), the yield point is generally defined by drawing a line parallel to the elastic line but displaced by an offset strain of 0.2%. The value of stress obtained in

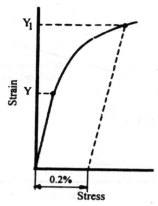

Fig. 3.3 Yield point location.

this manner will produce a given but tolerable amount of permanent deformation.

The load-extension curve (Fig. 3.1) shows that at the point of instability E, the rate of increase in load due to strain-hardening is just balanced by the rate of decrease in load due to diminishing area of cross-section since the load is maximum, that is, $dP = 0$. This condition defines the point' of instability B (Fig. 3.2) on the true stress-true strain curve.

From equation (3.1),

$$\frac{dP}{dl} = \sigma \frac{dA}{dl} + A \frac{d\sigma}{dl} = 0 \qquad (3.5)$$

at B. Now, the incompressibility (volume constancy) condition, $A_o l_o = A l$, gives

$$\frac{dA}{dl} = -\frac{A}{l} \qquad (3.6)$$

and equation (3.5) reduces to

$$\frac{d\sigma}{\sigma} = \frac{dl}{l} = de \qquad (3.7)$$

or

$$\frac{1}{\sigma} \frac{d\sigma}{de} = 1 \qquad (3.8)$$

where de is the incremental strain.

If we now draw a tangent at the point of instability I (Fig. 3.4), the length DF will be 1 ($Z=1$) and the strain at instability e_c can be evaluated.

The total plastic work W_p upto the point of instability is

$$W_p = \left[\int_0^{e_c} \sigma de\right] \qquad (3.9)$$

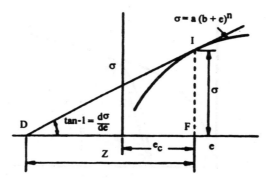

Fig. 3.4 Point of instability.

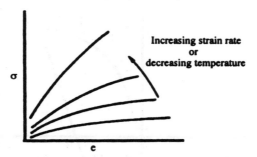

Fig. 3.5 Effects of strain rate and temperature.

Several attempts have been made to suggest an empirical equation for the true stress-true strain curve and relationship most commonly used is of the form

$$\sigma = a(b + e)^n \qquad (3.10a)$$

where a, b and n are constants for a given material and their values can be evaluated experimentally. Since $b \approx 0$ for most metals, the above relationship reduces to the form

$$\sigma = ae^n \qquad (3.10b)$$

The stress-strain curve of a material depends on the type of loading, rate of straining and deformation temperature. The type of loading may be tensile, compressive, bending, shearing or any combination of these, and these influence the yield stress of the material. In general, the yield strength of material decreases with increase in temperature, while the rate of straining or speed of deformation causes an increase in the yield strength (Fig. 3.5).

In a simple tensile test, if the applied load is removed after the material has been stretched beyond the yield point and loaded again,

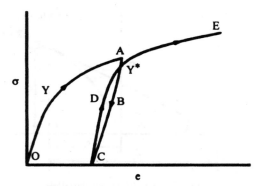

Fig. 3.6 Hysterises loop.

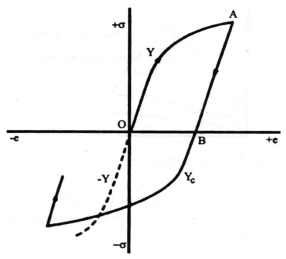

Fig. 3.7 Bauschinger effect.

a *hysterises loop* is formed (Fig. 3.6). On unloading from point A, the material follows a curve (ABC) which is almost parallel to the elastic loading path (OY). The total strain e is now reduced to e_p only because of release of elastic strain or elastic recovery e_r. This *elastic recovery*, sometimes called *springback*, is greater in materials that have higher yield stress, and lower elastic modulus. On reloading from point C, the path followed is CDY*, giving hysterisis loop. Yielding of the material now occurs at point Y^*, a value larger than that obtained at Y.

Similarly, if a metal plastically deformed to point A (Fig. 3.7) and unloaded and then subjected to a compressive load, yielding occurs at a lower stress value ($Y_c < Y$). This is because of residual stress developed in the metal due to loading and unloading. This *Bauschinger effect* is present in all plastic deformation processes involving reversal

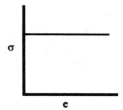

Fig. 3.8 Stress-strain curve for a rigid, perfectly-plastic material.

of stresses.

The loading pattern in forming processes vary considerably. The type of loading may be tensile, compressive, shearing, bending or any combination of these. Thus, plastic deformation may occur in three-dimensions and under a complex set of stresses.

In order to get an estimate of the load required to cause plastic deformation in metal forming, the effects of several parameters on yield strength of material are generally not considered. This is done in order to arrive at a solution. Often the effects of work-hardening is ignored and the stress-strain curve is idealised as shown in Figure 3.8 which represents the behaviour of a rigid, perfectly-plastic material. Also the total strain e, which is a sum of elastic strain e_e and plastic strain e_p, is approximated as equal to e_p only since e_e in forming operations is much smaller than e_p. Thus, $e \approx e_p$.

The strength of a material is usually described in terms of yield stress (σ_y) and the ultimate stress (σ_u). The term *ductility* is often used to describe the ability of a material to undergo plastic deformation before fracture and is usually expressed as the percentage elongation or the percentage strain at fracture. Thus, a larger percentage strain at fracture would mean higher ductility. A brittle material, on the other hand, fractures at a very small plastic strain. A material is generally considered brittle or nonductile if it fractures at a percentage elongation of less than 5%.

Toughness is the other mechanical property which describes the ability of a material to absorb energy in the plastic range. Toughness is therefore a function of both strength and ductility. The index commonly used to define toughness is the total area under the stress-strain curve which represents the energy required to produce fracture in a unit volume of material.

It is clear from the stress-strain curve (Fig. 3.2) that metals can be plastically deformed between yield point and point of instability. The yield point defines the minimum stress required to cause plastic deformation and the instability point represents the maximum strain a material can withstand before the onset of necking or local-

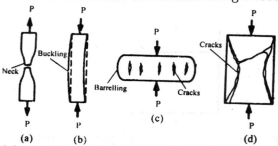

Fig. 3.9 (a) Necking and fracture of ductile materials, (b) buckling of ductile materials, (c) barrelling and cracking of ductile materials and (d) fracture of brittle material.

ized deformation. The strain at the onset of localized deformation (instability) is sometimes used as an index of the formability of the material.

The state of stress has a profound influence on the extent of plastic deformation that can be achieved. Plastic deformation is limited by necking and fracture of ductile material under a tensile load, buckling of ductile materials under a compressive load, fracture of brittle materials under a compressive load and cracking of the barrelled surface of ductile materials under compressive load. These are illustrated in Figure 3.9. Thus the forming limit is that at which uniform flow ceases and is determined by whichever of the above failures occur first and it obviously depends on the state of stress.

As mentioned earlier, plastic deformation in metal forming generally takes place under complex set of stresses and in three-dimensions. Such problems are difficult to analyze and often a two-dimensional (plane strain) model is considered. In *plane strain deformation*, plastic flow occurs entirely in one plane with no deformation in the direction perpendicular to the plane. Consider the case of compression of a plate between two flat dies (Fig. 3.10). When the width W_1 is much smaller than W_2, the lateral strains (strains along z-direction) are negligible and the deformation everywhere is parallel to (x, y) plane. Thus, plastic strain e_z is zero and volume constancy condition (Eq. 3.4) gives $e_x = -e_y$.

3.2 Mechanism of Plastic Deformation

When metals solidify from molten state, the atoms arrange themselves in well-ordered patterns called crystals. Such solids are called crystalline solids. The whole solid is seldom composed of one single crystal, but a very large number of small, randomly-oriented crystalline grains form the whole solid. Such materials are called

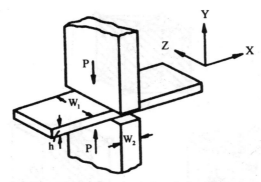

Fig. 3.10 Plane strain deformation.

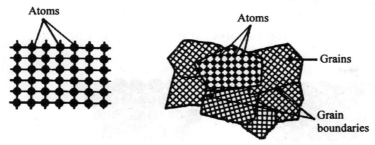

Fig. 3.11 (a) Single crystal and (b) polycrystalline solid.

polycrystalline solids. Figure 3.11 shows a single-crystal and a poly-crystalline solid. The patterns generally found in most metals are:

(a) Body-centred cubic (bcc)
(b) Face-centred cubic (fcc)
(c) Hexagonal close-packed (hcp)

Table 3.1 Crystal structure of some common metals.

bcc	fcc	hcp
• Chromium	• Aluminium	• Cobalt
• Iron (below 910°C)	• Copper	• Magnesium
• Molybdenum	• Iron	• Zinc
	(between 910-1400°C)	• Zirconium
• Tungsten	• Lead	
• Vanadium	• Nickel	

These *crystal structures* are shown in Figure 3.12.

These structures are formed on the basis of energy minimization. Tungsten forms a bcc structure and aluminium forms an fcc structure because less energy is required to form these structures. The

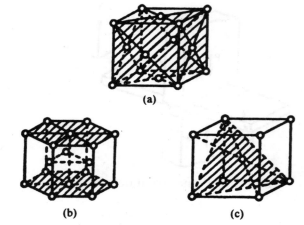

(a)

(b)   **(c)**

Fig. 3.12 Crystal structures (a) bcc, (b) fcc and (c) hcp.

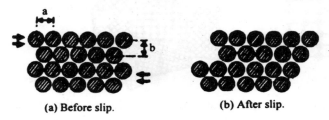

(a) Before slip.   **(b) After slip.**

Fig. 3.13 Plastic deformation in perfect crystal.

same metal at different temperature can form different structures. Iron, for example, forms bcc structure below 910°C and an fcc structure between 910 to 1400°C. The crystal structures found in some common metals are indicated in Table 3.1.

Plastic deformation is primarily due to shearing of atomic planes over one another, similar to the distortion of a pack of cards when one card slides over the another. Consider a crystal lattice with regularly spaced atoms (Fig. 3.13a). When sufficiently high shear force is applied as shown, the upper layer of atoms move to the right and the lower layer to the left and finally settle down as shown in Figure 3.13(b). The atoms are again in equilibrium and will remain so even after the external force is removed. The crystal lattice, therefore, undergoes a permanent deformation, termed as plastic deformation which cannot be recovered upon withdrawal of the external force.

The shear stress (τ) required to cause slip in single crystals is directly proportional to a, representing the atomic density of the plane, and inversely proportional to b, the distance between the atomic

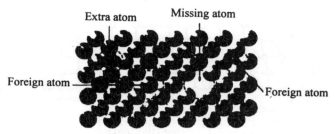

Fig. 3.14 Imperfections in crystal structure.

planes, that is $\tau \propto a/b$. The shear stress required to cause slipping therefore decreases as a/b decreases. This will cause slip to occur along planes of maximum atomic density, or on planes with large interplanar spacing.

Defining slip system as a combination of slip plane and its direction of slip, the number of slip systems in a bcc structure is 48. That is, an external shear force can operate on any one of these systems and cause slip. The required force to effect plastic deformation is, however, large because of relatively high a/b ratio. Materials with such structures (tungsten and molybdenum) will, therefore, possess high strength and moderate ductility.

In fcc structure there are 12 slip systems (four close-packed planes, each containing three close-packed directions). Here the probability of a system being oriented for slip is moderate but the required shear stress is relatively low since a/b ratio is smaller. Materials in this group (aluminium and copper) will therefore have moderate strength but excellent ductility.

The fcc crystals have only three slip systems, so the probability of slip is also low but because of closed-packing of atoms the shear force required for plastic deformation is rather low. Such materials (magnesium and zinc) are generally brittle or have low ductility.

The experimental values of shear stress required to produce a slip in metal crystals have been found to be one or two orders of magnitude less than theoretically estimated values. This discrepancy has been explained in terms of imperfections which are always present in the crystal structure. These defects and imperfections could be line defects (dislocations), point defects (vacancy or missing atom, interstitial atom or extra atom, and impurity or foreign atom), bulk imperfections (voids, and inclusions or non metallic elements) and planer imperfections (grain boundaries). Some of these defects are shown in Figure 3.14.

Dislocations are localized imperfections or disruptions in the regular, symmetrical arrangement of atom in the structure of metals.

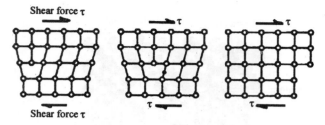

Fig. 3.15 Edge dislocation.

Consider a simple example of edge dislocation (Fig. 3.15) which shows the movement of an edge dislocation across the crystal lattice when a shear force is applied. The shear force required to cause slip on a slip plane containing a dislocation is much less than the shear force required for slip on a perfect plane. The action is similar to moving a carpet by forming a hump at one end and moving it to the other end. The force required to move the carpet in this manner is much less than the force required to slide the carpet.

Although dislocations help in slip, but with increasing deformation, more and more dislocations move and interfere with each other or become entangled. The movement of dislocations is also impeded by barriers such as impurities, inclusions and grain boundaries. Because of these impediments in the movement of various dislocations, the shear stress required for slip increases, resulting in increase in the strength of the material. This increase in the strength due to entanglements is known as *strain hardening* or *work hardening*.

Metals commonly used for manufacturing are polycrystalline, that is, they are composed of many randomly oriented crystals. The deformation within each crystal of a polycrystalline metal, however, proceeds in the manner described above. Since the lattice structure grains are not aligned in the same orientation, the applied force causes different deformation in various crystals. Also the slip lines do not cross over from one grain to another since grain boundaries act as a barrier to dislocation movement. Therefore polycrystalline solid with finer grain structures (more grains per unit area) will have higher strength. Larger grain size, on the other hand, provides small boundary area and results in lower strength.

3.3   Hot and Cold Working

Metal forming processes have been generally classified as hot or cold working. When the working temperature of the material is above its recrystallization temperature, the process is called *hot working* and

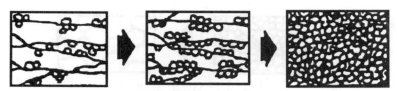

Fig. 3.16 Recrystallization.

when the operation is carried out below the recrystallization temperature, the process is called *cold working*. Often *warm working* is also classified which refers to operations carried out in the transition zone between hot and cold working. The classification, hot, warm and cold working, is therefore essentially on the basis of working temperature.

Plastic deformation results in deformation of grains and grain boundaries and a general increase in strength by creating many additional dislocations which increases the internal energy of metal being deformed. If this plastically deformed metal is heated to a specific temperature for a certain length of time, new, equi- axed, unstrained grains are formed-replacing the original grains (Fig. 3.16).

This process is called *recrystallization*. The temperature at which recrystallization takes place depends upon the degree of cold work (work-hardening) and is different for each metal. In general, the higher the degree of cold work, the lower the temperature required for recrystallization. This is because the number of dislocations and the energy stored in these dislocations increase as the amount of cold work increases and this energy becomes available for recrystallization. Recrystallization is also a function of time, because it involves movement and exchange of atoms across grain boundaries.

Table 3.2 Recrystallization temperature of some common metals.

Metal	Recrystallization temperature ($^\circ C$)
Aluminium	150
Copper	200
Iron	450
Lead	Room temperature
Silver	200
Tin	Room temperature

The recrystallization temperature for most metals is around 0.5 T_m, T_m being the melting temperature and is generally defined as the temperature at which recrystallization is completed in about an

Fig. 3.17 Grain growth.

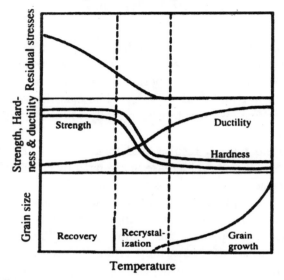

Fig. 3.18 Effects of recovery, recrystallization and grain growth (After Kalpakjian, 1995).

hour. Recrystallization temperature of some common metals as given in Table 3.2.

If the temperature of metal is held above the recrystallization temperature, the new grains formed begin to grow in size and even exceed the original grain size (Fig. 3.17). This phenomenon is called *grain growth* and has adverse affect on the mechanical properties and produce rough surface when deformed.

If the temperature of the metal is held in a certain range below the recrystallization temperature, the stresses in the highly deformed regions are relieved. This recovery process generally occurs in the range of 0.3 to 0.5 T_m and restores some of the original softness with visible change in grain structure.

It now appears that for hot working the temperature must be above 0.5 T_m and for cold working the temperature should be below 0.3 T_m. The transition zone of 0.3 to 0.5 T_m now represents the warm working region. Figure 3.18 summarizes the effect of recovery, recrystallization and grain growth on mechanical properties of material in cold, warm and hot working regions. Considering these effects the advantages and disadvantages of hot and cold working can be summarized as given below.

Hot working: Advantages:

1. Very high reduction is possible without fear of fracture.

2. Deformation energy required is low, hence less powerful equipment are required.

3. The process is faster, hence high production rate.

4. Metal is made tougher because pores get closed and impurities are segregated.

5. The process doesnot change hardness or ductility of the metal since distorted grains soon change into new undeformed grains.

6. Structure can be altered to improve final properties.

Disadvantages:

1. High temperature may promote undesirable reactions.

2. Metallurgical structure may be non-uniform because of cooling history after deformation.

3. Heat-resistant tools are required which are expensive.

4. Close tolerances can not be held because of non-uniform cooling and thermal contraction.

5. Surface finish obtained is poor because of scale formation.

6. Handling of material is not so easy.

Cold Working: Advantages:

1. Good surface finish and better dimensional accuracy is obtained.

2. Strength, fatigue and wear properties are improved.

3. Minimum contamination because of low working temperature.

4. Energy saving since heating is not required.

5. Handling of material is easy.

Disadvantages:

1. Deformation energy required is high, so rugged and more powerful equipment are required. Thus equipment cost is high.

2. Strain-hardening limits deformation.

3. Ductility of metal is reduced.

The popularity of hot-working processes has been primarily due to the fact that metals become softer and more ductile at elevated temperatures. Thus massive deformation can be achieved without loss of plasticity. Cold working - on the other hand - is used mainly to achieve better dimensional accuracy and good surface finish. In fact many cold-working processes have identical hot-working counterparts and in most cases even the equipment are identical, except that cold-working machines are more rugged and powerful. Hot-worked products are invariably the starting material for subsequent cold working.

3.4   Primary Metal-forming Processes

Practically all metals which are not used in cast form are reduced to some standard shapes for subsequent processing. Manufacturing companies producing metals (steel, copper and aluminium) supply metals in the form of ingots which are obtained by casting liquid metal into a square cross-section (approximately 600x600 mm) metallic container. These ingots are then hot rolled to get slabs (500-1800 mm wide and 50 to 300 mm thick), billets (40 to 150 sq mm) and blooms (150 to 400 sq mm). Sometimes continuous casting method is used to directly cast the liquid metal into slabs, billets or blooms. These shapes are then further processed, usually through hot rolling, forging or extrusion, to produce materials in standard forms such as plates, sheets, rods, tubes and structural sections. These standard shapes can be further reduced by using one of the cold working operations such as cold rolling, cold extrusion, deep drawing, wire drawing and tube drawing. to get the final configuration. In fact there are a large number of cold-working processes in use now and invariably more than one process is required to be used for achieving the desired surface finish and dimensional accuracy. The sequence of operations for obtaining some of the standard shapes is depicted in Figure 3.19.

Common primary metal-working operations are rolling, forging, extrusion, tube and wire drawing and deep drawing and these will be briefly described in this chapter. Punching and blanking operations, although not a metal-forming process, have also been included primarily because of their similarity with the deep drawing operation.

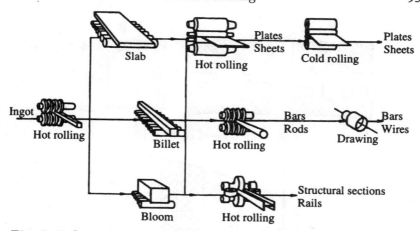

Fig. 3.19 Sequence of operations for obtaining standard shapes.

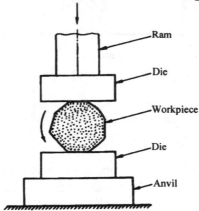

Fig. 3.20 Open-die forging.

3.4.1 Forging

Forging is perhaps the oldest metal working process and was known even during prehistoric days when metallic tools were made by heating and hammering. Forging basically involves plastic deformation of workpiece by compressing it between two dies to achieve the desired configuration. Depending upon the complexity of the part to be produced, forging may carried out with open or closed dies. Simple components can be made by *open-die forging* by compressing the workpiece between two flat plates. Often open-die components are produced by repeated blows imparted by a mechanical hammer. The desired shape in this case is obtained by manually manipulating the workpiece between blows (Fig. 3.20).

In *closed-die forging* (Fig. 3.21) the desired configuration is obtained by squeezing the workpiece between two shaped and closed

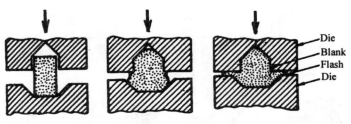

Fig. 3.21 Closed-die forging.

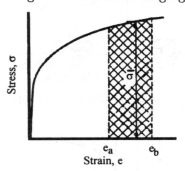

Fig. 3.22 Mean yield stress.

dies. The upper half of the die is attached to the ram and the lower
one to the anvil. On squeezing the die cavity gets completely filled
and the excess metal comes out around the periphery of the die as
flash which is later trimmed off from the forged component. Instead
of press forging, drop forging is also used for close-die forging. In the
latter case, the workpiece kept in the lower die is forged by one or
more blows by a guided falling hammer or ram. In press forging, a
mechanical or a hydraulic press is used to slowly squeeze the workpiece. In this case forging is completed in a single closing of dies,
hence the dimensional accuracy obtained is much better than that
from drop forging.

Both open-die and closed-die forgings can be carried out in hot or
cold state. Cold forging obviously requires higher deformation energy
and is usually carried out for only those materials which are sufficiently ductile at room-temperature. Cold forged parts have better
dimensional accuracy and have good surface finish. Hot forged parts
although require lower forces but give inferior finish and dimensional
accuracy.

The load required for compressing a plate between two parallel
flat dies (Fig. 3.10) can be estimated using the work formula. Assuming no change in volume, the work done per unit volume W/V
in homogeneous deformation is equal to the area of the stress-strain
curve between appropriate strain values (Fig. 3.22).

Thus,

$$\frac{W}{V} = \int_{e_a}^{e_b} \sigma de \qquad (3.11)$$

Here *homogeneous deformation* means that the principal stresses are uniform across the section of the deforming material and that the friction at the interfaces are negligible. The section of material therefore remains geometrically similar and does not distort during deformation.

Equation (3.11) can be simplified if a mean yield stress $\bar{\sigma}$ is considered and e is evaluated from dimension changes. Thus, if a plate of original thickness h_o is compressed to thickness h,

$$\frac{W}{V} = \bar{\sigma} \int_{h_o}^{h} \frac{dh}{h} \qquad (3.12)$$

In terms of incremental work dW, equation (3.12) becomes

$$dW = V\bar{\sigma}\frac{dh}{h} = \bar{\sigma}Adh \qquad (3.13)$$

The external work required to deform the plate through the same height gives

$$dW = pAdh \qquad (3.14)$$

where p is the pressure applied on the die plate. Equating (3.13) and (3.14) the load P required for compression is

$$P = A\bar{\sigma} \qquad (3.15)$$

If the forging conditions are taken to approximate plane strain deformation (negligible lateral spread), then for better approximation $\bar{\sigma}$ may be increased by 15%. Also, 20% increase in load may be allowed as a rough guide for including frictional contribution. Thus,

$$P = 1.2(1.15\bar{\sigma})A \qquad (3.16)$$

3.4.2 Rolling

Rolling is the most extensively used metal forming process and it accounts for almost 90% of the metal produced by forming. In this process, the material to be rolled is drawn by means of friction into the gap between two revolving rolls (Fig. 3.23). The compressive forces applied by the rolls reduce the thickness of the material or changes its cross-sectional area. The shape and size of the product

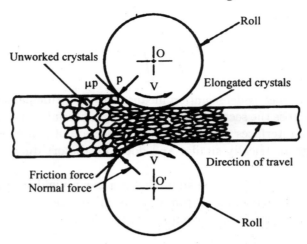

Fig. 3.23 Rolling process.

coming out of the rolls depend upon the roll gap and the contour of the rolls. Various flat and shape rolling processes are depicted in Figure 3.19. Hot rolling is carried out to roll ingots into slabs, blooms or billets. On further hot rolling, plates, bars, rounds, structural shapes and rails are obtained. Because of limitations in equipment and workability of metals, rolling is done in progressive steps, that is, a number of passes through the rolls may be required to get the required configuration.

For example, ten roll passes are required to get a 100×100 mm billet reduced to a 12 mm rod (Fig. 3.24). The initial few passes are designed to merely reduce the cross-sectional area, while the intermediate passes not only reduce the area but also try to bring the shape closer to the final shape. Final or finishing passes bring the material to the required shape and size.

Bars, rods, sheets and strips of most common metals are finished by cold rolling. The main reasons for cold rolling are better dimensional accuracy, good surface finish and improved physical properties.

A variety of roll configurations are used in rolling mills (Fig. 3.25) and they are commonly designated by the number and arrangement of rolls. Two-high and three-high mills are generally used for initial and intermediate passes during hot rolling, while four-high and cluster roll arrangements are used for final passes. The last two arrangements are also preferred for cold rolling because rolls in these arrangements are supported by back-up rolls which minimize roll deflections and produce better tolerance.

Roll materials commonly used are cast iron, cast steel and/or

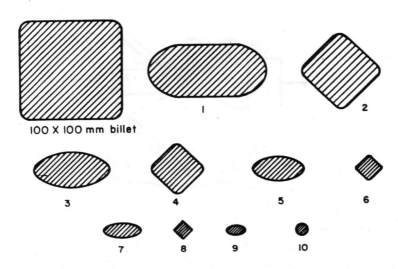

100 X 100 mm billet

Fig. 3.24 Roll passes to get a 12mm rod from 100 X 100 mm billet (After Amstead et al., 1987).

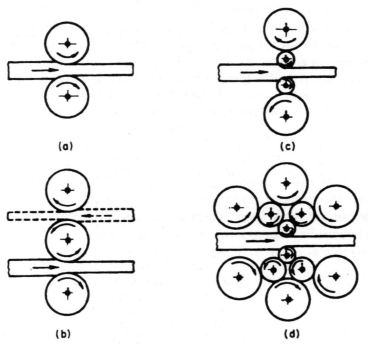

Fig. 3.25 Roll configurations: (a) two-high (b) three-high reversible (c) four high and (d) cluster arrangements.

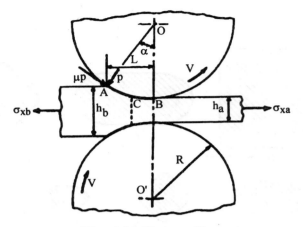

Fig. 3.26 Sheet rolling.

forged steel because of high strength and high wear resistance requirements. Hot rolls are generally rough so that they can bite the
work, but cold rolls are ground or polished to impart good finish.

During rolling the crystals get elongated in the rolling direction
(Fig. 3.23) and the material emerges at a higher speed than it enters. In cold rolling the crystals more or less retain the elongated
shape, but in hot rolling they start to reform after coming out of the
deformation zone.

The peripheral velocity of rolls at entry A (Fig. 3.26) exceeds
that of the strip, which is dragged in if the interface friction is high
enough. In the deformation zone the thickness of strip gets reduced
and it elongates. This increases its linear speed and at exit B it
travels faster than the rolls. Thus there exists a *neutral point* C at
which the surface velocity of strip and rolls are the same and there is
no slip. At this neutral point the direction of friction force reverses.
When the angle of contact α exceeds the angle of friction λ, the
rolls can not draw fresh material into the roll gap. In other words,
the longitudinal component of friction μp must exceed that of radial
pressure p at entry A. Therefore,

$$\mu p \, dA \cos \alpha > p \, dA \sin \alpha \qquad (3.17)$$

or

$$\tan \lambda > \tan \alpha \qquad (3.18)$$

The maximum value of α, say $\alpha^* = \lambda$ is often called the *angle of
bite*. The maximum reduction or draft $(\Delta h = h_b - h_a)$ possible can
be obtained as

$$(\Delta h)_{max} = \mu^2 R \qquad (3.19)$$

since

$$L \approx \sqrt{\Delta h R}; \quad \tan \alpha \approx \sqrt{\frac{\Delta h}{R}} \tag{3.20}$$

Here R is the roll radius and μ is the coefficient of friction.

It is possible to roll with greater draft if the strip is forced into the roll gap. This external pressure is generally limited, so that the angle of contact or angle of nip (α) is not greater than twice the angle of bite (α^*).

An estimate of roll load during rolling of flats can be obtained by considering the process as homogeneous compression. Since α in rolling seldom exceeds 7 degrees, the rolls may be considered to be flat platens of length L, the projected length of the arc of contact. If the width of the strip is w and $\bar{\sigma}$ is the mean yield stress, the load P required to compress the strip can be estimated as

$$P = \bar{\sigma} L w \tag{3.21}$$

$$\text{or} \quad P = \bar{\sigma} w \sqrt{\Delta h\, R} \tag{3.22}$$

Assuming plane strain deformation and allowing for frictional contribution as in Sec. 3.4.1,

$$P = 1.2(1.15\bar{\sigma})w\sqrt{\Delta h\, R} = 1.38\bar{\sigma}w\sqrt{\Delta h\, R} \tag{3.23}$$

The roll torque T can be estimated if the moment of the resultant vertical force about the axis is considered. Taking the perpendicular distance from the line of action of the resultant to the axis to be aL,

$$T = aL\, P \tag{3.24}$$

The fraction a is generally in the range of 0.45 to 0.5. Taking a to be 0.5, the torque required for rolling can be estimated from

$$T = (0.5\sqrt{\Delta h\, R})(1.38\bar{\sigma}w\sqrt{\Delta h\, R}) \tag{3.25}$$

or

$$T = 0.69\bar{\sigma}w\Delta h\, R \tag{3.26}$$

3.4.3 Extrusion

Extrusion is a relatively new process and its commercial exploitation started early in the nineteenth century with the extrusion of lead pipes. Extrusion of steel, however, was possible only after 1930 when extrusion chambers could be designed to withstand high temperature and high pressure.

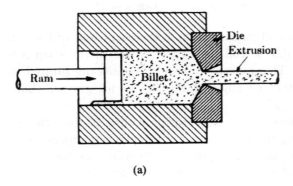

(a)

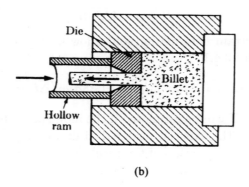

(b)

Fig. 3.27 (a) Direct and (b) indirect extrusion processes.

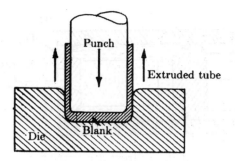

Fig. 3.28 Impact extrusion.

In the extrusion process (Fig. 3.27), the material is compressed in a chamber and the deformed material is forced to flow through the die. The die opening corresponds to the cross-section of the required product. Products having constant cross-section can be produced by this method since the die geometry remains the same during the entire operation. It is basically a hot working process, but cold extrusion is also carried out – particularly for softer materials.

In hot extrusion, a round billet which has been heated above the recrystallization temperature is compressed inside a cylindrical chamber by moving a ram and forced to flow through a die. The die opening may be round, or it may have other shapes. Hot extrusion is usually carried out by direct or indirect extrusion methods, also called forward and backward/reverse extrusion (Fig. 3.27a and b). In *direct extrusion* the metal flow is in the same direction as that of the ram and is the most extensively used extrusion method. Because of relative motion between the heated billet and the chamber walls, friction is severe and this is generally reduced by using molten glass as lubricant – particularly during extrusion of steels. At lower working temperatures, a mixture of oil and graphite is often used. The *indirect extrusion* process where metal flow is in the opposite direction to that of ram movement, is relatively more energy efficient since it reduces friction considerably because there is no friction to overcome along the chamber walls. The process, however, is not used extensively because it restricts the length of extruded components. Also, handling of extruded products through a moving ram is not very convenient.

Two cold extrusion processes that are commonly used are direct extrusion and impact extrusion. *Direct cold extrusion* is similar to direct hot extrusion, except that higher extrusion pressures are required. Because of this the process finds applications in the manufacturing of cams, brackets and small components for automobiles,

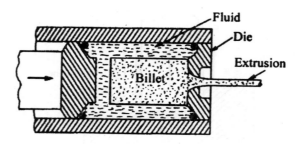

Fig. 3.29 Hydrostatic extrusion.

bicycles and appliances where the pressure required is not very high.

Impact extrusion is somewhat similar to indirect extrusion. Here the punch descends rapidly on to the blank (Fig. 3.28) which gets indirectly extruded on to the punch and to give a tubular section. The length of the tube formed is controlled by the amount of metal in the slug or by the blank thickness. The most common example of parts formed by this method are collapsible tubes for pastes.

Advantages of cold extrusion over hot extrusion are essentially in terms of improved mechanical properties, good control of dimensions, better surface finish and higher production rates.

Hydrostatic extrusion is another method where the required pressure is applied through a fluid medium surrounding the billet Fig. 3.29. Although the presence of fluid inside the extrusion chamber eliminates the container wall friction, the process finds limited industrial application because of need for specialized equipment and toolings and low production rate (high set-up time).

Assuming homogeneous deformation and zero friction, the extrusion pressure p for direct extrusion can be estimated equating the external work to the deformation work. The work done by the ram W_1 in moving through a distance ℓ_o while applying pressure p on the billet of cross-section area A_o is given by

$$W_1 = pA_o\ell_o \qquad (3.27)$$

The deformation work

$$W_2 = V\bar{\sigma}\ln\frac{\ell_1}{\ell_o} = V\bar{\sigma}\ln\frac{A_o}{A_1} \qquad (3.28)$$

where V is the volume of material being deformed from length ℓ_o to ℓ_1 or from cross-sectional area A_o to A_1. Equating (3.27) and (3.28) gives

$$p = \bar{\sigma}\ln\frac{A_o}{A_1} \qquad (3.29)$$

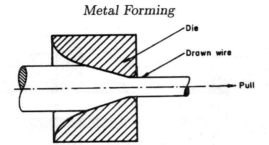

Fig. 3.30 Wire drawing.

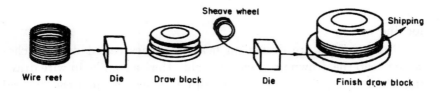

Fig. 3.31 Sequence used for making wires.

since $V = V_o = A_o\ell_o = A_1\ell_1$ from volume constancy condition. For plane strain deformation, the mean yield stress may be increased by 15% and 20% extra work may be included to account for friction. Thus,

$$p = 1.8\bar{\sigma} \ln \frac{A_o}{A_1} \qquad (3.30)$$

3.4.4 Drawing

Large quantities of wires, rods, tubes and other sections are produced by the drawing process which is basically a cold working operation. In this process the material is pulled through a die in order to reduce it to the desired shape and size. In a typical *wire drawing* operation (Fig. 3.30), one end of the wire is reduced and passed through the opening in the die, gripped and pulled to reduce its diameter. Drawing wire gets wrapped round a power-driven capstan which provides the required frictional drag to pull the wire through the die. By successive drawing through dies of reducing diameter the wire can be reduced to a very small diameter. Annealing before each drawing operation permits large reduction in area and descaling treatments prolong the life of the dies. The sequence used for making wires is shown schematically in Figure 3.31. Tungsten carbide dies are generally used for drawing of hard wires, and diamond dies is the choice

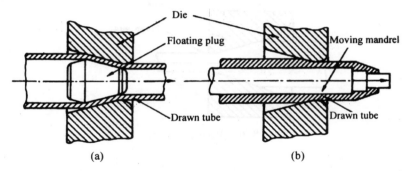

Fig. 3.32 Tube drawing.

for fine wires.

Rods or bars are drawn on heavy benches called drawbenches which keep the drawn products straight. Here also, like in wire drawing, the rod is pointed so that it can be passed through the die and gripped by the jaws which is attached to an endless chain, and travels along a straight track. The drawbenches are usually driven hydraulically for smoother starting action. Bars are generally drawn in short lengths, but smaller diameter rods can be drawn in coiled form.

Tube drawing is also similar to wire drawing, except that a mandrel of appropriate diameter is required to form the internal hole. Two arrangements are shown in Figure 3.32, (a) with a moving mandrel and (b) with a floating plug. Here also the tube is pointed to pass through the die opening and then gripped and drawn in a similar manner as in drawing of rod/bars. The process reduces the diameter and thickness of the tube.

The drawing stress in wire or rod drawing operations can also be estimated by equating external work and deformation work. For homogeneous, frictionless wire drawing, the work done by the drawing force F_1 in moving to the full length ℓ_1 of the drawn wire is given by

$$W_1 = F_1\ell_1 \qquad (3.31)$$

The deformation work or the work done in deforming the wire is

$$W_2 = V\bar{\sigma}\ln\frac{\ell_1}{\ell_o} = V\bar{\sigma}\ln\frac{A_o}{A_1} \qquad (3.32)$$

Hence,

$$F_1 = \frac{V}{\ell_1}\bar{\sigma}\ln\frac{A_o}{A_1} = A_1\bar{\sigma}\ln\frac{A_o}{A_1} \qquad (3.33)$$

since $V = V_o = A_o\ell_o = A_1\ell_1$.

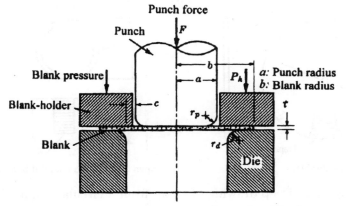

Fig. 3.33 Deep drawing of circular blank.

The reduction in area r is given by

$$r = \frac{A_o - A_1}{A_o} = 1 - \frac{A_1}{A_o} \qquad (3.34)$$

Equation (3.33) now gives

$$F_1 = A_1 \bar{\sigma} \ln \frac{1}{1-r} \qquad (3.35)$$

and the drawing stress

$$\sigma_1 = \frac{F_1}{A_1} = \bar{\sigma} \ln \frac{1}{1-r} \qquad (3.36)$$

Allowing 20% for friction, σ_1 can be taken as

$$\sigma_1 = 1.2\bar{\sigma} \ln \frac{1}{1-r} \qquad (3.37)$$

The maximum reduction is limited by the tensile failure of the drawn section. Neglecting strain-hardening, the failure will occur when the drawing stress equals the yield stress of the drawn wire, that is, when $\sigma_1 = \bar{\sigma}$.

3.4.5 Deep Drawing

Deep drawing is one of the most extensively used operation for making cylindrical shaped parts such as cups and shells from sheet metal. In this process (Fig. 3.33), the blank is placed on top of a die block and the punch pushes the blank into the die cavity. As the blank is drawn into the die cavity compressive stress is set up around the

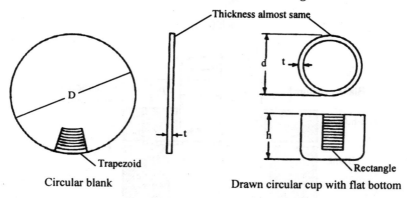

Fig. 3.34 Deep drawing of a cup from a circular blank.

flange and it tends to wrinkle or buckle the flange. This is seen from the way a trapezoid on the outer edge of the blank is stretched in one direction and compressed in another direction to become a rectangle on the cup drawn (Fig. 3.34).

This wrinkling of the blank is prevented by applying a blank-holding force P_h (Fig. 3.33) through a blankholder. Introduction of blankholding force increases friction and hence the required punch load F. Therefore, P_h should be just enough to prevent wrinkling of the flange. The edges of the punch and the die are rounded with radii r_p and r_d for smooth flow of metal. Sufficient clearance (c) is also provided between punch and die so that formed sheet metal (thickness t) could be easily accommodated, that is, $c > t$. Insufficient clearance c and too small corner radii r_p and r_d may cause shearing or tearing of the blank. A drawn cup can be redrawn into a smaller cup but it must be annealed to prevent failure.

Most common punch and die materials are tool steels and cast irons but carbides are also used sometimes.

The size of the blank required for drawing can be estimated from volume constancy. For the circular cup (Fig. 3.34), neglecting thinning and thickening of cup walls, the volume V of blank metal required is obtained from

$$V = \frac{\pi D^2}{4}t = \frac{\pi d^2}{4}t + \pi d\, th \qquad (3.38)$$

or,

$$D = \sqrt{d^2 + 4dh} \qquad (3.39)$$

where D and t are the diameter and thickness of the blank, and d and h are the diameter and height of the drawn cup.

Deep drawing is a complex operation and its not possible to derive an expression for drawing force in a simple manner. The maximum

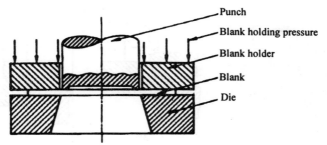

Fig. 3.35 Punching and blanking.

drawing force F_{max} that can be applied for drawing a cup, neglecting friction at the blank-die interface can, however, be estimated from

$$F_{max} = 2\pi dt\sigma_t \qquad (3.40)$$

where σ_t is the tensile strength of the material. An empirical relationship for estimating drawing force F gives

$$F = \pi dt\sigma(\frac{D}{d} - 0.7) \qquad (3.41)$$

where σ is the yield stress of blank material. The relationship takes into account the effects of friction and bending.

3.4.6 Punching and Blanking

Punching and blanking operations are not metal-forming (constant mass) operations but are discussed here mainly because of their similarity with deep drawing. These operations are similar, except for the corner radii and the clearance between punch and die. Like the deep drawing operation, here also the blank is held between punch and die (Fig. 3.35) with the help of a blankholder to prevent wrinkling of the flange. Since the objective of punching and blanking is to remove material from the sheet metal (blank) by causing rupture, the punch and die corners are not provided any radius. As the punch enters the blank, it pushes the material down into the die opening. The stresses developed in the material is highest at the edges of punch and die and the material starts to rupture at these points. If the clearance c between the punch and the die is correct, the two cracks meet to give a clean cut (Fig. 3.36a). If the clearance is too large or too small, the cracks do not meet (Fig.3.36b and c), resulting in unclean edges.

Punching and blanking are identical processes. When the peered sheet metal is the final product, then the operation is called *punching*, and when the final product is removed portion of the sheet, the

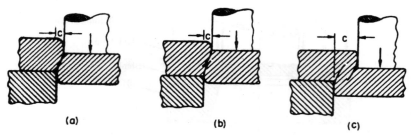

Fig. 3.36 Effect of clearance during blanking and punching.

operation is known as *blanking*. In other words, blanking cuts a whole piece from sheet metal to get a product, punching cuts a hole and the removed material is scrap.

Tool steel is the most common material for punch and die. Carbides are also used, particularly when high production rates are required.

The force required for punching or blanking basically depends on the shear strength of material σ_s and the area to be sheared (tL). The punching force F can, therefore, be estimated from

$$F = \sigma_s t L \tag{3.42}$$

where L is the length of the cut edge and t is the blank thickness.

3.5   Comparison of Metal-forming Processes

The advantages and limitations of primary forming processes described in this chapter are summarized in Table 3.3.

Numerical Examples

Q.1 The true stress-true strain curve of a metal is given as $\sigma = ae^n$, where $a = 850$ MPa and $n = 0.3$. Determine the mean yield stress when a 100 mm long specimen of this metal is stretched to 157 mm.

Solution:

Referring to Figure 3.22,

$$e_a = ln\left(\frac{157}{100}\right) = 0.45; e_b = 0$$

Table 3.3 Comparison of metal forming processes.

Metal Forming Process	Advantages	Limitations
Open-die forging	• Inexpensive tooling and equipment • Simple to operate • Wide range of workpiece sizes can be used • Suitable for low production volume	• Can be used for simple shapes only. • Fairly skilled operators are required. • Production rate is low. • Dimensional accuracy and surface finish achieved are poorer. • Finishing required for achieving final shape.
Closed-die forging	• Suitable for high production rate • Can be used for production of complex shapes • Good dimensional accuracy and reproducibility.	• High equipment and tooling cost. • Appropriate die set for production of each component • More than one step required for each forging • Finishing required for achieving final shape
Hot rolling	• High production rate • Suitable for large reduction • Wide range of shapes (Billets, blooms, slabs, sheets, bars, tubes and structural sections) can be produced.	• High equipment cost. • Suitable for production of large sections • Poor dimensional accuracy and finish

Cold rolling
- High production rate.
- Suitable for production of plates, sheets and foils.
- Good dimensional accuracy and finish.

- High equipment cost.
- Deformation limited to small reductions.

Hot extrusion
- Moderate cost of equipment and toolings.
- Suitable for large reduction.
- Complex sections and long products can be produced.

- Only constant cross-section can be produced.
- Components with thin walls are difficult to produce.
- Lubrication is necessary.
- Dimensional accuracy and finish achieved are not good.

Impact extrusion
- High production rate.
- Good finish and dimensional accuracy.
- Generally no finishing is required.
- Suitable for production of thin sections.

- Suitable for production of light components from softer materials.
- Deformation limited to small reductions.

Process	Advantages	Limitations
Drawing	• Low equipment and tooling cost. • Good surface finish and dimensional accuracy. • High production rate. • Long lengths of rounds, tubings, square and angles can be produced.	• Deformation limited to small reductions. • Production of constant cross-sections only. • Lubrication is necessary.
Deep drawing	• High production rate. • Moderate equipment and tooling cost. • Good surface finish.	• Limited to forming of thin sheets. • Forming of shallow or deep parts of simple shapes only. • Finishing required
Punching and blanking	• High production rate. • Low cost of labour. • Almost any shape can be obtained. • Moderate equipment cost.	• Limited to thin sheet applications. • Cost of tooling can be high.

Mean yield stress e_a

$$\bar{\sigma} = \frac{1}{e_a - e_b} \int_{e_b}^{e_a} \sigma de$$

$$= \frac{1}{e_a - e_b} \int_{e_b}^{e_a} ae^n de$$

$$= \frac{1}{e_a - e_b} \left[\frac{ae^{n+1}}{n+1} \right]_{e_b}^{e_a}$$

$$= \frac{1}{0.45} \cdot \frac{850(0.45)^{1.3}}{1.3} = \frac{850(0.45)^{0.3}}{1.3} = \frac{669.4}{1.3}$$

$$= 514.9 MPa$$

Q.2 What will be value of strain hardening exponent n of a metal that will give a mean yield stress value which is three-quarters the final stress value after deformation?

Solution:

Given $\bar{\sigma} = 0.75\sigma f$

$$\bar{\sigma} = \frac{1}{e_f} \int_0^{e_f} ae^n de$$

$$= \frac{ae_f^n}{1+n}$$

Therefore,

$$\frac{ae_f^n}{1+n} = 0.75\sigma f = 0.75ae_f^n$$

or

$$0.75(1+n) = 1$$
$$n = 0.33$$

Q.3 A 5 mm diameter rod of a metal that has true stress-true strain relationship, $\sigma = 895e^{0.5}$ MPa, is subjected to tensile forces. What is the minimum diameter that can be achieved?

Solution:

The specimen can be stretched upto the point of instability where

$$\frac{1}{\sigma}\frac{d\sigma}{de} = 1$$

From equation $\sigma = ae^n$,

$$\frac{1}{\sigma}\frac{d\sigma}{de} = \frac{nae^{n-1}}{ae^n} = \frac{n}{e} = 1$$

or

$$e_I = n = 0.5$$

The final diameter d_f achievable can be evaluated as

$$e = ln\left(\frac{l_f}{l_o}\right) = ln\left(\frac{A_o}{A_f}\right) = ln\left(\frac{d_o^2}{d_f^2}\right)$$

Therefore,

$$\frac{d_o^2}{d_f^2} = \exp(0.5)$$

and

$$d_f = \sqrt{25/\exp(0.5)}$$
$$= 3.89 \text{ mm}$$

Q.4 A cylindrical workpiece of diameter 30 mm and height 30 mm is to be cold forged in a press to a height of 20 mm. The press is capable of exerting a maximum force of 1,000,000 N. If the true stress-true strain curve of the material is $\sigma = 400e^{0.2}$ and $\mu = 0$, indicate whether or not this can be achieved on this press.

Solution:

Load required for compression

$$P = A_f\bar{\sigma} \quad (A_f : \text{final area}; \bar{\sigma} : \text{mean yield stress})$$

$$A_f = \frac{V}{h_f}$$

$$= \frac{\pi(30)^2 30}{4 \times 20} \quad (V : \text{Volume}; h_f = \text{final height})$$

and

$$e_f = ln\left(\frac{30}{20}\right) \quad (e_f : \text{final strain})$$

$$\sigma = ae^n$$

Therefore,

$$\bar{\sigma} = \frac{1}{e_f} \int_o^{e_f} ae^n de = \frac{ae_f^n}{1+n} = \frac{400(ln1.5)^{0.2}}{1.2}$$

$$P = \frac{\pi(30)^2 30}{4 \times 20} \cdot \frac{400(ln1.5)^{0.2}}{1.2}$$
$$= 294,898.7 \text{ N}$$

Since P is less than 10,00,000 N, the deformation required can be achieved on this press.

Q.5 A 40 mm flat plate is to reduced to 30 mm in a single pass cold rolling operation. Determine the minimum required coefficient of friction if the roll diameter is 600 mm.

Solution:

Maximum reduction $(\Delta h)_{max} = \mu^2 R$

Given $\Delta h = t_o - t_f = 40 - 30 = 10$ mm

$$R = \frac{600}{2} = 300 \text{ mm}$$

Therefore,

$$\mu = \sqrt{\frac{\Delta h}{R}} = \sqrt{\frac{10}{300}} = 0.183$$

the required value of μ.

Q.6 The thickness of a plate is to be reduced from 50 mm to 25 mm in a number of cold rolling passes. The roll radius is 350 mm and the coefficient of friction is estimated to be 0.15. For equal draft for each pass determine the number of passes required and the draft for each pass.

Solution:

Maximum permissible draft for each pass

$$(\Delta h)_{max} = \mu^2 R = 0.15^2 \times 350 = 7.88 \text{ mm}$$

Minimum no. of passes required

$$(n)_{min} = \frac{h_o - h_f}{(\Delta h)_{max}}$$
$$= \frac{50 - 25}{7.88}$$
$$= 3.17 \text{ or } 4 \text{ passes}$$

Draft per pass

$$\Delta h = \frac{50 - 25}{4} = 6.25 \text{ mm}$$

Q.7 A 20 mm plate is to be reduced to 18 mm in a single rolling pass. Determine the roll force and torque per unit width when roll diameter is 500 mm and the stress-strain curve of work material is $\sigma = 600e^{0.22}$ MPa.

Solution:

Roll load/unit width

$$\frac{P}{w} = \bar{\sigma}\sqrt{\Delta h R}$$

$$\Delta h = 20 - 18 = 2 \text{ mm} = 0.002 \text{ m}$$

$$R = 250 \text{ mm} = 0.25 \text{ m}; \quad e_f = ln\left(\frac{20}{18}\right) = 0.105$$

$$\bar{\sigma} = \frac{1}{e_f}\int_o^{e_f} ae^n de = \frac{ae_f^n}{1+n}$$

$$= \frac{600(0.105)^{0.22}}{1.22}$$

$$= 300 \text{ MPa}$$

Substituting these values,

$$\frac{P}{w} = 300\sqrt{0.002 \times 0.25} = 3.36 \text{ MN}$$

$$= 3,360,000 \text{ N}$$

Roll torque per unit width

$$\frac{T}{w} = \alpha L \frac{P}{w}$$

Here

$$\alpha = 0.5$$
$$L = \sqrt{\Delta h R} = \sqrt{0.002 \times 0.25} = 0.0112 \text{ m}$$
$$\frac{P}{w} = 3.36 \text{ MN} = 3,360,000 \text{ N}$$

Substituting these values,

$$\frac{T}{w} = 0.5 \times 0.0112 \times 3,360,000$$

$$= 18816 \text{ N-m}$$

Q.8 A 75 mm long billet that has a 35 mm diameter is reduced to a diameter of 20 mm through direct extrusion. If $\sigma = 750e^{0.25}$ MP is the stress-strain relationship for the work material, determine the extrusion ratio and the ram pressure.

Solution:

Extrusion ratio r is defined as

$$
\begin{aligned}
r &= \frac{A_o}{A_f} \\
&= \frac{d_o^2}{d_f^2} \\
&= \frac{(35)^2}{(20)^2} \\
&= 3.06
\end{aligned}
$$

Strain

$$
\begin{aligned}
e_f &= ln\left(\frac{l_f}{l_o}\right) \\
&= ln\left(\frac{A_o}{A_f}\right) \\
&= ln3.06 \\
&= 1.12
\end{aligned}
$$

$$
\begin{aligned}
\bar{\sigma} &= \frac{1}{e_a - e_b}\int_{e_a}^{e_b} ae^n de \\
&= \frac{1}{e_f}\int_o^{e_f} ae^n de \\
&= \frac{ae_f^n}{1+n} \\
&= \frac{750(1.12)^{0.25}}{1.25} = 493.7
\end{aligned}
$$

Therefore, extrusion pressure

$$
\begin{aligned}
p &= \bar{\sigma}ln\left(\frac{A_o}{A_f}\right). \\
&= 4937 \times 1.12 \\
&= 552.94 \text{ MP}
\end{aligned}
$$

Q.9 A 3.0 mm diameter wire is drawn to a diameter of 2.5 mm. If the stress-strain curve of wire material is given by $\sigma = 500e^{0.3}$ MPa, determine the drawing stress required to achieve this reduction.

Solution:

$$\text{Reduction} \quad r = \frac{A_o - A_f}{A_D}$$

$$= 1 - \frac{d_f^2}{d_o^2} = 1 - \frac{(2.5)^2}{(3.0)^2}$$

$$= 0.306$$

$$\text{Drawing stress} \quad \sigma_d = \bar{\sigma} ln \frac{1}{1-r}$$

$$\bar{\sigma} = \int_o^{e_f} ae^n de = \frac{ae_f^n}{1+n}$$

$$e_f = ln\left(\frac{l_f}{l_o}\right) = ln\left(\frac{A_o}{A_f}\right) = ln\left(\frac{d_o^2}{d_f^2}\right)$$

$$= ln\left(\frac{3.0^2}{2.5^2}\right) = ln 1.44 = 0.365$$

Therefore,

$$\bar{\sigma} = \frac{500 \times (0.365)^{0.3}}{1+0.3} = 284.26 \text{ MPa}$$

and

$$\sigma_d = 284.26 \times ln\left(\frac{1}{1-0.306}\right)$$

$$= 284.26 \times 0.365$$

$$= 103.84 \text{ MPa}$$

Q.10 A flat bottom cup of inside diameter 70 mm and height 50 mm is to be deep drawn from a blank of 3 mm thickness. Determine the required diameter of blank.

Solution:

Equating blank and cup volume,

$$\frac{\pi D^2 t}{4} = \frac{\pi d^2 t}{4} + \pi dht$$

where D is the blank diameter, and d and h are cup diameter and height, and t is the blank thickness. The above equation assumes that thickness t remains constant. Therefore,

$$
\begin{aligned}
D &= \sqrt{d^2 + 4dh} \\
\text{or} \quad D &= \sqrt{(70)^2 + 4(70 \times 50)} \\
&= 137.5 \text{ mm}
\end{aligned}
$$

Q.11 What is the maximum possible reduction that can be achieved when the work material is perfectly plastic metal and the interface is frictionless?

Solution:

The drawing stress

$$\sigma_d = \bar{\sigma} ln \frac{1}{1-r}$$

The maximum possible draw stress is equal to yield strength of material. Therefore,

$$\frac{\sigma_d}{\bar{\sigma}} = 1 = ln \frac{1}{1 - r_{max}}$$

or

$$
\begin{aligned}
r_{max} &= \frac{2.72 - 1}{2.72} \\
&= 0.63
\end{aligned}
$$

Q.12 A blanking operation has to be performed on a 2 mm thick steel to obtain 75 mm diameter pieces. If the shear strength of the material is 450 MPa, determine the blanking force required for this operation.

Solution:

The blanking force

$$F = \sigma_s t L$$

where

$$\sigma_s = 450 \text{ MPa} ; t = 2 \text{ mm}; L = \pi d = 75\pi$$

Substituting these values,

$$
\begin{aligned}
F &= 450 \times 2 \times (\pi \times 75) \\
&= 212057.5 \text{ N}
\end{aligned}
$$

Review Questions

3.1 What is instability point of stress-strain cruve? How this point can be identified?

3.2 What is the significance of point of instability in metal-forming processes?

3.3 Why polycrystalline materials exhibit strain-hardening when subjected to plastic deformation?

3.4 Explain briefly the mechanism of plastic deformation.

3.5 Distinguish between cold, warm and hot working.

3.6 What is the significance of recrystallisation temperature in metal forming?

3.7 What is plane strain deformation? How this can be achieved during compression between two flat dies?

3.8 Why is cold-worked metal annealed?

3.9 Why is 'springback' an important consideration in cold-forming processes?

3.10 Compare open and closed die forging.

3.11 Why is flash desirable in closed-die forging?

3.12 How roll force can be reduced in flat rolling?

3.13 Why are hot rolled products generally limited to standard shapes and sizes?

3.14 Why are a number of rolling passes required to obtain a rolled rod/bar?

3.15 What is neutral point in rolling process?

3.16 What is angle of bite and what is its significance in the rolling process?

3.17 Why advantages are gained by using cluster arrangement of rolls or cluster mill for rolling?

3.18 List the common ways of extruding metals.

3.19 Distinguish between direct and indirect extrusion.

3.20 What is the primary shape limitation of extrusion process?

3.21 What are the important variables that affect the extrusion pressure?

3.22 What are commonly used materials for making wire drawing dies?

3.23 Why are rods drawn in draw benches?

3.24 Why the drawing stress should never exceed the yield strength of material during wire drawing?

3.25 What is the primary benefit of tube drawing with floating plug?

3.26 What happens when a cup is drawn from sheet metal?

3.27 What purpose is served by blank-holding force?

3.28 How is the clearance between punch and die decided for deep drawing?

3.29 Why are blanked edges generally not smooth?

3.30 What measures can be taken to improve the quality of sheared edges in blanking?

Chapter 4

Processing of Plastics

4.1 Introduction

Plastics are organic solids (natural or synthetic resins, or their compounds) that can be made to flow easily by heat or by pressure or by a combination of both to form definite shapes. Properties of plastic materials substantially differ from those of metal and hence their processing also differs. Plastic components are generally fabricated by a single operation rather than a sequence of operations as in the case of metals. With plastics, large and complex shapes can be formed as a single unit, thus eliminating various complicated assembly operations. Plastic fabrication processes often provide the required surface finish and precision eliminating the need for additional finishing operations.

Plastics are polymer materials and the properties of the finished product greatly depend upon the choice of their manufacturing process which, in turn, depends on the type or nature of polymer. Polymers, as indicated in Chapter 1 (sec. 1.4.5), are broadly classified as thermoplastics, thermosets and elastomers. The first two are commonly called plastic, while the third one as rubber. *Plastic*, therefore, refers to a group of engineering materials consisting of large macromolecules that exhibit plastic characteristics, that is, they can be shaped or formed by inelastic deformation.

Plastics (derived from the Greek word, *plastikes*, means it can be moulded and shaped) find wide application in consumer and industrial products because of their unique and diverse properties. Plastics are light in weight, with an average specific gravity of 1.4, which makes these materials suitable for producing light-weight components used in automobiles, aircrafts and sporting goods. Although tensile strength of some plastics is low, their strength-to-weight ra-

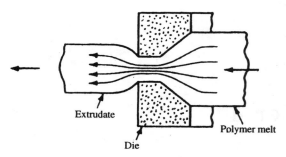

Fig. 4.1. Die swell.

tio is often comparable with heat treated alloy steels and titanium alloys.

Plastics are, however, inferior to metals from the point of view of their mechanical properties. Most of the plastics are prone to dimensional instability with substantial creep and cold flow at all temperatures. Some plastics get affected by moisture. Operating temperature of most of the plastic materials is low, generally ranging from 65 to 315°C, which is considerably lower than the operating temperature of metals. Rigidity and fatigue strength of plastics are also substantially lower than most of metals.

The behaviour of plastics becomes more and more prominent as the temperature increases. Its viscoelastic behaviour manifests itself in the form of shape memory during forming and shaping. Thus, when the polymer melt is transformed from one shape to another, it tends to remember its previous shape and attempts to regain its original shape. Figure 4.1 illustrates this during extrusion of polymer melt. Here the extruded material tends to grow in size, indicating the tendency to return to its original shape. This behaviour is commonly known as *die swell*. The amount of swelling depends on the time the polymer melt spends in the die cavity and the land. The longer the time it spends in the die, the lower is the amount of swelling. Thus, viscosity and viscoelasticity behaviour of polymer melt are important considerations in the selection of material, processing technique, and process parameters.

All plastic forming and shaping processes require heating of plastic so that it flows. This liquid plastic or *polymer melt* has two important properties — viscosity and viscoelasticity — which are important for forming and shaping of plastics. *Viscosity* is defined as resistance to flow and is a measure of internal friction that arises when velocity gradient is present in fluid. Thus, the more viscous the fluid is, the higher is the internal friction and the greater is the resistance to flow. *Viscoelasticity*-as the name suggests — is a combination of viscosity and elasticity and this property determines the strain experienced by a material when subjected to a combination of stress and temperature over time. Figure 4.2 shows the response of a viscoelastic material when subjected to stress below yield point. Here the strain gradually increases under applied stress and also decays gradually when stress is removed.

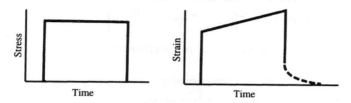

Fig.4.2. Viscoelastic properties.

4.2 Forming and Shaping of Plastics

A wide range of plastic materials are available and the fabrication method to be used for converting them into the desired shape depends upon the type or nature of polymer. A large number of different processes are used for processing of plastics. Since plastic materials are converted into finished product in a single operation, the selection of material-process combination is extremely important for achieving the final shape and the desired properties. The commonly used methods for processing of plastics are:

- Extrusion
- Injection moulding
- Blow moulding
- Thermo-forming
- Compression moulding
- Transfer moulding
- Casting

4.2.1 Extrusion

In this method grannules of plastics are allowed to fall from a hopper into the extruder barrel (Fig. 4.3). As the screw extruder is rotated the material passes through a preheating zone, where it is heated, homogenized and compressed, and is finally forced through the die. The extruded material comes on to a conveyer where it is cooled by air or water sprays. The extruder screw clearly has three distinct sections — the feed section, the compression section and the melting

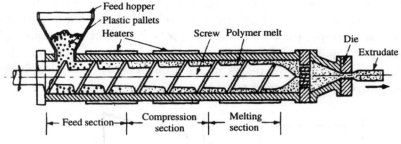

Fig. 4.3. Screw extruder.

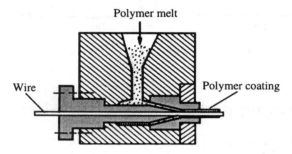

Fig. 4.4. Wire coating.

section. The lengths of these section are varied to suit the melting characteristics of the extruded material. Owing to the continuous nature of the process, it is extensively used for producing long products of uniform cross-section such as rods, tubes and channels from thermo-plastics. Plastic coated wires and cables are also produced using this technique. For this purpose, the wire is fed into the die opening at a controlled rate as shown in Figure 4.4.

4.2.2   Injection Moulding

Figure 4.5 shows a schematic diagram of injection moulding process and an injection moulding machine (Fig. 4.6). Raw thermoplastic grannules are placed in a hopper located above a reciprocating plunger (Fig. 4.5a). As the plunger is withdrawn, plastic grannules fall into the chamber under gravity. During the forward stroke the plunger forces the raw material into the heating zone for preheating. Further movement of the plunger causes the preheated material to move into the injection section where it is melted and superheated to a temperature of 200-300°C. The molten material is finally forced into the closed mould cavity under a pressure of around 35-140 MPa, through sprue, runners and gates. The mould is kept cool by circu-

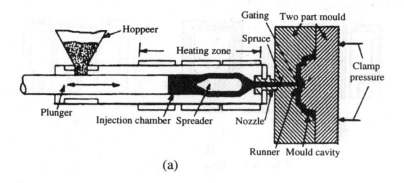

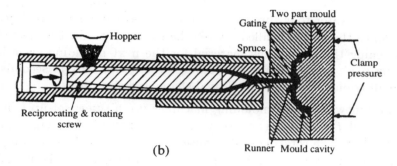

Fig. 4.5. Injection moulding with (a) a reciprocating plunger and (b) reciprocating and rotating screw.

Fig. 4.6. Injection moulding machine.

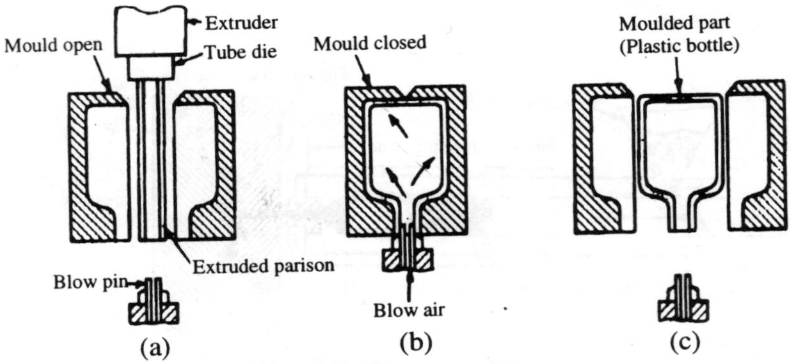

Fig. 4.7. Blow moulding.

lating cold water to ensure that the thermoplastic material solidifies as soon as the mould is filled. While the moulded product is ejected by opening the mould, the material for the next moulding cycle is getting ready. The complete moulding cycle takes 1 to 45 seconds, depending on the material and final shape and size.

Most new injection moulding machines use a screw set-up (Fig. 4.5b), similar to those on extrusion machines, instead of a reciprocating plunger. The rotating screw causes the material to pass through the preheating zone, the injection section and finally into the mould cavity as in the case of reciprocating plunger. On these machines (Fig. 4.5b), as pressure at the mould entrance builts up, the reciprocating screw moves backwards to precisely control the volume of material to be injected. The screw now stops rotating and is pushed forward to force the molten plastic into the mould cavity.

Large quantities of thermoplastic components are produced by injection moulding with relatively lower cost per piece. Complex parts can be produced with very close tolerance and practically no finishing requirements.

4.2.3   Blow Moulding

In blow moulding a hot tube of plastic material is placed between two halves of the mould. The mould is closed and air or a non- reactive gas like argon is blown under pressure of 20-40 MPa which expands the hot tube outwards to fill the mould cavity. The mould is then opened and the product, hollow in shape, is removed from the mould (Fig. 4.7). The process is commonly used for making plastic bottles and containers.

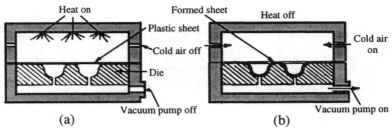

Fig. 4.8. Thermoforming.

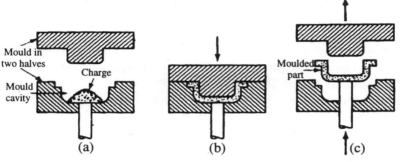

Fig. 4.9. Compression moulding

4.2.4 Thermoforming

The process, also known as thermoforming, is depicted schematically in Figure 4.8. In this process a sheet of thermoplastic material is placed over a die and heated until it becomes soft. A vacuum is then created inside the die cavity which draws down the heated plastic sheet into the shape of the die. The material is then cooled, the vacuum is released and the final product is taken out. Because of low strength of plastic materials, the pressure differential is generally sufficient for most forming operations. Sometimes air pressure or mechanical means are applied to increase the pressure differential. The cycle time of the process is generally a few minutes only and is quite economical since high strength dies are not required. It finds extensive use in making of plastic advertising signs, liners, panels and housings.

4.2.5 Compression Moulding

In compression moulding (Fig. 4.9) the raw plastic material in the form of solid grannules is placed in the cavity of an open mould which has been preheated to a temperature of 120 to 240°C. A punch, also heated· upto the same temperature, squeezes the material into the mould cavity. The plastic material melts at this temperature and

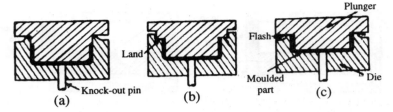

Fig. 4.10. Compression moulds: (a) positive type, (b) semi-positive type and (c) flash-type

under the pressure of punch it flows into all portions of the mould cavity. Pressures used in compression moulding varies from 7 to 140 MPa, depending upon the size and nature of material. The material is kept inside the mould for some time to allow it to cure under continued exposure of heat and then removed to obtain the final product.

Compression moulding is performed mostly for thermosetting plastics which require pressure in the range of 7-15 MPa. Parts produced are simple with uniform walls, thickness of which are generally not more than 3 mm. Sometimes the raw plastic material (charge) is preheated to reduce the curing time.

Three types of compression moulds used for this process are:

• Positive-type

• Semi-positive type

• Flash type

In *positive-type moulds* the plunger fits snugly in the mould. In this case (Fig. 4.10a) the force exerted by the plunger is fully utilized to fill the mould. The amount of raw plastic material or charge should, therefore, be precisely controlled to produce a part of accurate size.

In *semipositive-type moulds* (Fig. 4.10b) the plunger makes a close fit only during the last few millimeters of its travel. Full pressure is, therefore, exerted only during the final closing of the mould and excess material appears as a small flash.

In *flash-type moulds* (Fig. 4.10c) the plunger closes the mould bearing on a narrow flash ridge. In this case, the excess material is squeezed out around the cavity as flash and results in some wastage of material. This kind of moulds are, however, cheapest to fabricate since a close fit of the plunger is not required.

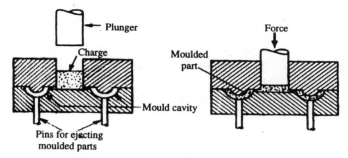

Fig. 4.11. Transfer moulding.

4.2.6   Transfer Moulding

Compression moulding often results in turbulence and uneven flow of liquid plastic in the mould because of non-uniform pressure. This phenomenon can be avoided using transfer moulding. In this process the raw plastic material is heated and compressed in a chamber and then forced into the mould cavity (Fig. 4.11). Pressures in the range of 30-100 MPa, depending upon the polymer properties, are generally used.

The process provides relatively close tolerances and fairly uniform density. Walls of thin sections can also be obtained using this process. The process is, however, relatively more expensive primarily because of the cost of mould.

4.2.7   Casting

Casting is the simplest and cheapest process when the number of parts required is small. Here no fillers are used and no pressure is required while pouring the liquid plastic into the mould. For making moulds for small products, a steel pattern is dipped into molten lead, removed and allowed to cool. The lead shell when removed from the sides of pattern becomes the mould for casting. The casting process is a slow process. Thermoset resins, while in the mould, are required to be heated for hours or days at 65° to 95°C to harden. Other types of plastics can be cured at room temperature. Hollow shapes in the plastic components can be obtained by centrifugal casting. Thick plates can be obtained by casting in glass plate moulds. The casting process is commonly used for producing sheets, gears, lenses, ornaments, prototypes and dies.

4.3   Comparison of Plastic Forming Processes

The advantages and limitations of plastic forming processes described in this chapter are compared in Table 4.1.

Review Questions

4.1 What is the difference between thermoplastic and thermosetting polymers?

4.2 What is die swell and how can this be controlled?

4.3 Why long and uniform cross-section plastic products can be conveniently produced by the extrusion process?

4.4 Identify the three sections of a screw extruder. How are their lengths decided?

4.5 How plastic coated wires are obtained?

4.6 How long a typical moulding cycle takes in the injection moulding of thermoplastics?

4.7 Why injection moulding process is capable of producing complex shapes with practically no finishing requirements?

4.8 Why argon gas under pressure is used in the blow moulding process?

4.9 Describe the sequence of operations for thermoforming.

4.10 What are the three basic types of moulds used for compression moulding?

4.11 Identify the similarities between compression moulding and closed-die forging.

4.12 Why should the amount of material introduced into the plunger for positive-type compression moulding be precisely controlled?

4.13 Compare transfer moulding with compression moulding to identify the attractive features of transfer moulding.

4.14 How moulds for smaller products are made for the casting process?

4.15 Why the casting process is not popular for thermoset resins?

Table 4.1 Comparison of plastic forming processes.

Process	Advantages	Limitations
Extrusion	• Relatively inexpensive, tooling. • High production rate.	• Suitable for forming of long uniform sections. • High production volume is required. • Dimensional accuracy not very good.
Injection moulding	• Complex shapes of various sizes can be obtained. • Good dimensional accuracy.	• High tooling cost. • High volume production is required.
Blow moulding	• High production rate. • Hollow shapes of various sizes with thin walls can be produced. • Low cost for making hollow shapes.	• Limited to production of hollow shapes.
Thermo-forming	• Low tooling cost. • Shallow and deep cavities can be produced. • High production rate. • Quite economical.	• Dimensional accuracy not so good.

Compression moulding
- Simple setting.
- Relatively inexpensive tooling.
- Used mainly for thermosetting plastics.
- Medium production rate.
- Dimensional accuracy not so good.

Transfer Moulding
- Relatively more complex parts can be produced.
- High production rate.
- Medium tooling cost.
- Relatively better dimensional accuracy and uniform density.
- Walls of thin sections can be obtained.
- Loss of material as scrap.
- Relatively more expensive.

Casting
- Simple or intricate shapes can be produced.
- Very economical.
- Low production rate.

Chapter 5

Powder Metallurgy Processing

5.1 Introduction

The term powder metallurgy (P/M) broadly covers manufacturing of components from metal powders and certain non-metallic powders. The process has been known for a very long time and the earliest use of iron powder dates back to 3000 BC. The modern era of powder metallurgy began when tungsten lamp filaments were developed for Edison. Earlier powder-based components were selected mainly because of their low costs, but now the basis of selection is better quality, uniform properties and low production cost.

The process basically involves compacting of fine-powdered materials in a die under relatively high pressure to get the desired shape. The pressed component is then sintered (heated without melting) which provides high strength and desired density to the component.

The process is now widely used for manufacturing of gears, cams, bushings, cutting tools, piston rings, connecting rods and impellers. The components can be made from pure metals, alloys, or mixture of metallic and non-metallic powders. The commonly used materials are iron, copper, aluminium, nickle, titanium, brass, bronze, steels and refractory metals.

The stages in producing a component by powder metallurgy processing are:

(a) Production of the powder
(b) Mixing and blending of the powder
(c) Pressing or compacting the powder in a die
(d) Sintering of compacted powder
(e) Finishing or secondary manufacturing

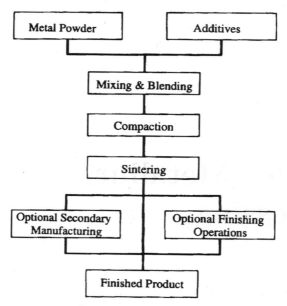

Fig. 5.1 Powder metallurgy processing.

A simplified flow chart of powder metallurgy processing is presented in Figure 5.1.

5.2 Production of Powder

All powder metallurgy processing start with powder and the properties of P/M products depend upon the characteristics and properties of the powder used. The parameters that are important include particle shape, size and its distribution, surface texture and chemistry and internal particle structure. Several methods are now available for powder metal production, each imparting special physical properties. The choice of a particular method is, therefore, on the basis of the desired properties and characteristics and the cost of production.

The basic methods for producing metal powders are:
- Mechanical fabrication techniques
- Electrolytic fabrication techniques
- Chemical fabrication techniques
- Atomization fabrication techniques

Mechanical fabrication of powder involves crushing or grinding of brittle or less ductile metals into powder particles. In *electrolytic fabrication* the powder is precipitated at the cathode of an electrolytic cell under certain operating conditions. This technique produces powders of high purity. In *chemical fabrication*, powders are formed

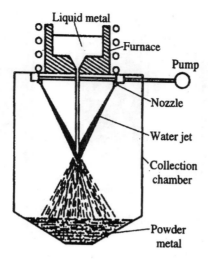

Fig. 5.2 Atomization process.

by gas-solid, liquid, or vapour phase reactions. The technique which is extensively used is reduction of metal oxides using hydrogen or carbon monoxide as reducing agents. The powder obtained using this technique are spongy and uniformly sized. The purity of powder, however, depends on the purity of the oxide.

There are several powder fabrication methods which fall under the general category of *atomization*. These techniques provide majority of powders used for P/M processing. In *atomization process*, the metal in the liquid state is forced through an orifice into a stream of gas or water under high pressure (Fig. 5.2).

The gas may be air or one of the inert gases (nitrogen, helium or argon). The process causes extremely rapid cooling and disintegration of molten metal into powder form. The size of particle formed depends on the temperature of the molten metal and its flow rate, the size of the nozzle and the jet characteristics.

5.3 Mixing and Blending

Mixing and blending are two important pre-compacting steps. The starting material for P/M processing is almost always a mixture of powder of various sizes, or powders of different composition. The purpose of *blending and mixing* is to combine these powders into a homogeneous mass. Here blending refers to the combination of powders of different sizes but of the same composition, while mixing implies powders of different composition. Blending causes powders

Metal powder

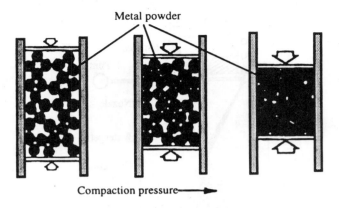

Compaction pressure

Fig. 5.3 Metal powder compaction.

of different sizes to flow and compact into a higher density. Mixing of powders of different chemistry imparts special physical and mechanical properties to the product. In order to improve the flow characteristics and compressibility of the powders, lubricants (graphite and stearic acid) are added to the mixture. The proportion of lubricant is less than 5% by weight so that the green strength does not get adversely affected. Blending and mixing are generally carried out in air or in inert atmospheres to avoid oxidation, and in liquids for better mixing, elimination of dust and reduced explosion hazards.

5.4   Compaction

After blending and mixing, the powders are pressed into the desired shape and size in dies using a hydraulic or mechanical press. The resulting compaction deforms the powder into a high density mass.

Figure 5.3 shows the stages of metal powder compaction. Initially the loose array of metal particles get a closer packing. On further compaction, the point contacts between particles begin to deform and finally extensive plastic deformation causes densification. Thus, increasing compaction pressure provides better packing of particles and leads to decreasing porosity (Fig. 5.4a). Also with increasing pressure, the localized deformation allows new contacts to be formed which eventually tend to saturate giving the flattened part of the curve (Fig. 5.4b).

The green density of the powder compact depends on the compaction pressure and at higher pressures it tends to approach the strength of the metal in the bulk form (Fig. 5.5). The pressed density of over 90% is, however, difficult to obtain. The compaction

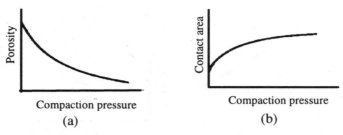

Fig. 5.4 Effect of compaction pressure on (a) porosity and (b) contact area.

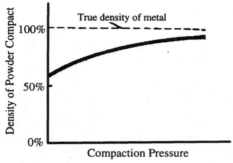

Fig. 5.5 Effect of compaction pressure on green density.

pressure is selected on the basis of desired density and porosity. The range of compaction pressure used for some common materials are given in Table 5.1.

Table 5.1 Compaction pressure for some metal powders.

Metal powder	Compaction pressure (MPa)
Aluminium	75-275
Aluminium Oxide	100-150
Brass	400-700
Carbon	140-170
Iron	400-800
Tungsten	75-150
Tungsten Carbides	150-400

The effect of particle size on the strength of powder compact (Fig. 5.6a) shows that smaller particles provide better strength mainly due to reduction in porosity (Fig. 5.6b).

Friction between the punch and the die wall and between the powder particles may cause the green density of the part to vary

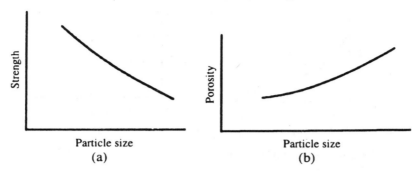

Fig. 5.6 Effect of particle size on (a) green strength and (b) porosity.

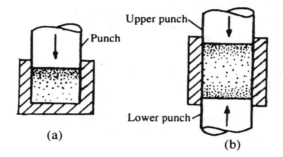

Fig. 5.7 Compaction with single and two moving punches.

considerably (Fig. 5.7a). This can be improved by pressing between two punches (Fig. 5.7b) in a double-acting press.

5.5   Sintering

The green compact obtained after compaction is brittle and its strength is low. In the *sintering process*, these green compacts are heated in a controlled-atmosphere furnace to temperatures of 70 to 90% of their melting point temperatures to allow packed metal powders to bond together.

Sintering operations are generally carried out in three stages (Fig. 5.8). During the first stage (pre-heating or burn-off stage), the temperature is slowly increased so that all volatile materials in the green compact that would interfere with good bonding are removed. Rapid heating at this stage may entrap gases and produce high internal pressure which may fracture the compacts. The second stage, the sintering or high-temperature stage, causes solid-state bonding of powder particles as a result of atomic diffusion. Diffusion is a time-temperature sensitive phenomenon. Therefore sufficient time must be provided to obtain the desired density. Table 5.2 gives sintering

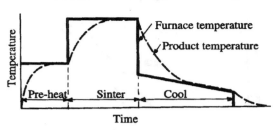

Fig. 5.8 Three stages of sintering.

temperature and time for common metals.

Table 5.2 Sintering temperature and time for some metals.

Metal powder	Sintering temperature °C	Sintering time (min)
Brass	850-900	10-45
Bronze	750-880	10-20
Copper	850-900	10-45
Iron	1000-1150	10-45
Nickel	1000-1150	30-45
Stainless steel	1100-1300	30-60
Tungsten	2350	480
Tungsten carbide	1420-1500	20-30

The third stage is the cooling stage where the sintered product is allowed to cool while maintaining controlled atmosphere. This is done primarily to prevent oxidation and thermal shock. An oxygen-free atmoshpere is, therefore, essential not only during the cooling stage but throughout the sintering process. The gases commonly used for sintering are hydrogen, nitrogen, inert gas, dissociated or burned ammonia and partially combusted hydrocarbons, otherwise it is carried in vacuum.

The mechanisms involved in sintering are quite complex and depend upon various process parameters. Diffusion, recrystallization, grain growth and densification, however, appear to be the mechanisms principally involved in sintering, while sintering temperature, sintering time and sintering atmosphere appear to be the important process parameters controlling sintering. The increase in density and strength of the powder compact during sintering is mainly due to disappearance of particle boundaries as a result of atomic diffusion and recrystallization. Higher sintering temperature or longer sintering time increases the strength and density of the compact. However, increasing the sintering temperature and time beyond a certain point

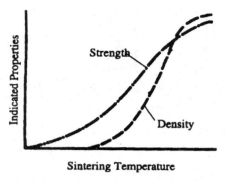

Fig. 5.9 Effect of sintering temperature on strength and density.

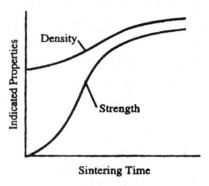

Fig. 5.10 Effect of sintering time on density and strength.

have only marginal effect on both strength and density (Figs. 5.9 and 5.10). The increase in density of the compact during sintering is accompanied by shrinkage, hence appropriate allowances should be provided for shrinkage.

During sintering of powder compacts that have particles of two different metal (one with a lower melting point), a liquid phase may exist. In this case alloying may take place at the particle-particle interfaces, and the particle that has melted may surround the particle that has not melted. In such cases, high compact density can be quickly attained. In products of this type, the nature of alloy formed, the ability of the liquid metal to wet the solid particles, and the capillary action of the liquid in the solid compact play important roles.

Presintering, wherein the compacted parts are heated for a short time at a temperature considerably below the sintering temperature, is employed when some machining is required on parts made of difficult-to-machine materials. Presintering provides sufficient strength to parts so that they can be machined. Final sintering is given to these products after machining.

Sometimes compacting and sintering are carried out concurrently rather than consecutively. In other words, sintering of powder is carried out while the compact is under compaction pressure. One such technique is *hot isostatic pressing* (HIP) where the powder is sealed in a flexible, airtight container and subjected to high pressure and high temperature concurrently. The pressure and temperature used is typically around 100 MPa and 1200°C, respectively. High cost of sealing the powder in flexible containers which can withstand high pressure as well as high temperature has made the process less attractive. Further, relatively long cycle time for HIP has made the process unattractive for high-volume production.

In *spark sintering*, a variant of HIP, the metal powder placed in a graphite mould is heated by a high alternating current and compacted simultaneously. Rapid electric discharges activate the surface of the particles by removing any oxide coating, and thus promote good bonding during high temperature compaction.

5.6   Secondary and Finishing Operations

For many applications, powder metallurgy products are ready for use after sintering. In some cases, however, secondary and/or finishing operations are carried out after sintering to improve the properties of the product, or to improve the dimensional accuracy and surface finish, or for providing special characteristics. The operations that are generally carried out include, coining and sizing, impregnation and infiltration, machining and grinding, plating and heat treatment.

Coining and *sizing* are compacting operations where the product is placed in a die and subjected to high pressure to improve dimensional accuracy, surface finish and strength of sintered parts. These are basically cold working operations.

Porosity of powder metallurgy products permits impregnation and infiltration. In *impregnation*, fluid (generally oil) is forced into the porous network of P/M product by immersing the part in heated fluid and applying pressure. Internally lubricated bearings made by this method may contain upto 40% oil by volume and require no lubrication during their service life.

In the *infiltration process*, a slug whose melting point is lower than that of the P/M constituent, is placed close to the sintered product and the assembly is heated to melting temperature of the slug. The molten metal is then forced into the sintered product under pressure or it is made to flow into the pores by capillary action. The process provides relatively pore-free P/M product of good density and strength.

P/M products may also be subjected to finishing operations such as machining and grinding for improving dimensional accuracy and surface finish, plating for wear and corrosion resistance, and heat treatment for improving strength and hardness.

5.7   Characteristics of P/M Processing

The powder-metallurgy processing, like other manufacturing processes, has some distinct advantages and limitations. These are summarized below.

Advantages:

1. A wide range of compositions can be used to obtain wide variation in mechanical and physical properties.

2. Complex shapes can be produced.

3. The process is suitable for high production volume with uniformity and reproducibility.

4. Good dimensional accuracy and surface finish obtained reduces or eliminates machining or finishing in many applications.

5. No material is wasted in P/M processing.

Limitations:

1. High material cost (cost of powder metals).

2. High tooling and equipment cost.

3. Mechanical properties such as strength and ductility of P/M parts are relatively inferior to cast or forged products.

4. Shape of P/M product is limited to those which can be ejected from the die. Thin sections are difficult to produce and the overall size is limited by press capacity.

5. Non-uniform density leads to property variations in P/M products.

Numerical Examples

Q.1 A green compact that has 90% Fe, 8% Cu and 2% C by weight is sintered to 96% theoretical density. What is the theoretical density of compact? (Densities of Fe, Cu and C are 7.87, 8.96 and 2.25 gm/cm³, respectively.)

Solution:

Volume of 100 g of powder is

$$\frac{90}{7.87} + \frac{8}{8.96} + \frac{2}{2.25} = 13.2 \text{ cm}^3$$

Therefore, theoretical density of compact

$$= \frac{100}{13.2} = 7.57 \text{ g/cm}^3$$

Q.2 During sintering of a metal-powder green compact, the linear shrinkage was 5%. If the desired density of compact is 96% of the theoretical density, what should be the density of green compact?

Solution:

If linear shrinkage is taken at $(\Delta l/l_o)$, where l_o is the original length, then the volume after sintering,

$$V_s = V_c \left(1 - \frac{\Delta l}{l_o}\right)^3$$

where V_c is the volume of green compact. This expression can be rewritten in terms of densities ρ_s and ρ_c after sintering and compaction respectively as

$$\rho_s = \rho_c \left(1 - \frac{\Delta l}{l_o}\right)^3$$

since mass does not change. Thus,

$$\rho_s = 0.96(1 - 0.05)^3 = 0.82 \text{ or } 82\%$$

Review Questions

5.1 Summarize the stages involved in powder metallurgy processing?

5.2 What are the basic methods of producing metal powders? On what parameters does the selection of a particular method depend?

5.3 What purpose does mixing and blending serve?

5.4 What is the purpose of adding lubricants to the metal powder during mixing and blending? How the green strength of mixture gets affected by the addition of lubricants?

5.5 Explain why compaction leads to high density mass and better packing of particles?

5.6 On what considerations the compaction pressure is selected?

5.7 Why smaller particles of powder provide better strength to the powder metallurgy products?

5.8 What is the purpose of sintering? How the sintering process is performed?

5.9 Why rapid heating is avoided during sintering?

5.10 Explain why sintering process has to be performed in an oxygen-free atmosphere? Can the process be carried out in vacuum?

5.11 What are the mechanisms involved in sintering?

5.12 What are the important process parameters to be controlled during sintering?

5.13 On what considerations the sintering temperature and sintering time are decided?

5.14 Why a reasonably high compact density is achieved in case of powder compacts that have particles of two different metals, one with a lower melting point?

5.15 What is hot isostatic pressing? Why is this process less popular?

5.16 What is pre-sintering? What purpose does it serve?

5.17 What kind of operations are carried out after sintering to improve the dimensional accuracy and surface finish of the product?

5.18 List the main advantages of powder metallurgy processing?

Chapter 6

Heat Treatment of Metals

6.1 Introduction

Metals and alloys may not possess all the desired properties in the finished product. Alloying and heat treatment are two methods which are extensively used for controlling material properties. Alloying elements are added to impart specific properties to the original material. For example, addition of 4-8% of Cr in steel improves the corrosion and wear resistance significantly. Similarly, addition of 0.2-5% of Mo increases the strength and toughness of steel. When Cr, Mn and V are added alongwith Mo, hot hardness and hot strength improves considerably.

Heat treatment is a constant mass operation which is used extensively for modifying the microstructure of engineering materials. The resulting phase transformation influences the mechanical properties such as strength, ductility, toughness, hardness and wear resistance. In fact *heat treatment* is defined as a process of controlled heating and cooling for the purpose of altering the physical and mechanical properties of metals and alloys. The purpose of heat treatment is to increase the service life of a finished product by increasing its strength and hardness, or to prepare a material for easier fabrication by improving machinability and formability. Thus, through a particular heat treatment a given material can be softened to ease machining and through another heat treatment, it may be hardened to increase its wear resistance and improve the service life.

6.2 Phase Diagram

The basis of changing properties through heat treatment is essentially through modification of internal structure of the material which is characterized in terms of phases present, their size, shape and distribution in the material. The nature of phases present at different temperatures can be predicted from its *phase diagram* or *equilibrium diagram* or *equilibrium phase diagram* which shows the relationship between temperature, composition and phases present in a particular alloy. The phase diagram, therefore, indicates the temperatures that must be attained in order to achieve a desired structure and the change that will occur on subsequent cooling. Most heat treatment operations generally involve slow cooling or holding at elevated temperatures for a certain length of time. Thus it tends to approximate equilibrium conditions and the resulting structure can be predicted reasonably well by the phase or equilibrium diagram. Since steel is the most important engineering material, the iron-carbon phase diagram is of utmost interest in manufacturing and is also the most frequently used phase diagram.

6.2.1   Iron-Carbon Phase Diagram

Figure 6.1 shows the iron-carbon phase diagram. This shows C variation up to 6% only since commercially pure iron contains up to 0.008% C, steels up to 2.11% C and cast irons up to 6.67% C. Pure iron melts at 1538° C, as indicated near the left boundary of the figure, and as it cools, it first forms delta ferrite (δ), then austenite (ν) and finally alpha ferrite (α).

Alpha ferrite or *ferrite* is a solid solution of body-centred cubic (bcc) iron with a maximum solid solubility of 0.022% C at a temperature of 727°C. *Delta ferrite* is of no practical significance since it is stable only at very high temperatures. *Ferrite*, derived from latin word *ferrum* meaning iron, is a relatively soft and ductile material, and is magnetic upto 768°C. Although very little carbon can be dissolved in bcc iron, the presence of carbon can significantly change the mechanical properties of ferrite. Iron, between 1394°C to 912°C, undergoes transformation from bcc to fcc structure to give *gamma iron*, commonly known as *austenite*. The solid solubility of austenite is much higher than that of ferrite with solid solubitily of up to 2.11% C. Austenite is denser than ferrite and is ductile at elevated temperatures. Steel in austenitic form is non-magnetic. *Cementite*, represented by the right hand boundary of Figure 6.1, is 100% iron carbide (Fe_3C) with 6.67% C. Cementite is a very hard and brittle intermetallic compound and has significant influence on the mechanical properties of steel.

The iron-carbon diagram for steel can be simplified considerably since the region with carbon greater than 2% is of little significance

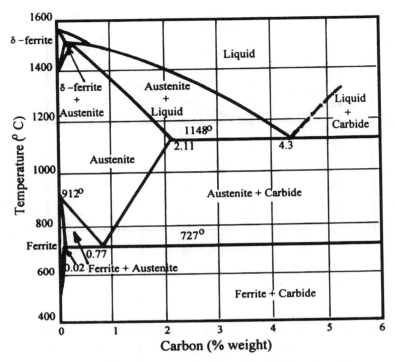

Fig. 6.1 Iron-carbon phase diagram.

and can be deleted. The resulting diagram is shown in Figure 6.2 which indicates that various microstructures can be developed, depending upon the carbon content and the heat treatment method. For example, when iron with less than 0.77% C is slowly cooled from 1100° C in the austenite phase (line XX), a reaction takes place when the temperature reaches 727° C which transforms austenite into alpha ferrite (bcc) and cementite. Since the solid solubility of carbon in ferrite is only 0.022%, the extra carbon which does not get dissolved in ferrite forms cementite. This reaction is called *eutectoid reaction* indicating that at a certain temperature, a single solid phase, that is austenite, is transformed into two other solid phases – ferrite and cementite. The resulting structure of eutectoid steel is called *pearlite* whose microstructure consists of alternate layers of ferrite and cementite. The mechanical properties of pearlite is, therefore, something, between soft and ductile ferrite and hard and brittle cementite.

Similarly when the carbon content is less than 0.77% (line YY) the material is entirely austenite at higher temperature, but on cooling it enters the region of stable ferrite and austenite phases. At 727°C the austenite is of eutectoid composition and has 0.77%C, and

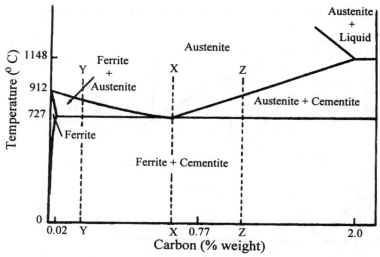

Fig. 6.2 Iron-carbon diagram for steel.

on further cooling the remaining austenite transforms into pearlite. The resulting structure is now a mixture of proeutectoid ferrite (ferrite formed before the eutectoid reaction) and pearlite.

When steel cools along ZZ (Fig. 6.2), the proeutectoid phase is cementite instead of ferrite. As the carbon-rich phase forms, the remaining austenite decreases in carbon content and reaches eutectoid composition at 727°C. Any remaining austenite, as before, transforms into pearlite on further cooling. The resulting structure has continuous network of cementite which causes the material to be extremely brittle.

Steels with carbon content from 0.025 to 0.77% are called hypoeutectoid steels, while those with carbon content greater than 0.77% are called hypereutectoid steels. Steels with carbon content of 0.77% are called eutectoid steel. Thus lines XX, YY and ZZ in Figure6.2 represent transformation of eutectoid, hypoeutectoid and hypereutectoid steels, respectively.

The transitions described above are for equilibrium conditions which are achieved during slow cooling. The material during slow heating will also achieve equilibrium condition and the same transitions will occur, but in the reverse manner. When the alloy is cooled or heated rapidly, entirely different results may be obtained since sufficient time is not available for the phase reactions to occur. In these cases the phase diagram described is no longer useful.

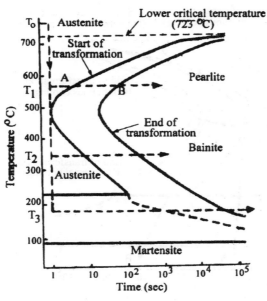

Fig. 6.3 TTT-diagram for eutectoid steel.

6.3 TTT-diagram for Carbon Steel

The information on the change of phase with cooling rate can be obtained from the *time-temperature-transformation diagram*, commonly known as the *TTT-diagram*. Here the temperature is plotted along y-axis using a linear scale, while x-axis represents the time on a logarithmic scale. The TTT-diagram for eutectoid steel is shown in Figure 6.3.

The curves (continuous lines) represent the time required to start and complete the transformation from austenite to pearlite. Thus, when austenite is rapidly cooled ($t = 0$) from temperature T_0 to T_1, the transformation to pearlite begins at point A after a lapse of time t_1 and ends at B after time t_2. This transformation takes place at constant temperature and is known as *isothermal transformation*. Similarly, the transformations taking place at temperatures T_2 and T_3 can be obtained as shown. When the temperature is near the nose part of the diagram, the transformation starts almost immediately or after a minimum lapse of time. At temperatures below this, say at T_2, austenite transforms into *bainite* (mixture of ferrite and cementite). At temperatures T_3 which is below 220°C, there is no curve indicating the beginning of transformation. Thus at temperatures below 220°C, the transformation from austenite to martensite is almost instantaneous.

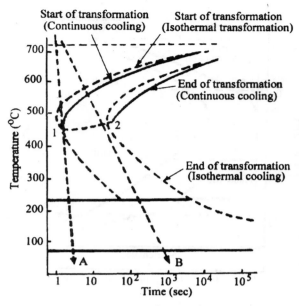

Fig. 6.4 Modified TTT-diagram.

It must be pointed out that the transformations indicated by the TTT-diagram is valid only for isothermal transformation. When the cooling is continuous, a modified TTT-diagram is used (Fig. 6.4). Consider two cooling rates: (i) rapid cooling rate represented by curve A and (ii) moderate cooling rate represented by curve B. During rapid cooling the entire austenite is transformed into martensite because curve A does not enter the pearlite transformation region (the area between the two continuous curves). The moderate cooling rate curve, on the other hand, enters the pearlite region causing a part of austenite to be transformed into pearlite and the remaining into martensite. The quantity of pearlite produced will depend upon the point of intersection of curve B and line 1-2. When the intersection point is nearer to point 1, lesser pearlite will be produced. The structure of steel will, therefore, depend on the manner of cooling after it has been heated to achieve stable austenite phase (above 725°C).

6.4 Heat Treatment Processes

The commonly used heat treatment processes for steels include:
- Hardening
- Annealing
- Normalizing

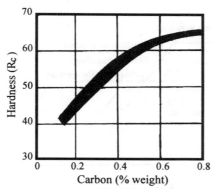

Fig. 6.5 Variation of hardness of 99.9% martensite with carbon. (After DeGarmo et al., 1988)

- Tempering
- Surface hardening

6.4.1 Hardening

Hardening is performed to impart strength and hardness to alloys by heating upto a certain temperature, depending on the material, and cooling it rapidly.

While heating a solid solution of alloying elements is formed at high temperature which becomes supersaturated upon cooling. Under certain conditions the solute gets dispersed as fine particles in the crystal lattice which helps in blocking the dislocation movements when stresses are applied. As a result the metal becomes stronger and harder. When steel is heated to the austenite region (above 725°C) and held there until its carbon is dissolved and then cooled rapidly (quenching), the carbon does not get sufficient time to escape and gets dissipiated in the lattice structure. The martensite structure thus formed is quite hard and strong but brittle. Figure 6.5 shows the variation in hardness of 99.9% martensite with carbon.

Quenching is performed to cool the hot metal rapidly and is performed by immersing it in brine (salt water), water, oil, molten salt, air or gas. Quenching invariably sets up residual stresses in the workpiece, sometimes resulting in cracks. Residual stresses are removed by a process called annealing.

6.4.2 Annealing

Annealing is performed to reduce hardness, remove residual stress, improve toughness, restore ductility and to alter various mechanical,

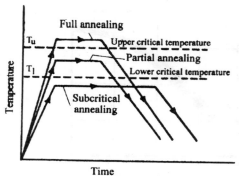

Fig. 6.6 Annealing processes.

electrical or magnetic properties of the material through refinement of grain structure.

Annealing consists of heating the workpiece to a predetermined temperature, holding it at that temperature for a definite period of time and then cooling it slowly. The process is generally carried out in a controlled atmosphere of inert gas or at a lower temperature to prevent oxidation of the surface layer.

On the basis of treatment temperature, annealing can be classified as:

- Full annealing
- Partial annealing
- Subcritical annealing

These processes are shown in Figure 6.6.

Annealing of ferrous alloys, generally low and medium carbon steels, is usually known as full annealing. *Full annealing* consists of heating the material from 10 to 45°C above the upper critical temperature, maintaining the temperature for a definite period of time for complete transformation into austenite and then cooling slowly in the furnace itself, after turning it off. The rate of cooling is generally around 10°C per hour. As a result of full annealing the material becomes soft and ductile with small uniform grains since a structure with coarse pearlite is obtained after this process.

Partial annealing is basically incomplete annealing since only partial transformation is achieved, while in subcritical annealing no phase transformation takes place.

Annealing can also be classified on the basis of the purpose of treatment. For example, a process anneal may be used for restoring ductility in severely strain-hardened (cold worked) steel so that further working may be carried out. It is a *subcritical annealing* process since steel is heated to a temperature slightly below the lower critical temperature, held at this temperature for sufficient time for softening to occur and then cooled at the desired rate, usually in air. A stress-relief anneal is employed to remove residual stresses.

6.4.3 Normalizing

Normalizing is very similar to annealing and is performed to avoid excessive softness in the material. In this process, the material is heated beyond the upper critical temperature to transform the structure to austenite and then allowed to cool in air. This increases the rate of cooling and results in slight hardening and loss of ductility. Relatively higher rate of cooling decomposes austenite at relatively lower temperature resulting in better dispersion of ferrite-carbide aggregate. Also the amount of pearlite is more and grain size is finer. These result in enhanced mechanical properties.

Annealing is more expensive than normalizing mainly because of prolong heating time and higher energy consumption. Besides cooling rates are not critical in normalizing. Normalizing, however, causes properties to vary between surface and interior primarily because of difference in cooling at different locations.

The selection heat treatment operations discussed above is strongly influenced by the carbon content in the steel. *Process annealing* or normalizing is usually preferred for low carbon steels (less than 0.3%C), while medium carbon steels (0.3 to 0.6%C) are full-annealed. *Spheroidization anneal* is carried out only when the carbon is above 6%. A graphical summary of these processes for steels on phase diagram is shown in Figure 6.7.

6.4.4 Tempering

As discussed earlier, when an austenite structure is rapidly cooled after heating, martensite is formed. This improves the strength, hardness and wear resistance of steel but adversely affects ductility and toughness and also imparts brittleness due to internal stresses developed during quenching. Steel in this state is unsuitable for some service conditions. The decrease in internal stress and reduction is brittleness is achieved through *tempering* which consists of secondary heating of hardened steel upto the lower critical temperature of 723°C and then cooling at a prescribed rate. This process also improves ductility and toughness and marginally lowers strength, hardness and wear resistance. In general, the higher the tempering temperature, the higher is the ductility and toughness but decreases the hardness and strength. Thus tempering temperature should be selected to

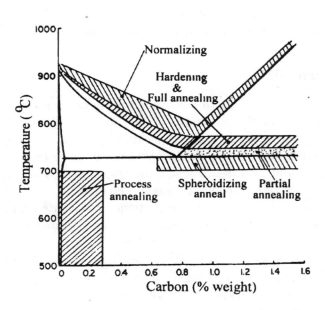

Fig. 6.7 Heat treatments of steel on phase diagram.

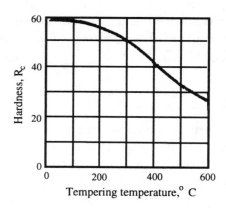

Fig. 6.8 Effect of tempering temperature on hardness of steel. (After Rao, 1987)

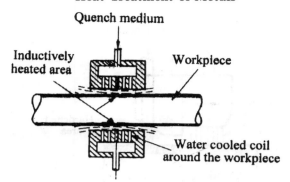

Fig. 6.9 Induction hardening.

get the optimum combination of mechanical properties. Figure 6.8 shows the effect of tempering temperature on hardness of steel.

6.4.5 Surface Hardening

The heat treatment methods covered above are meant to be effective for the entire material, whereas surface-hardening methods are meant for improving the hardness and wear resistance of outer layers only. Hardening, for example, improves the hardness and wear resistance of the material but also reduces the shock and fatigue resistance. In many applications we desire greater surface hardness to improve the wear resistance on the surfaces, and a soft and ductile core for shock resistance. For such cases, surface hardening treatment is carried out. Basically there are two methods for achieving this. The first method involves phase transformation by rapid heating and cooling of the outer surface (induction hardening and flame hardening), while the second method involves thermochemical treatment where the surface composition of steel is changed by diffusion of carbon and/or nitrogen or other elements (carburizing, nitriding and cyaniding).

In *induction hardening* heating is done by passing a high-frequency current through a water-cooled coil wrapped around the workpiece (Fig. 6.9). The magnetic field generated induces current that heats the workpiece surface. The depth of penetration δ of current (hence heat) can be estimated from

$$\delta \approx 2\sqrt{\frac{\rho}{\mu f}} \tag{6.1}$$

where ρ and μ are the resistivity and permeability of material, and f is the frequency in hertz. Thus, the higher the frequency, the greater is the depth of penetration.

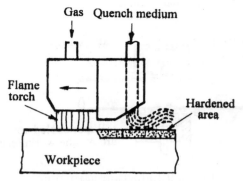

Fig. 6.10 Flame hardening.

Induction heating is usually carried for a few seconds only and immediately after heating the surface is quenched by a jet of cold water. Quenching causes the austenitized surface layer to change to martensitic structure giving hard and wear resistant outer layer.

Surface hardness of 50 to 60 Rockwell C up to a depth of 0.6-6 mm can be easily achieved by this technique. Induction hardening is used for surface hardening of gears and sprocket teeth, shafts, piston rods, lathe beds and centres and crank shafts. The process is basically performed for medium carbon steel and cast irons.

In *flame hardening* the surface of the workpiece is heated locally or progressively by a gas flame, usually an oxy-acetylene flame. The shape of the flame torch head is usually made to match the workpiece contour for homogeneous heating of the entire surface. Quenching is normally performed by cold water sprayed from a nozzle which follows the flame torch head as shown in Figure 6.10.

The characteristics and the field of use of this process are the same as that for induction hardening.

Laser and electron beams have also been used to produce hardened surfaces. In *laser beam hardening* the surface of the workpiece is scanned with laser beam of chosen intensity and size at the desired scanning speed. Often a coating of zinc or manganese phosphate is applied before laser scanning for better efficiency of converting light energy into heat. The depth of heat penetration is governed by both time and energy density. Water or oil quenching is generally not required in laser hardening since heat is quickly removed by the cool mass of surrounding metal. The microstructure of laser-heated steel is generally bainite and ferrite at the heated surface and pearlite and ferrite in the interior. A 0.4% carbon steel can be easily hardened to Rockwell C 65 using this treatment. The treatment produces practically no distortions and induces no residual stress and can, therefore,

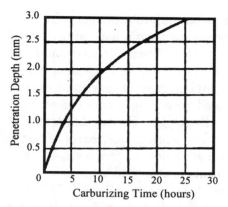

Fig. 6.11 Effect of carburizing time on penetration depth. (After Rao, 1987)

be safely used to harden selected surface areas leaving the remaining surface areas unaffected.

Electron beam hardening is very similar to laser beam hardening, except that the heating is obtained by a beam of high-energy electrons, rather than a beam of light. The electron beam is focussed by means of electromagnetic controls on to the surface area to be heated. The depth of penetration of heat depends upon the power input and the time duration. Depth up to 0.75 mm can be easily achieved by this method. Since electrons cannot travel in air, this treatment is carried out in vacuum which is a major limitation of the process.

Carburizing is the most widely used thermo-chemical treatment for surface hardening of steels. The process involves heating of low-carbon (0.2% carbon) and alloy steels (0.08-0.2% C) up to 870-950°C in a sealed container with carbon atmosphere, holding the specimen at the desired temperature for about 4-10 hours depending on the depth of penetration required, and then quenching. As a result of heating the specimen in an atmoshpere of carbon, carbon diffuses into the surface layer of steel making it harder. In this process a hard, high-carbon surface is produced with hardness of Rockwell C 55-65. The depth of penetration depends on the carburizing time (Fig. 6.11) and is usually in the range of 0.5 to 3 mm. This process is effectively used for case hardening of gears, cams, shafts, bearings, piston pins, sprockets, clutches and plates.

The nitriding process is effectively used for case hardening of chromium-molybdenum alloy steels, stainless steels and high-speed tool steels containing nitride-forming elements. In *nitriding* the specimen is heated in a furnace up to a temperature of 500-600°C in an atmosphere of ammonia gas or in a bath of molten cyanide salts for 10-40 hours. Nitrogen gets diffused into steel and forms alloy nitrides penetratng the metal upto a depth of 0.6 mm, depending upon the nitriding time. The process gives a very hard case (Reckwell C 60-70) which does not need quenching or subsequent thermal processing. The process is normally applied for case hardening of gears, shafts, sprockets, valves, cutters, boring bars, parts of fuel injection pump and antifriction bearings. Since the process uses lower temperatures, distortion of components is also reduced.

Cyaniding involves heating of steel to 760-845°C in a molten bath of cyanide solutions (30% sodium cyanide or other salts) holding the part for about 30 to 60 minutes at the desired temperature and then quenching in water or oil. Carbon and nitrogen formed during the process diffuse to give a thin wear resistant layer of carbonitride. Surface hardness of up to Rockwell C 65 at a depth of 0.025 to 0.25 mm can be obtained by this process. The process is generally used for low-carbon (0.2% C) and alloy steels (0.08-0.2% C) components.

6.5 Summary

The main features of the heat treatment processes described in this chapter are summarized below:

- Hardening: Imparts hardness throughout the part. Lacks toughness.

- Annealing: Reduces hardness and strength. Improves ductility. Relieves stress in cold worked parts.

- Normalizing: Avoids excessive softness.

- Tempering: Reduces brittleness. Increases ductility and toughness.

- Induction hardening/Flame hardening: Increases surface hardness to R_C 50-60 from 0.6 to 6mm depth.

- Carburizing: Produces high carbon surface layer with hardness R_C 55-65. Case depth 0.5 to 2.5 mm.

- Nitriding: Produces surface hardness of R_C 60-70. Case depth 0.1 to 0.6 mm.

- Cyaniding: Produces surface hardness upto R_C 70. Case depth 0.025 to 0.25 mm.

Review Questions

6.1 What is heat treatment?

6.2 What is an equilibrium phase diagram?

6.3 In what way phase diagrams help in designing the processing for heat treatment?

6.4 What is a TTT-diagram and what does it show?

6.5 What are the characteristics of ferrite, austenite and cementite?

6.6 What is pearlite? What is its structure?

6.7 What is isothermal transformation?

6.8 In what way the modified TTT-diagram is useful?

6.9 Explain how the structure of steel depends on the manner of cooling from its stable austenite phase.

6.10 Why quenching performed in oil is less likely to produce cracks than water or brine?

6.11 What are the major mechanisms available to increase the strength of metals?

6.12 What is the basic mechanism of hardening of steel?

6.13 What is the purpose of annealing? How this heat treatment process is carried out?

6.14 Why annealing is performed in a controlled atmosphere of inert gas?

6.15 What is the main difference between annealing and normalizing?

6.16 What is tempering and why is it done?

6.17 What is the purpose of surface hardening? In induction hardening which parameters control the depth of heat penetration?

6.18 Which surface hardening process is most suitable for the heat treatment of gear teeth and why?

6.19 What processes are used for hardening of low carbon steels? Explain why?

6.20 How is laser hardening carried out? Why water or oil quenching is not required in laser hardening?

6.21 Why low carbon steels do not respond to hardening by quenching?

6.22 What are the functions of artificial atmosphere used during heat treatment of metals?

Chapter 7

Metal Cutting

7.1 Introduction

Machining processes are material removal operations in which the desired shape, size and surface finish on the finished product are obtained by removing surplus material. Machining is undoubtedly the most important of all manufacturing processes because almost every manufactured product requires machining at some stage of their production. Parts produced by casting or forging have some or all of their surfaces refined by machining processes. In other cases these processes are used to finish surfaces more closely to the desired dimensions and surface finish.

A wide variety of machining processes are now available and these can be put in the following three broad categories:

- Metal-cutting processes
- Grinding and finishing processes
- Unconventional machining processes

While machining, a generic term, refers to all material removal processes, *metal-cutting* refers to only those processes where material removal is effected by the relative motion between tool made of harder material and the workpiece. Metal-cutting processes can be further classified on the basis of type of tool used. The tool could be a single-point cutting tool as used in operations like turning or shaping, or a multi-point tool as used in milling or drilling operations.

Grinding and *finishing* processes are those where metal is removed by a large number of hard abrasive particles or grains which may be bonded as in grinding wheels, or be in loose form as in lapping.

Unconventional machining processes are those which use electrical, chemical and other means of material removal for shaping high strength materials and for producing complicated shapes.

Table 7.1 gives the classification details of machining processes.

7.2 Metal Cutting

As mentioned earlier, material removal in metal-cutting operations is effected by the relative motion between a hard tool and the workpiece. The interaction between tool and workpiece causes the tool to be driven through the workpiece material and remove a layer of metal in the form of a chip. The kind of shape produced by this tool-workpiece interaction depends upon the tool shape and the path it traverses through the workpiece material. For example, when the workpiece is rotated about an axis and the tool is traversed in a definite path relative to the axis, a·surface of revolution is produced. When the tool path is parallel to the axis of rotation, the surface produced is a cylinder as in straight turning (Fig. 7.1a). If the tool path is straight but inclined to the axis, a conical surface is obtained as in taper turning (Fig. 7.1b). In boring an inside cylindrical surface is produced just as in straight turning except that the tool is located inside the hole (Fig. 7.1c).

A plane surface can be obtained by revolving the workpiece and traversing the tool at right angle to the axis as in facing (Fig. 7.1d). Flat surface can also be produced by reciprocating the workpiece and providing a cross-feed to the tool at the end of stroke as in planing (Fig. 7.1e). In shaping, the tool is reciprocated and cross-feed is provided to the workpiece at the end of stroke to get a flat surface.

Cylindrical and flat surfaces can also be produced by multi-point tools. In drilling a twin-edged tool is rotated and fed into the workpiece to get a cylindrical hole (Fig. 7.1f). A flat surface is produced during milling when the multi-point rotary cutter removes material from the workpiece fed parallel to its axis of rotation (Fig. 7.1g).

A contoured surface can be produced by rotating the workpiece and traversing the tool along a curved path as in contour turning (Fig. 7.1h). If the length of the contoured surface required is short, contour forming may be carried out by using a profile tool corresponding to the required form and traversing it perpendicular to the axis of rotating workpiece (Fig. 7.1i).

Table 7.2 summarizes the basic metal-cutting operations described above in term of shape produced, type of cutting tool, and the tool and workpiece motions. It is clear that various types of surfaces can be produced, depending on the nature of relative motion between the tool and the workpiece. The line generated by the primary or

Table 7.1 Classification of machining processes.

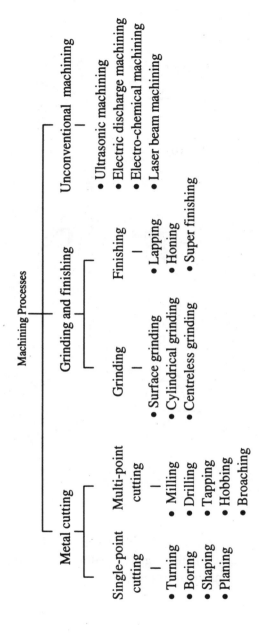

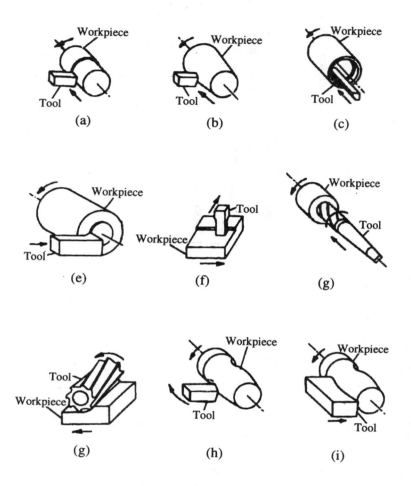

Fig. 7.1 Tool-work interaction: (a) straight turning, (b) taper turning, (c) boring, (d) facing, (e) planing, (f) drilling, (g) milling, (h) contour turning and (i) contour forming.

cutting motion is called the *generatrix*, while the line depicting sec-
ondary·or feed motion is called the *directrix*. Most of the geometrical
shapes can be produced by the geometrical generating lines, generatrix and directrix, with appropriately chosen relative motions. For
example, when the generatrix (cutting motion) is rectilinear and the
directrix (feed motion) is also rectilinear, a flat surface is obtained
as in shaping or planing. Similarly, when the generatrix is a circle
and the directrix is along a line perpendicular to the plane of generatrix, the surface obtained is a cylinder as in turning. When the
circular generatrix and rectilinear directrix are in the same plane, a
plane surface is obtained is in milling. These three cases are shown
in Figure 7.2.

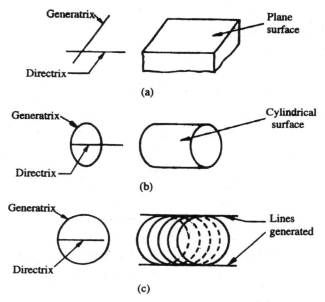

Fig. 7.2 Production of geometrical shapes. (a) plane surface, (b)
cylindrical surface and (c) plane surface.

· In Figs. 7.2(a) and (b) the surfaces produced are by direct tracing of generatrices, while in Figure 7.2(c) the surface produced is
an envelope of the generatrices. Thus the methods of producing
machined surfaces can be classified into two broad categories: the
tracing method, and the generation method. When the surface is
produced by direct tracing of the generatrices the method is known
as *tracing*, whereas in the *generation* method the surface produced
is essentially an envelope of generatrices.

Table 7.2 Classification of machining processes.

Operation	Shape obtained	Cutting tool	Tool motion	Work motion
Turning	Cylindrical	Single point	Translation	Rotary
Boring	Cylindrical	Single point	Rotation	Forward translation
Shaping	Flat	Single point	Translation	Intermittent translation
Planing	Flat	Single point	Intermittent translation	Translatory
Milling	Flat & contoured	Multi-point	Rotation	Translatory
Drilling	Cylindrical	Multi-point	Rotation & translatory	Stationary

7.3   Chip Formation

Metal-cutting is basically a chip-forming operation where the required workpiece configuration is obtained by removing excess material in the form of chip. The mechanics of chip formation in these processes are quite complex since two or more cutting edges are involved in cutting and the deformation takes place in three dimensions. The basic mechanics involved in these processes can, however, be understood by examining the cutting mechanism with a single-edge wedge tool. When the workpiece is pushed into this tool, a layer of material is removed from the workpiece and it slides over the front face of the tool called the rake face. When the cutting edge of the wedge is perpendicular to the cutting velocity vector (Fig. 7.3), the process is called *orthogonal cutting*. In this case, the material gets deformed under plane strain conditions since strain in the y-direction is zero and the width of the chip formed is the same as the width of the workpiece. To ensure plane strain (two-dimensional) deformation the width of workpiece w must be much greater than the thickness of layer t removed from the workpiece ($w > 20t$). Also the width of tool must be greater than the width of workpiece so that end or edge effects could be neglected (Fig. 7.3).

In most practical metal-cutting processes, the cutting edge of the tool is not perpendicular to the cutting velocity vector but set at an angle i with the normal to the cutting velocity vector (y-direction). Cutting in this case takes place in three-dimensions and represents the general case of *oblique cutting* (Fig. 7.4).

When the inclination angle i is zero, the two-dimensional machining or orthogonal cutting situation is obtained. From Figs. 7.3 and 7.4, it is clear that the chip slides directly up the tool face in orthog-

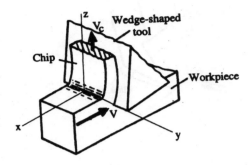

Fig. 7.3 Orthogonal cutting.

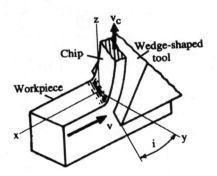

Fig. 7.4 Oblique cutting.

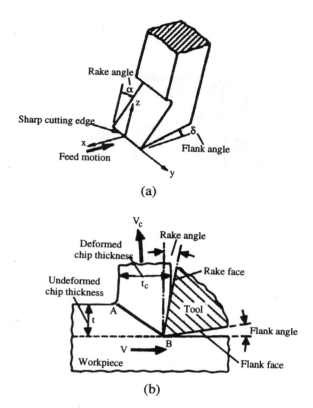

Fig. 7.5(a) Wedge-shaped tool and (b) orthogonal cutting.

onal cutting, while a lateral direction of chip movement is obtained in oblique cutting.

In order to understand the basic mechanics of the cutting process, the simple case of two-dimensional or orthogonal cutting will be considered. Here a rectangular workpiece, with width large enough so that plane strain deformation is achieved, is cut by a wedge-shaped tool (Fig. 7.5a) of rake angle α (angle of the tool face from normal to the machined surface) and flank angle δ (angle of the back face of tool from normal to the machined surface). Cutting can be achieved either by moving the tool or the workpiece. In both cases, the principle involved is the same.

During tool-work interaction the workpiece material is severely compressed and the material in a narrow zone extending from the tool tip (B) to the free surface of the workpiece (A) gets plastically deformed (Fig. 7.5b). The deformation occurs due to intense shearing in this narrow zone, called the *shear zone*. This shear zone is

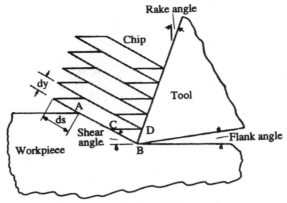

Fig. 7.6 Card analogy.

usually very narrow, except at low cutting speeds, and is generally approximated by a plane, called the *shear plane*. The angle that this shear plane makes with the surface of the workpiece is called the *shear angle* (ϕ).

The chips are thus produced by the shearing process along the shear plane and the chips formed slide up the tool face as cutting progresses. Imagine a pack of playing cards stacked parallel to the shear plane AB (Fig. 7.6). On shearing these cards will slide one after the other and climb up the tool face. During shearing each card slides through a distance just sufficient to maintain contact with the tool. If these cards were infinitesimally thin, shearing will appear to occur in a continuous manner. In a similar manner, thin layers of metal are removed from the workpiece and the chip is formed continuously.

7.3.1 Types of Chips

Due to variations in material behaviour and cutting conditions, widely different types of chips are obtained during metal cutting. These, however, can be broadly classified into the following three categories:
1. Continuous chips
2. Continuous chips with built-up-edge
3. Discontinuous chips.

The process of chip formation described above produces continuous chips provided the resistance to sliding between the chip and the tool is negligible. Continuous chips (Fig. 7.7a) are generally obtained when ductile materials are machined at high cutting speed and low feed. It also produces good surface finish on the workpiece. These

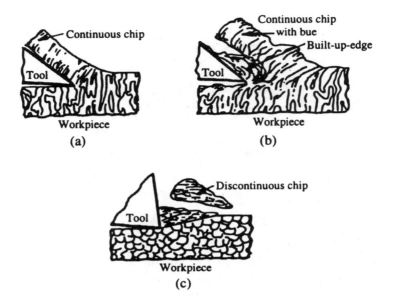

Fig. 7.7 Types of chips: (a) continuous chip, (b) continuous chip with BUE and (c) discontinuous chip.

long ribbon-like chips sometimes create handling problem because they tend to get tangled around the tool holder.

Under certain machining conditions, the resistance to sliding of the chip over the rake face is so severe that instead of sliding, a thin layer of metal is ruptured from the chip surface. This occurs when the temperature and pressure conditions at the chip-tool interface are such that the surface layer on the underside of chip gets welded to the tool face which on rupture leaves a layer of chip material welded to the tool face forming the *built-up-edge* (BUE). The presence of BUE material further increases friction resulting in piling of another layer of chip material on the rake face. The process continues and layer after layer of chip material piles up until it becomes unstable and breaks off. Most of the broken pieces are carried away by the underside of the chip, while some escape under the flank face of the tool (Fig. 7.7b).

It is clear that built-up-edge formation involves welding and rupture of chip materials. While welding is affected by temperature and pressure, strain hardening and thermal softening are important for rupture. The underside layer of chip gets severely deformed during machining and the resulting strain hardening causes the hardness of this layer to increase significantly. As the chip flows, the bonding between this hardened layer and the tool breaks at a softer layer some distance inside the chip. A thin layer of chip material thus sticks to the rake face and BUE formation gets initiated.

The built-up-edge formation generally occurs in a certain speed range. At speeds beyond a certain value when the recrystalization temperature of chip material is reached, strain hardening is negligible and no BUE is formed. At low cutting speeds, the temperature is low and severe strain hardening causes the chip to fracture in the deformation zone itself. In general low cutting speed, high feed and small rake angle are conducive to BUE formation. Presence of BUE increases power consumption during machining and results in poor surface finish.

Discontinuous chips are formed when the work material gets fractured in the shear zone itself due to high strain. Thus for brittle materials like cast iron which cannot withstand high strain, the chips will come out in small segments (discontinuos chips) and are merely pushed away by the tool (Fig. 7.7c). Discontinuous chips are also formed during machining of ductile materials when cutting conditions are such that they are plastically deformed beyond the fracture strain. Low cutting speed, high feed and small rake angle generally produce discontinuous chips.

The conditions that generally influence the formation of three types of chips described above are summarized in Table. 7.3.

Table 7.3 Factors influencing formation of various types of chips.

Factors	Continuous	Continuous with BUE	Discontinuous
• Work material	Ductile	Ductile	Brittle
• Cutting speed	High	Medium	Low
• Feed	High	Low	Low
• Rake angle	Large	Small	Small
• Cutting edge	Sharp	Dull	-
• Friction	Low	High	-
• Cutting fluid	Efficient	Poor	-

7.4 Cutting Forces and Power

The knowledge of the magnitude and variation of cutting forces is necessary for rational design of machine for cutting operations. It helps the designer in deciding the dimensions of various machine

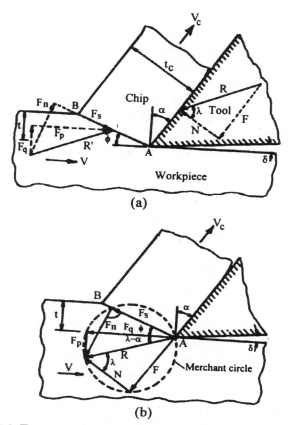

Fig. 7.8 Forces acting on the tool in orthogonal cutting; (a) Equilibrium of chip and (b) Force components superimposed at the tool tip.

components and the power required to drive the tool and the machine table.

The forces acting on the tool during orthogonal cutting can be obtained by considering the chip as a free body held in equilibrium by the forces transmitted across the shear plane and the chip-tool contact interface (Fig. 7.8a). For equilibrium R must be equal, opposite and collinear to R'. R' can be resolved into two components F_p and F_q, the cutting force in the direction of cutting velocity V and the thrust force normal to the direction of cutting velocity. Alternatively R' can be resolved as shear force and normal force F_s and F_n, along the shear plane and perpendicular to the shear plane. Similarly, R can be resolved as friction and normal forces, F and N on the rake face.

Forces F_p and F_q can be easily measured during cutting by means of a suitably designed froce dynmometer. F and N can, therefore, be evaluated from

$$F = F_p \sin \alpha + F_q \cos \alpha \qquad (7.1)$$

$$N = F_p \cos \alpha - F_q \sin \alpha \qquad (7.2)$$

where α is the rake angle of the tool. Hence the coefficient of friction on the rake face

$$\mu = \tan \lambda = \frac{F}{N} \qquad (7.3)$$

or

$$\mu = \frac{F_q + F_p \tan \alpha}{F_p - F_q \tan \alpha} \qquad (7.4)$$

where λ is the friction angle.

The value of μ in metal cutting operations is generally in the range of 0.5 to 2.0. Thus, the chip while flowing up the rake face encounters considerable frictional resistance. The chip-tool contact length is typically of the order of 1 mm.

Forces F_s and F_n can be obtained from

$$F_s = F_p \cos \phi - F_q \sin \phi \qquad (7.5)$$

$$F_n = F_p \sin \phi + F_q \cos \phi \qquad (7.6)$$

provided ϕ is known.

From the geometry of Figure 7.8,

$$AB = \frac{t}{\sin \phi} = \frac{t_c}{\cos(\phi - \alpha)} \qquad (7.7)$$

or

$$\tan \phi = \frac{r \cos \alpha}{1 - r \sin \alpha} \qquad (7.8)$$

where r is the chip-thickness ratio.

By equating the volume of the undeformed chip (length l, thickness t, width b) and the deformed chip (length l_c, thickness t_c, width $b_c = b$) gives

$$r = \frac{t}{t_c} = \frac{l_c}{l} \qquad (7.9)$$

Thus by experimentally evaluating r, the shear angle ϕ can be estimated.

The total power P required for cutting can be evaluated from

$$P = F_p V \qquad (7.10)$$

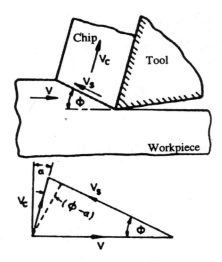

Fig. 7.9 Velocity diagram.

This power is mainly dissipated in shearing the material along the shear plane and in overcoming rake face friction. Thus,

Total power = Power for shearing + Power for friction

or

$$P = F_s V_s + F V_c \qquad (7.11)$$

From Figure 7.9, the shear velocity V_s and chip velocity V_c can be obtained as

$$V_s = \frac{V \cos \alpha}{\cos(\phi - \alpha)} \qquad (7.12)$$

and

$$V_c = \frac{V \sin \phi}{\cos(\phi - \alpha)} \qquad (7.13)$$

7.5   Cutting Temperature

The energy dissipated in metal-cutting operations gets converted into heat. In fact, there are three distinct regions where heat is generated. These are:

(a) The shear zone where energy needed to shear the chip is the source of heat. About 80-85% of the heat is generated in this region.

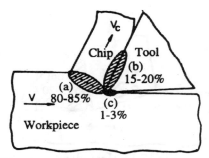

Fig. 7.10 Regions of heat generation.

(b) The chip-tool interface region where energy needed to overcome friction is the source of heat. Some plastic deformation also occurs in this region. About 15-20% of the heat is generated in this region.

(c) The tool-work interface region where energy needed to overcome frictional rubbing between flank face of the tool and the workpiece is the source of heat. Only 1-3% of the heat is generated in this region.

These heat sources are shown in Figure 7.10.

Heat generated during cutting may remain in the workpiece, or flow into the tool, or be carried away by the chip. Experiments show that about 80-85% of the heat generated is carried away by the chip, 15-20% flows into the tool, and less than 5% remains in the workpiece (Fig. 7.11). The temperature in the cutting zone, therefore, rises and may reach 500°C or more depending upon the cutting speed (Fig. 7.12). This temperature may adversely affect

(i) The hardness and wear resistance of tool,

(ii) The properties of workpiece material and in some cases cause thermal damage, and

(iii) The dimensional accuracy of the component.

Cutting speed is the most important parameter affecting the cutting zone temperature. Feed and depth of cut are other variables which affect the temperature but their influence is not pronounced.

The average shear plane temperature $\bar{\theta}_s$ can be estimated from the rate at which shear energy $(F_s V_s)$ is expended. Thus,

$$F_s V_s = \rho c V t b(\bar{\theta}_s - \theta_o) \qquad (7.14)$$

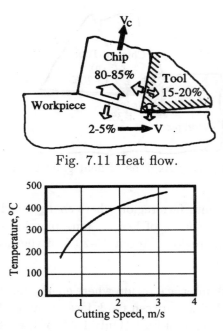

Fig. 7.11 Heat flow.

Fig. 7.12 Effect of cutting speed on temperature.

where ρ and c are density and specific heat of the work material and θ_o is the ambient temperature. If 80% of this heat is assumed to go into the chip, then

$$\bar{\theta}_s = \frac{\beta F_s V_s}{\rho c V t b} + \theta_o \qquad (7.15)$$

where β may be assumed to be 0.8.

The temperature at the tool face is obtained by adding to the shear plane temperature, the temperature rise due to rake face friction. Analysis for estimating temperature rise due to rake face friciton is available, but this is beyond the scope of this book.

The maximum temperature in the cutting zone (Fig. 7.13) occurs not at the tool tip but at some distance further up the rake face. Material at a point such as X gets heated as it passes through the shear zone and finally leaves as a chip. Points such as Z remain in the workpiece and their temperature rises merely due to conduction of heat into the workpiece. For points such as Y, heating continues beyond the shear plane into the frictional heat region. These points, however, loose shear zone heat to the chip while moving up but gain friction heat. These factors cause maximum tool temperature to occur some distance away from the cutting edge.

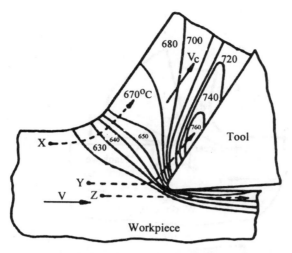

Fig. 7.13 Temperature in the cutting zone. (After Boothroyd, 1975)

7.6 Tool Wear and Tool Life

Wear of a cutting tool takes place in two distinct ways (Fig. 7.14). Due to rubbing of flank face against the machined surface, wear occurs on the flank face in the form of a wear land. Similarly, flow of the chip over the rake face causes rake face wear in the form of a crater. This crater is generally formed some distance up the rake face where cutting temperature is maximum. Flank wear is usually evaluated in term of wear-land size or length of wear land l_w, while depth of crater d_c is usually used for evaluating crater wear.

There are two basic causes of tool wear: (i) adhesion and (ii) diffusion. *Adhesion* occurs when two bodies come under intimate contact such that atoms come within interatomic distance to form strong bonds. During metal cutting, the chip-tool and tool-workpiece interfaces come under close contact. These contacts occur at the surface asperities only (Fig. 7.15), thus the real area of contact A_r is only a fraction of the total or apparant area A. In such a situation the normal load at the junction is supported by minute asperities in contact with each other. The contact pressure thus reaches a high value causing plastic deformation and welding of the junctions. If a sliding force is now applied to the junction, shearing of the welded joint may occur at the junction, below the junction, or above the junction, depending upon the fracture strength of the joint and the strength of the sliding bodies. Welding or adhesive bonding at the junction is usually stronger than the base metals because of strain hardening and diffusion and sliding causes the fracture to occur in

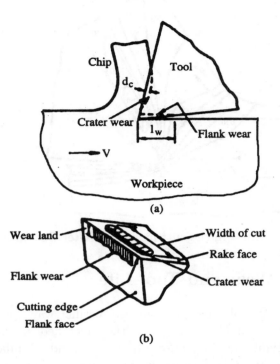

(a)

(b)

Fig. 7.14 Tool Wear.

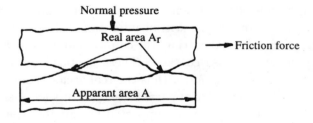

Fig. 7.15 Contact on surface asperities.

the weaker material. Although the fractured fragment gets attached to the stronger or harder material, it eventually gets dislodged during further sliding and comes out as a loose fragment or wear particle. As the normal load is increased, A_r increases and the sliding force required to shear the junction increases.

Diffusion is the mechanism by which atoms in a metallic crystal move from one lattice point to another causing transfer of an element. This transfer takes place from a region of high concentration to that of low concentration with the rate of diffusion depending on the concentration gradient. Diffusion is a time-temperature dependent process and its rate increases exponentially with rise in temperature. During sliding contact of two dissimilar metals, atoms may diffuse across the contacting asperities leading to wear.

In metal cutting diffusion may be regarded as an integral part of adhesion wear process. At chip-tool and tool-workpiece interfaces, diffusion of atoms from tool material to work material or chip may cause weakening of the tool surface structure leading to increase in tool wear. A typical example of this is diffusion of cobalt from tungsten carbide tool into the steel workpiece causing weakened tool surface layer. Similarly, diffusion of carbon onto the inside surface of chip during machining of a ferrous alloy with tungsten carbide tool strengthens the surface which in turn increases wear rate.

As indicated earlier, diffusion is temperature as well as time dependent phenomenon. Thus, at higher cutting speeds diffusion rate increases because of higher temperature but contact time, an inverse function of speed, causes reduced diffusion rate. This relationship between wear rate and sliding/cutting speed as influenced by diffusion is a complex one but it appears that diffusion plays a significant role in the formation and development of crater on the rake face, particularly in the higher range of cutting speeds where higher temperatures are obtained. Also, the formation of crater some distance up the rake face where temperature is maximum supports the argument that diffusion has strong influence on crater wear.

Abrasion (ploughing of grooves on softer material by the surface asperities of harder material or by loose hard particles trapped at the sliding interface), chemical action (oxidation and electrochemical action) and fatigue also occur at the chip-tool and tool-workpiece interfaces but there contribution to tool wear is small.

Experimental studies indicate that the wear land on flank face increases with cutting time. A typical wear land growth pattern (Fig. 7.16) indicates three distinct regions. Initially the wear rate is high because the sharp tool edge quickly breaks down due to high

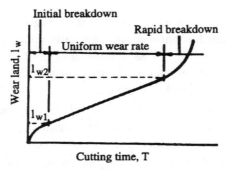

Fig. 7.16 Typical wear-land growth pattern.

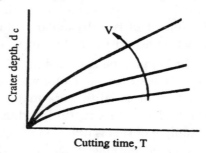

Fig. 7.17 Crater wear-cutting time curves.

initial stress (nominally zero contact area). Once a finite wear land size lw_1, is established, wear increases at a uniform rate for a considerable period. When the wear-land size reaches a critical value lw_2, the interface temperature and the normal pressure become sufficiently high to cause sub-surface plastic flow and rapid growth of wear. The cutting tool, therefore, must be regrounded before wear-land size lw_2 is reached.

Crater wear is generally evaluated in terms of depth of crater d_c and its variation with cutting time and cutting speed is shown in Figure 7.17. As the crater depth increases, the strength of the tool decreases and may eventually cause catastropic failure (rupture) of the tool.

Metal-cutting operations are generally carried out to obtain the desired geometrical configurations, tolerances, and surface finishes often unobtainable by any other technique. A tool that is no longer able to provide the desired output in terms of accuracy and finish is said to have failed. Thus, one never waits for the total destruction of tool but removes and resharpens the tool when its performance is unsatisfactory. *Tool life* therefore represents the useful life of a cutting tool from the start of a cut to some end-point defined by a failure criterion. The life of a tool is generally specified in terms of

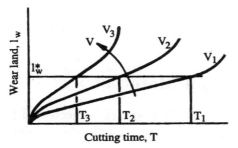

Fig. 7.18 Wear land - cutting time curves.

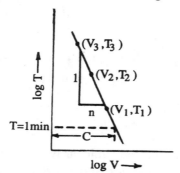

Fig. 7.19 Taylor tool life equation.

cutting time to failure.

The failure criterion most commonly used is the wear-land size, not only becuase it can be easily measured but because it is related to output parameters such as tolerance and surface finish. The critical wear-land size $(l_w^\star)$ recommended for tool made of different materials is 0.3 mm for finishing operations and 0.6 mm for roughing operations. Limiting value of crater depth $d_c^\star$ is sometimes used as a failure criterion during machining at high cutting speeds.

When the wear land-cutting time curves obtained at various cutting speeds are plotted (Fig. 7.18), it is found that the wear rate increases with increasing cutting speed. From curves such as these, the tool life at various cutting speeds in terms of critical wear-land size $l_w^\star$ can be obtained. When these tool life values (T) are plotted against speed (V) using log-log co-ordinates (Fig. 7.19), the curve obtained is linear giving a relationship of the form

$$VT^n = C$$

where n and C are constants for a given tool and work materials, and machining conditions other than cutting speed. This equation has come to be known as the *Taylor tool life equation* since F.W. Taylor was the first to suggest this relationship. Since T is usually measured in minutes, C is the cutting speed that gives a tool life of one minute.

7.7   Cutting Tool Materials

During chip formation cutting tools are subjected to high pressures and temperatures. The tool materials, therefore, must meet the following basic requirements:

(i) The tool material must be strong and hard enough to withstand high pressures.

(ii) The tool materials must be able to retain the strength and hardness at high operating temperatures (hot hardness).

(iii) The tool material must have sufficient wear resistance so that tool life obtained is acceptable.

(iv) The tool material must be sufficiently tough to withstand the impact forces, absorb shock and prevent chipping of cutting edges.

(v) The tool material must have thermal-shock resistance to absorb rapid heating and cooling during interrrupted cutting operations.

The other characteristics that are considered are grindability, weldability, hardenability, chemical stability and thermal properties.

The basic requirements indicated above are clearly conflicting and no tool material can satisfy all the requirements. This has led to the development of a wide variety of tool materials over the years and many of them are still in use. Some of the common ones are discussed below.

Carbon tool steels with a typical composition of 0.8-1.3% carbon, 0.1 to 0.4% silicon and 0.1-0.4% manganese are still in use for machining of softer materials. This is the oldest cutting tool material and, in fact, until about 1870 this was the only tool material in use. These tools have low hot hardness and soften above 250°C.

High-speed steel, an alloy steel, with a typical composition of 18% tungsten 4% chromium, 1% vanadium and 5% cobalt was introduced around 1910 and was capable of machining upto 35 m/min. Because of their ability to machine at higher cutting speeds, these alloy steels came to be known as high-speed steel (HSS). 'Moly' HSS was introduced around 1925 and had a composition of 0.8% carbon, 4%

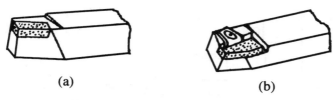

(a)   (b)

Fig. 7.20 Tungsten carbide tools.

chromium, 2% vanadium, 6% tungsten and 5% molybdenum. Partial replacement of tungsten by molybdenum enabled these tools to be operated at more than twice the speeds of earlier HSS tools.

Cast non-ferrous alloys such as stellites have also been used as cutting tool materials. These alloys typicaly have 40-50% cobalt, 27-32% chromium, 14-29% tungsten and 2-4% carbon. Increased hardness of these tools permitted use of still higher speed (100 m/min) but at the cost of reduced toughness.

Cemented carbide, developed around 1930 using powder metallurgy technique, had tungsten carbide powder sintered with cobalt (3-12%) binder. These tools were mainly used for machining cast iron and non-ferrous materials because diffusion during machining of steels caused rapid cratering. For machining of steels 10-40% titanium carbide or tantalum carbide (or both) are substituted for tungsten carbide to develop diffusion-resistant interface. Thus, there are two types of sintered tungsten carbides — one for machining cast iron and non-ferrous materials (K-type) and the other for machining ferrous metals (P-type). An intermediate category of M-type containing smaller quantity of mixed cabides is also available for machining of ductile iron, hard steels and high temperature alloys. Carbide tools work well at high cutting speeds (250-1500 m/min) and retain their hardness upto 900°C.

Tungsten carbide tools are relatively very expensive and are used only as thick wafers attached to steel shanks. Earlier these wafers were brazed (Fig. 7.20a) but now they are available as inserts which can be mechanically clamped onto the tool shank (Fig. 7.20b). Inserts have the advantage that it can be rotated for a new edge after one edge becomes dull.

Carbides are very brittle and sensitive to thermal shocks. That is why cutting fluids are rarely used during intermittent cutting operations with carbide tools.

In *coated carbides*, developed around 1970, a thin layer of ceramic material is deposited on steel cutting grade carbide tools to reduce the tendency of cratering so that tools could be used for machining

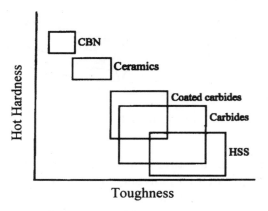

Fig. 7.21 Variation in toughness with increasing hot hardness of tool materials.

at higher speeds. The coating materials that are commonly used are titanium carbide (TiC), titanium nitrite (TiN) and aluminium oxide (Al_2O_3). Composite or multilayer coatings are also used because they prolong tool life through formation of stronger metallurgical bond between coating and the carbide substrate. Such tools can be used for machining of different materials because the desirable properties can be combined and optimized in two or three layers of coatings of different materials. The coating thickness on carbide tools are generally in the range of 5 to 10 μm with single layer seldom exceeding 5 μm.

Ceramic tools are made from pure aluminium oxide (Al_2O_3) in the form of insert tool tips. These tools are made from very fine Al_2O_3 powder using PM processing. They are very hard (harder than carbide) but very brittle and do not soften at elevated temperatures. Such tools are, therefore, suitable for very high speed cutting, but under light loads and continuous machining conditions because of their poor shock resistance.

Cubic boron nitride (CBN) cutting tools were introduced around 1970 by bonding a 0.5 mm thick layer of polycrystalline CBN onto a carbide substrate through sintering under pressure. It retains its hardness upto 1000°C and because of low chemical reactivity it reduces cratering. CBN has a hardness second only to that of diamond and can be efficiently used for machining of difficult-to-machine materials at much higher speeds than carbides. CBN is also used for making tool inserts.

Diamond, the hardest material, is used primarily for high-speed finishing of non-ferrous materials. Its use as a metal-cutting tool is limited mainly because it changes into graphite at high temperature

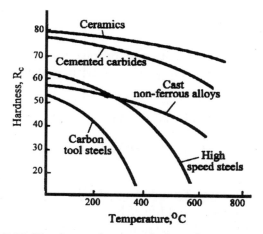

Fig. 7.22 Hardness characteristics of common tool materials.

(700°C) which diffuses into iron and makes it unsuitable for machining of steels. Polycrystalline diamond tools are available as inserts or as 0.5-1 mm thick layer sintered onto a carbide substrate.

Table 7.4 Recommended speed range for various tool materials.

Tool material	Typical cutting speed, (m/min)	Speed range
Carbon tool steels	10	Low speed
High-speed steels	40	Medium speed
Cast non-ferrous alloys	60	Medium speed
Cemented carbides	150	Medium speed
Coated carbides	350	Medium to high speed
Ceramic tools	550	High to very high speed
Cubic boron nitride	250	Medium to high speed
Diamond	650	High to very high speed

Hot hardness and toughness are two important requirements for cutting tool materials. These are two conflicting requirements and the choice of a particular tool material is essentially a compromise between these two requirements. Figure 7.21 shows how the toughness decreases with increasing hot hardness of tool materials. The hardness characteristics of the existing tool materials (Fig. 7.22) dictate the typical cutting speed range that can be used with a particular tool (Table 7.4).

7.8   Cutting Fluids

Cutting fluids, also called coolants and lubricants, are extensively used in machining operations. The primary functions of cutting fluids are:

(i)   To act like a coolant and cool the cutting zone, and

(ii) To act like a lubricant and reduce to friction at the tool- chip and tool-work interfaces.

Reduction in cutting zone temperature aids in retaning the hardness of the tool and increases tool life. Also removal of heat from the cutting zone reduces thermal distortion of the workpiece and better dimensional accuracy is achieved.

For the cutting fluid to act as an effective lubricant it must penetrate the chip-tool and tool-work interfaces. High stresses on the tool rake face and rapid sliding of the chip away from the tool tip make it rather difficult for the cutting fluid to enter the interface, particularly at higher cutting speeds. However, some fluid does get into the interface from the sides of the chip, while some may get drawn between the surface asperities by the capillary action. These effects, however, reduce friction only marginally since full fluid film formation at the chip-tool interface is rather remote. Use of additives such as carbon tetrachloride have been rather effective in reducing chip-tool interface friction through formation of a low shear strength film on the inner surface of the chip.

The access of cutting fluid in the tool-work interface region is possible and this helps in improving surface finish.

The cutting fluids also perform two secondary functions: (i) removal of chips from the cutting zone, and (ii) protecting the finished surface from corrosion.

Considering the actions and functions of the cutting fluids, an ideal cutting fluid should have the following:

(a) Large specific heat and thermal conductivity for efficient cooling.

(b) Low viscosity and low molecular size for effective penetration at the tool-chip interface.

(c) Suitable additives for forming low shear strength film on the inner chip surface for reducing friction.

(d) Non-corrosive to prevent corrosion of machine components and finished workpiece.

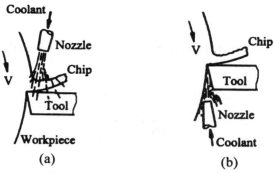

Fig. 7.23 Injecting cutting fluid.

(e) Inexpensive and readily available because of large quantity requirements.

Cutting fluids in use can be broadly classified into two categories: (i) water-based fluids, and (ii) oil-based fluids. Additives are added to either of them for achieving the desired function. Water mixed with oils or chemicals is the best cooling medium. The most popular cutting fluid, the soluble oils, are emulsions of mineral oil with an emulsifier such as soap in water. The mixture ratio of water and oil vary from 5 to 100, depending upon the requirements.

Oil-based fluids, generally mineral oils with appropriate additives, are used at low cutting speeds only so that lubrication is effective.

Coolants are generally applied by flooding the cutting zone from the chip side. A better way is to inject the cutting fluid under pressure through the clearance area (Fig. 7.23) so that fluid access to the cutting edge is easier for more effective cooling and lubrication.

Numerical Examples

Q.1 During orthogonal machining of a steel workpiece with a single-point cutting tool of 10° rake angle, the following data were recorded:

Chip thickness = 1.5mm
Cutting force = 980 N
Thrust force = 440 N
Undefined chip thickness = 0.6 mm
Width of cut = 1.8 mm

Determine the shear strength of the material.

Solution:

$$\text{Chip thickness ratio,} \quad r = \frac{t}{t_c} = \frac{0.6}{1.5} = 0.4$$

Since,

$$\tan\phi = \frac{r\cos\alpha}{1 - r\sin\alpha} = \frac{0.4\cos 10°}{1 - 0.4\sin 10°} = 0.423$$

Therefore,

$$\phi = \tan^{-1}0.423 = 22.94°$$

Now,

$$A_s = \frac{bt}{\sin\phi} = \frac{1.8 \times 0.6}{\sin 22.94} = 2.77 \text{ mm}^2$$

and the shear force component,

$$
\begin{aligned}
F_s &= F_p\cos\phi - F_q\sin\phi \\
&= 980\cos 22.94 - 440\sin 22.94 \\
&= 731 \text{ N.}
\end{aligned}
$$

Therefore, the strength of the material,

$$
\begin{aligned}
k &= \frac{F_s}{A_s} \\
&= \frac{731}{2.77} \\
&= 263.9 \text{ N/mm}^2
\end{aligned}
$$

Q.2 During orthogonal cutting with a 0° rake angle tool, the cutting and thrust forces were measured as 968 N and 455 N, respectively. Determine the coefficient of friction.

Solution:

Friction and normal forces, F and N, are

$$F = F_p\sin\alpha + F_q\cos\alpha = F_q$$

$$N = F_p\cos\alpha - F_q\sin\alpha = F_p$$

since $\alpha = 0°$. Therefore,

$$\mu = \frac{F}{N} = \frac{455}{968} = 0.47$$

Q.3 During orthogonal cutting with a 0° rake angle tool, the following data were obtained:

$$F_p = 950 \text{ N}, \quad F_q = 475 \text{ N}$$

$$V = 200 \text{ m/min}; \quad \phi = 18.4°$$

Determine the total power required for machining.

Solution:

Total power = Power for shearing + Power for friction

or

$$P = F_s V_s + F V_c$$

Now,

$$
\begin{aligned}
F_s = F_p \cos\phi - F_q \sin\phi &= 950 \times 0.95 - 475 \times 0.32 \\
&= 750.5 \text{ N} \\
F &= F_p \sin\alpha + F_q \cos\alpha = 475 \text{ N}
\end{aligned}
$$

$$V_s = \frac{V \cos\alpha}{\cos(\phi - \alpha)} = \frac{200/60}{0.95} = 3.51 \text{ m/s}$$

$$V_c = \frac{V \sin\phi}{\cos(\phi - \alpha)} = \frac{200/60 \times 0.32}{0.95} = 1.12 \text{ m/s}$$

Therefore,

$$
\begin{aligned}
P &= 750.5 \times 3.51 + 475 \times 1.12 \\
&= 3166.26 \text{ n-m/s}
\end{aligned}
$$

Q.4 Estimate the average shear plane temperature for machining a mild steel workpiece at a cutting speed of 2 m/s with a 10° rake angle tool. The width of cut is 2 mm and the undeformed chip thickness is 0.25 mm. (Given: $\phi = 36.72°$, $\rho = 7200$ kg/m³, c $= 502$ j/kg°C, $\mu = 0.5$ and $k = 400 \times 10^6$ N/m²)

Solution: Shear force,

$$
\begin{aligned}
F_s &= \frac{kbt}{\sin\phi} \\
&= \frac{400 \times 10^6 \times 2 \times 10^{-3} \times 0.25 \times 10^{-3}}{\sin 36.72°} \\
&= 334.6 \text{ N}
\end{aligned}
$$

Shear velocity,

$$V_s = \frac{\cos\alpha}{\cos(\phi-\alpha)}.V = \frac{\cos 10°}{\cos 26.72°} \times 2$$
$$= 2.21 \text{ m/s}$$

Average shear plane temperature,

$$\bar{\theta}_s = \frac{\beta F_s V_s}{\rho tbcV} + \theta_0$$

Taking ambient temperature $\theta = 25°$, and $\beta = 0.85$,

$$\bar{\theta}_s = \frac{0.85 \times 334.6 \times 2.21}{7200 \times 0.25 \times 10^{-3} \times 2 \times 10^{-3} \times 502 \times 2} + 25°$$
$$= 173.9 + 25$$
$$= 198.9°C$$

Q.5 During straight turning of a 25 mm diameter steel bar at 300 rpm with an HSS tool, a tool life of 10 min was obtained. When the same bar was turned at 250 rpm, the tool life increased to 52.5 min. What will be the tool life at a speed of 275 rpm?

Solution: Given:

$$V_1 = \frac{\pi \times 25 \times 300}{1000} \text{ m/min}; \quad T_1 = 10 \text{ min}$$

$$V_2 = \frac{\pi \times 25 \times 250}{1000} \text{ m/min}; \quad T_2 = 52.5 \text{ min}$$

using Taylor Tool life equation:

$$V_1 T_1^n = V_2 T_2^n$$

Therefore,

$$n = \frac{log(V_2/V_1)}{log(T_1/T_2)} = \frac{log\left(\frac{250}{300}\right)}{log\left(\frac{10}{52.5}\right)} = 0.11$$

Now,

$$V_1 T_1^n = V_3 T_3^n$$

or

$$T_3 = \left(\frac{V_1 T_1^n}{V_3}\right)^{1/n} = \left(\frac{V_1}{V_3}\right)^{1/n} \times T_1$$
$$= \left(\frac{300}{275}\right)^{1/0.11} \times 10$$
$$= 22 \text{ min}$$

Q.6 During machining the wear land l_w (mm) was found to be related to tool life T (minutes) and cutting speed V (m/min) as

$$l_w = 56.5 \times 10^{-8} \quad V^{2.4} T^{0.6}$$

when critical weal-land size $l_w^\star = 1.5$ mm was used for tool failure. Evaluate the cutting speed to obtain a tool life of 30 minutes.

Solution:

When $l_w = l_w^\star = 1.5$ mm,

$$V^{2.4} T^{0.6} = \frac{1.5}{56.5 \times 10^{-8}}$$

or

$$V T^{\frac{0.6}{2.4}} = \left(\frac{1.5}{56.5 \times 10^{-8}} \right)^{1/2.4}$$

or

$$V T^{0.25} = 475$$

becomes the Taylor tool life equation. For $T = 30$ min,

$$(V)_{30\text{min}} = \frac{475}{30^{0.25}} = 202.96 \text{ m/mm}$$

Q.7 A mild steel workpiece is being machined by two different tools A and B under identical machining conditions. The tool life equations for these tools are:

$$\text{ToolA} \quad V T^{0.31} = 43.3$$
$$\text{ToolB} \quad V T^{0.43} = 89.5$$

where V and T are in m/s and s, respectively. Determine the cutting speed above which tool B will give better tool life.

Solution:

At break-even speed $V^\star$ both tool give the same tool life. Therefore,

$$(89.5/V^\star)^{1/0.43} = (34.3/V^\star)^{1/0.31}$$

or

$$\frac{(V^\star)^{3.23}}{(V^\star)^{2.23}} = \frac{(34.3)^{3.23}}{(89.5)^{2.23}}$$

or

$$(V^\star)^{0.9} = \frac{90991.33}{22519.84} = 4.04$$

Therefore,

$$(V^\star) = 4.71 \text{ m/s}$$

Review Questions

7.1 Describe the motions imparted to the workpiece and tool to produce a flat surface on lathe.

7.2 What are generatrix and directrix? What are the motion imparted to generatrix and directrix to obtain a tapered surface?

7.3 What is the difference between orthogonal cutting and oblique cutting? Which one is preferred in practice and why?

7.4 Explain briefly the process of chip formation.

7.5 How is built-up-edge formed? What conditions favour the formation of built-up edge? Explain briefly.

7.6 How are discontinuous chips produced? Under what conditions discontinuous chips are obtained during machining of ductile materials?

7.7 What forces are considered to be important during orthogonal cutting?

7.8 How is coefficient of friction in metal cutting evaluated?

7.9 What is shear angle and how this can be evaluated?

7.10 What are the sources of heat in metal cutting?

7.11 Why the maximum temperature in the cutting zone occurs at some distance up the rake face?

7.12 Explain briefly the causes of tool wear.

7.13 Sketch the wear-land growth pattern and explain why these distinct regions are obtained?

7.14 What is tool life? How is tool life evaluated?

7.15 Why crater is formed some distance up the rake face?

7.16 What are the requirements of an ideal tool material? Can any tool material satisfy all the requirements?

7.17 Explain why hot hardness and toughness are two conflicting requirements for tool materials?

7.18 What are the primary functions of cutting fluids? How injecting the cutting fluid under pressure improves its performance?

Chapter 8

Machining Processes

8.1 Metal-cutting Processes

The basic process of material removal was discussed in the previous chapter through the action of a wedge-shaped tool. It is clear that the orientation of the rake face, that is, rake angle has significant influence on the cutting process since it affects cutting forces, power and type of chip formed. The geometry of a wedge-shaped tool can be described in terms of rake angle α and flank angle δ (Fig. 7.5a), but to define these angles a set of reference planes with a set of axes are required. The plane normally considered for defining angles α and δ of a wedge-shaped tool is a plane normal to the cutting edge and perpendicular to the plane containing the cutting edge, that is, plane OABC in Figure 8.1. The figure depicts the general case of oblique cutting. In orthogonal cutting situation $i = 0$ and this plane (OABC) will contain the cutting and chip velocity vectors (V and V_c) also.

The geometry of cutting tools used in practice is much more com-

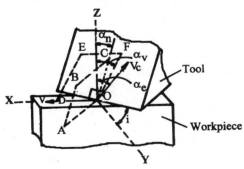

Fig. 8.1 Geometry of a wedge-shaped tool.

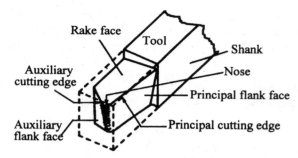

Fig. 8.2 Single-point cutting tool.

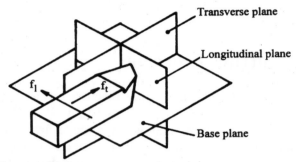

Fig. 8.3 Reference planes in the co-ordinate rake system.

plex since two or more cutting edges are invariably involved in the process. A typical single-point cutting tool (Fig. 8.2) has a rake face and two flank faces which give the principal and the auxiliary cutting edges. Since these tools have to be made in workshops, the inclination of various faces of the tools have to be defined with reference to a set of planes and axes. Over the years a number of reference systems have been suggested. These include the co-ordinate system, the orthogonal rake system and the normal rake system.

In the *co-ordinate system* (Fig. 8.3), also known as the American or *ASA system*, the horizontal plane containing the tool shank is the base plane. The second reference plane is the longitudinal plane perpendicular to the base plane but parallel to the longitudinal feed direction (f_l). The transverse plane, perpendicular to the above two planes, is the third reference plane.

In the *orthogonal rake system (ORS)* (Fig. 8.4), also known as the German or the *DIN system*, the base plane is the same as in the previous case but the second plane, the cutting plane, is perpendicular to the base plane and parallel to the cutting edge. The third reference plane, the orthogonal plane is perpendicular to the other two planes.

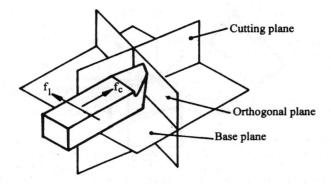

Fig. 8.4 Reference planes in the orthogonal rake system.

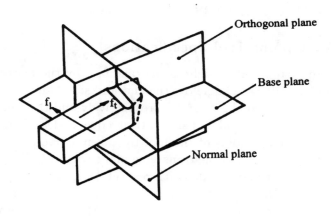

Fig. 8.5 Reference planes in the normal rake system.

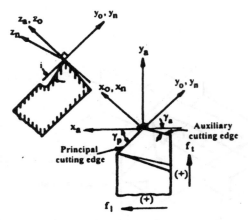

Fig. 8.6 System of axes for ASA, ORS and NRS systems.

In the *normal rake system (NRS)*, shown in Figure 8.5, the base and the cutting plane are the same as in the orthogonal rake system (ORS) but the third plane, the normal plane, is perpendicular to the cutting edge.

The system of axes for the three reference systems described are shown in Figure 8.6 as (x, y, z) axes with subscripts a, o and n referring to ASA, ORS and NRS systems, respectively.

8.1.1 Single-point Tool Specifications

The American system (ASA) defines the rake face by the back rake angle α_b and the side rake angle α_s, the end and side flank faces by the end and side flank angles δ_e and δ_s, respectively and the end and side cutting edges by the end and side cutting edge angles γ_e and γ_s, respectively. The nose radius of the tool tip taken as r on the base plane. Angle α_b is defined in the transverse plane with respect to y_a-axis, α_s in the longitudinal plane with respect to x_a-axis, δ_e in the transverse plane with respect to z_a-axis, δ_s in the longitudinal plane with respect to z_a-axis, and angles γ_e and γ_s on the base plane with respect to x_a and y_a axes, respectively. These angles are indicated in a special sequence as shown:

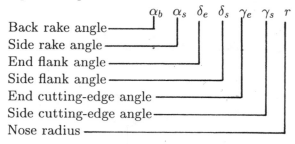

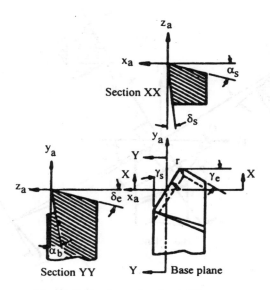

Fig. 8.7 Tool angles in ASA system.

The angles and the nose radius are shown in Figure 8.7.

Thus a tool geometry specified by 6°-6°-5°-8°-15°-5°-2 mm (ASA) would mean a single point cutting tool with back rake angle of 6°, side rake angle of 6°, end flank angle of 5°, side flank angle of 8°, end cutting-edge angle of 15°, side cutting-edge angle of 5° and nose radius of 2 mm.

The orthogonal rake system defines the rake face in terms of inclination angle i and orthogonal rake angle α_o, the principal and auxiliary flank faces by principal and auxiliary flank angles δ_p and δ_e, respectively, and the auxiliary and principal cutting edges by auxiliary and principal cutting-edge angles γ_a and γ_p, respectively. r as before is the nose radius of the tool.

The inclination angle i is defined on the cutting plane with reference to y_o-axis, while α_o is defined on the orthogonal plane with respect to x_o-axis. The principal flank angle δ_p is defined on the orthogonal plane with respect to z_o-axis, but the auxiliary flank angle δ_a is defined on a plane perpendicular to the auxiliary cutting edge, called the auxiliary orthogonal plane, and is evaluated with respect to z_{au}-axis. The principal cutting and auxiliary cutting-edge angles are defined on the base plane with respect to f_l-axis. These angles are shown in Figure 8.8.

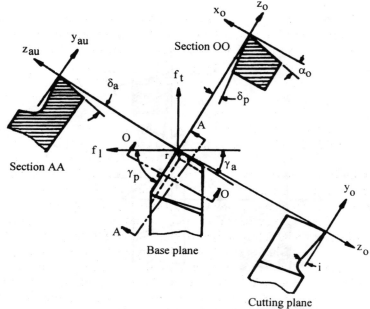

Fig. 8.8 Tool angles in ORS system.

The following is the tool specification in ORS system:

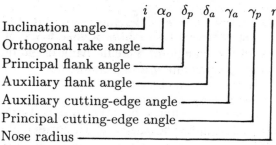

Inclination angle —— i
Orthogonal rake angle —— α_o
Principal flank angle —— δ_p
Auxiliary flank angle —— δ_a
Auxiliary cutting-edge angle —— γ_a
Principal cutting-edge angle —— γ_p
Nose radius —— r

The normal rake system of tool specification is an attempt by the International Standards Organization (ISO) to synthesize the different ways of specifying a single-point cutting tool. The ASA system described above is followed in the US and Canada, while the ORS system is used in Germany, Russia and other European countries. Until recently, the Orthogonal Rake System (ORS) was also followed in India but it has now adopted the system proposed by the International Standards Organization (ISO) which is the Normal Rake System (NRS).

The normal rake system (Fig. 8.9) also defines the inclination angle i, the auxiliary cutting-edge angle γ_a and the principal cutting-edge angle γ_p in the same manner as in the ORS system. The normal rake angle α_n and the principal normal flank angle δ_{pn} are measured

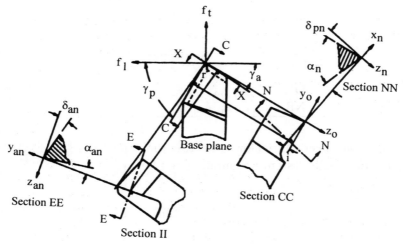

Fig. 8.9 Tool angles in NRS system.

on the normal plane with respect to x_n and z_n axes, respectively. The auxiliary normal flank angle δ_{an} is defined on the auxiliary normal plane with respect to z_{an}-axis.

In this system the reference planes and the axes are so chosen that every angle is a true angle. Tool grinding, therefore, becomes easy since no angle corrections are required during grinding. The sequence of angles in the normal rake system is given as

$$i \quad \alpha_n \quad \delta_{pn} \quad \delta_{an} \quad r_a \quad r_p \quad r$$

Inclination angle ———
Normal rake angle ———
Principal normal flank angle ┘
Auxiliary normal flank angle ———
Auxiliary cutting-edge angle ———
Principal cutting-edge angle ———
Nose radius ———

The tool specifications in the three systems described above are summarized in Table 8.1 and 8.2.

Table 8.1 Tool angles in different systems.

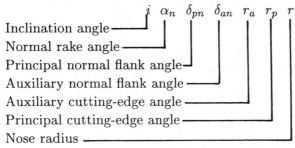

Tool Section	ASA	ORS	NRS
Rake face	α_b, α_o	i, α_o	i, α_n
Flank faces	δ_e, δ_s	δ_a, δ_p	δ_{an}, δ_{pn}
Cutting edges	γ_e, γ_s	γ_a, γ_p	γ_a, γ_p
Nose	r	r	r

Table 8.2 Tool sequence in different systems.

System	Sequence
ASA	$\alpha_b,\ \alpha_s,\ \delta_e,\ \delta_s,\ \gamma_e,\ \gamma_s,\ r$
ORS	$i,\ \alpha_o,\ \delta_p,\ \delta_a,\ \gamma_a,\ \gamma_p,\ r$
NRS	$i,\ \alpha_n,\ \delta_{pn},\ \delta_{an},\ \gamma_a,\ \gamma_p,\ r$

The equations required for converting tool angle in ASA and ORS systems into NRS system are summarized below:

ASA to NRS:

$$\tan i = \tan \alpha_b \cos \gamma_s - \tan \alpha_s \sin \gamma_s \tag{8.1}$$

$$\tan \alpha_n = \cos i (\tan \alpha_s \cos \gamma_s + \tan \alpha_b \sin \gamma_s) \tag{8.2}$$

$$\cot^2 \delta_p = \cot^2 \delta_e + \cot^2 \delta_s - \tan^2 i \tag{8.3}$$

$$\cot \delta_{pn} = \cos i \cot \delta_p \tag{8.4}$$

$$\gamma_p = 90 - \gamma_s \tag{8.5}$$

ORS to NRS:

$$\tan \alpha_n = \cos i \tan \alpha_o \tag{8.6}$$

$$\cot \delta_{pn} = \cos i \cot \delta_p \tag{8.7}$$

One simple method of obtaining these angle relationships is the vector method, illustrated through an example. Consider the convertion for obtaining α_b of ASA system from angles in ORS system. Taking P, Q and R vectors on the rake face of the tool with P along the cutting edge (shown on cutting plane), Q at right angle to the cutting edge (shown on orthogonal plane) and R on the transverse plane (Fig. 8.10), the vectors can be written as

$$\begin{aligned} P &= i \cos \gamma_p - j \sin \gamma_p - k \cos i \\ Q &= -i \sin \gamma_p - j \cos \gamma_p - k \tan \alpha_0 \\ R &= -j - k \tan \alpha_b \end{aligned} \tag{8.8}$$

in terms of unit vector i, j, k along x_a, y_a, z_a - axes. The mixed product of these vectors will be zero since they lie on the same plane. Thus,

$$\begin{bmatrix} \cos \gamma_p & -\sin \gamma_p & -\tan i \\ -\sin \gamma_p & -\cos \gamma_p & -\tan \alpha_0 \\ 0 & -1 & -\tan \alpha_b \end{bmatrix} = 0 \tag{8.9}$$

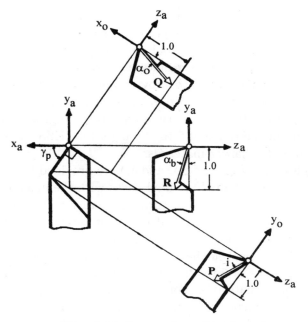

Fig. 8.10 Convertion of tool angles.

and its solution gives the required relationship as

$$\tan \alpha_b = \sin \gamma_p \tan i + \cos \gamma_p \tan \alpha_o \qquad (8.10)$$

Through appropriate choice of planes and axes, the other relationships can also be obtained.

8.1.2 Selection of Tool Angles

Tool angles depend on the tool-work combination and the output parameters of machining such as cutting forces, heat generated, dimensional accuracy, surface finish and tool life. The value selected is often a compromise between various conflicting parameters.

Rake face inclination controls the chip flow direction and also the direction of the resultant force. When the inclination angle is zero, the chip tends to flow parallel to the work surface and often creates removal problems and may even damage the finished work-surface. With suitable inclination angle i or back rake angle α_b, the chip is made to flow away from the workpiece. Inclination angle also increases the contact area and improves heat conduction. Large value of i, however, causes chatter and vibration problems. Rake angles α_n, and α_o and α_s influence cutting forces and power, and the surface finish. Larger values lower the forces and improves surface finish, but have adverse effect on the strength of the tool because less metal is available to support the tool. The optimum value of this angle is, therefore, a compromise between tool strength and efficient cutting. For brittle tool materials like carbides and oxides, this rake angle may be zero or even negative to provide adequate strength. The initial impact on tool with negative α_n or α_o or α_s occurs away from tool edge and prevent fracture or crumbling. Rake angles α_n, α_o and α_s are generally in the range of 5 to 15 degrees for HSS tools, lower values being used for harder materials.

Flank angles (δ_{pn}, δ_{an}, δ_p, δ_a, δ_e and δ_s) are provided to minimize rubbing of principal and auxiliary flank faces with the machined surface. For example, during straight turning operation the inclination of principal flank face (δ_{pn}, δ_p, and δ_s) must be greater than the helix angle of the cut. Higher values of flank angles will reduce rubbing but would also weaken the tool. For HSS tools, the values are generally in the range of 5 to 12 degrees with higher values used for machining of softer materials. For brittle tool materials the values are smaller. Flank angles have practically no influence on cutting forces and power, so an angle large enough to avoid rubbing is generally chosen.

Table 8.3 Typical tool angles.

Tool	Workpiece	Angles (degrees)					
HSS	Aluminium alloys	20	15	12	10	5	5
	Cast irons	5	8	5	5	15	15
	Copper alloys	10	10	8	8	5	5
	Mild steels	8	10	5	5	15	15
Cemented carbides (Brazed)	Aluminium alloys	3	15	5	5	15	15
	Cast irons	0	6	5	5	15	15
	Copper alloys	5	8	5	5	15	15
	Mild steels	0	6	5	5	15	15
Cemented carbides (Throwaway)	Aluminium alloys	0	5	5	5	15	15
	Cast irons	-5	-5	5	5	15	15
	Copper alloys	0	5	5	5	15	15
	Mild steels	-5	-5	5	5	15	15

Auxiliary and end cutting-edge angles γ_a and γ_e are essentially provided to prevent rubbing of tool against the machined surface so that chatter is minimized. Large value of these angles weaken the tool and also affect heat conduction because of reduced contact area. With principal or side cutting-edge angle (γ_p or γ_s), the initial contact with the tool is away from the cutting edge and prevents fracture or crumbling of cutting edge. Also, increase in the contact area improves heat conduction from the cutting zone. Large values of γ_p or γ_s weaken the tool and also cause tool chatter because the forces tend to separate the tool from the workpiece. For most machining conditions, values of γ_p or γ_s and also γ_a or γ_e in the range of 5 to 15 degrees have been found to be satisfactory.

Nose radius is provided on single-point cutting tools essentially to improve its tool life. It also improves the surface finish by smoothening the feed marks and increases conductivity. Large nose radius, however, will increase cutting forces and power, and also cause tool chatter. Nose radius in the range of 0.5 to 3 mm have been found to be satisfactory for most operations.

Tool angles for typical applications have been summarized in Table 8.3.

8.1.3 Single-point Cutting Operations

The primary machining processes that use single-point cutting tools are turning, boring, shaping and planing operations with turning as the most common operation.

The commonly used turning operations are shown in Figure 8.11. In these operations, the cutting or primary motion is provided by rotating the workpiece between centres or by holding it on one end in a chuck. The feed or the secondary motion is provided by traversing the tool in the longitudinal or transverse direction. For producing cylindrical surfaces, the tool is provided longitudinal feed parallel to the workpiece axis (Fig. 8.11a). When the feed motion is at an angle to the workpiece axis, a tapered surface is produced (Fig. 8.11b). Thread cutting is carried out by providing axial movement to the tool in relation to the rotation of the workpiece (Fig. 8.11c). Thus for a given cutting speed, finer threads can be produced by slower tool movement. The shape of the thread produced depends upon the shape of the tool used. If a normal feed motion is given to the axis of rotation, a flat end face can be produced (Fig. 8.11d). The radial movement of the tool can also be used for parting or cutting-off a piece from the end of a part (Fig. 8.11e). A profiled surface can be produced by feeding the tool radially into the workpiece (Fig. 8.11f) or by changing the distance of the tool from the workpiece axis while the tool is moving longitudinally (Fig. 8.11g).

Drilling is carried out by rotating the workpiece and feeding the

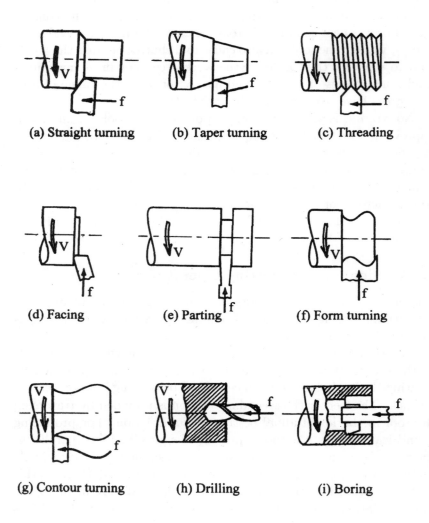

(a) Straight turning   (b) Taper turning   (c) Threading

(d) Facing   (e) Parting   (f) Form turning

(g) Contour turning   (h) Drilling   (i) Boring

Fig. 8.11 Commonly used turning operations.

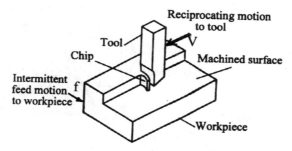

Fig. 8.12 Shaping operation.

drill held in the tailstock into the workpiece along its axis as shown in Figure 8.11h.

Boring is a variation of the turning operation. It is essentially an internal turning operation to enlarge an existing hole to a specific size (Fig. 8.11i). Boring can also be done by rotating the tool and keeping the workpiece stationary on boring machines.

Shaping and *planing* operations are used for producing flat or plane surface. In shaping operations (Fig. 8.12) the tool is given a reciprocating motion and at the end of return stroke, the workpiece is fed at right angle to the direction of cutting motion. This ensures that the tool always encounters a layer of uncut material during its cutting stroke. The reciprocating motion is obtained using a mechanical or hydraulic drive. Since return stroke is an idle stroke, these drives are designed to provide faster return strokes in order to reduce the total cutting time. Shapers are not suitable for producing long jobs (in excess of 1 m) because overhang of the ram limits the cutting stroke. For long jobs, the cutting motion is provided to the workpiece, and the tool is fed at right angles to the cutting motion at the end of each return stroke. This process is known as planing. Both shaping and planing operations are used for producing horizontal, vertical and inclined flat surfaces.

Figure 8.13 depicts the action of a single-point cutting tool during straight turning operation. The wedge-shaped primary cutting edge performs cutting through kinematic interaction and removes the excess material in the form of chips. The plan view of the set-up does not clearly show the chip forming action of the tool but the sectional view perpendicular to the cutting edge clearly shows the tool wedge and the chip produced. The undeformed chip-thickness t and the chip width b in this case can be obtained as

$$t = f \cos \gamma_s \quad \text{and} \quad b = d/\cos \gamma_s \qquad (8.11)$$

where f is the feed per revolution, d is the depth of cut and γ_s is the

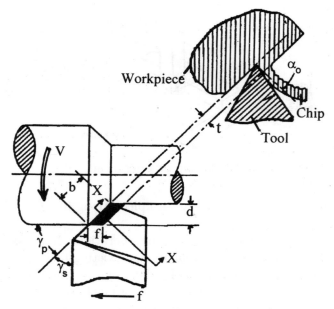

Fig. 8.13 Chip formation in turning.

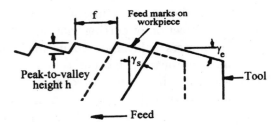

Fig. 8.14 Surface finish in turning with zero nose radius tool.

side cutting-edge angle (ASA system).

The material removal rate (MRR) is obtained as

$$MRR = \left(\frac{\pi D_i^2}{4} - \frac{\pi D_f^2}{4}\right) L/(L/fN)$$

or

$$MRR \approx Vfd$$

Here D_i and D_f are initial and final diameters of workpiece, L is the length of cut, and N and V are the rpm and the surface speed of the workpiece.

During continuous chip formation, the tool profile gets reproduced onto the work surface. How the profile gets transferred onto the work surface during straight turning with a sharp (zero nose radius) tool is shown in Figure 8.14. The resulting surface finish can

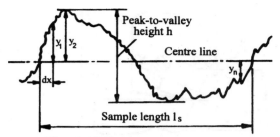

Fig. 8.15 Evaluation of surface finish.

be evaluated in terms of peak-to-valley height (root-to-crest value), centre line average (CLA) value or root mean square (RMS) value. Referring to Figure 8.15, the CLA value is

$$h_{CLA} = \frac{1}{n} \sum_{i=1}^{n} |y_i| \qquad (8.12)$$

and the RMS value is

$$h_{RMS} = \left[\frac{y_1^2 + y_2^2 + \ldots + y_n^2}{n} \right]^{1/2} \qquad (8.13)$$

where y_i; $i = 1, n$ are the ordinates of y.

The peak-to-valley height h for straight turning operation with sharp tool can be evaluated from

$$f = h \tan \gamma_s + h \cot \gamma_e \qquad (8.14)$$

or

$$h = \frac{f}{\tan \gamma_s + \cot \gamma_e} \qquad (8.15)$$

where γ_e is the end cutting-edge angle of the tool.

The action of a shaping/planing tool is very similar to that in turning. The cutting is mainly performed by the wedge-shaped primary or principal cutting edge as shown in Figure 8.16. The sectional view perpendicular to the primary cutting edge gives the undeformed chip thickness and chip width values as

$$t = f \cos \gamma_s \quad \text{and} \quad b = d/\cos \gamma_s \qquad (8.16)$$

The material removal rate (MRR) is

$$MRR = \frac{\text{Vol. of mat. removed}}{\text{Cutting time}} = LWd/(L/f)$$

$$= LWd/(L/f)$$

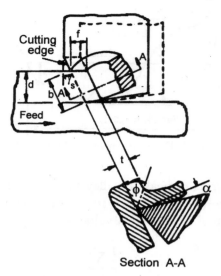

Fig. 8.16 Chip formation in shaping operation.

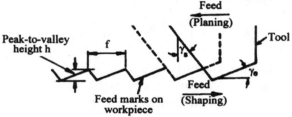

Fig. 8.17 Surface finish in shaping.

$$= \frac{Wd}{f}$$

where L and W are length and width of cut, d is the depth of cut and f is the table feed.

The surface roughness in terms of peak-to-valley height for shaping/planing with a sharp cutting tool (Fig. 8.17) gives

$$h = \frac{f}{\tan \gamma_s + \cot \gamma_e} \tag{8.17}$$

Equations (8.16) and (8.17) are the same as those for turning except that f here is the feed per pass.

8.1.4 Multi-point Cutting Operations

The two most commonly used cutting operations with multi-point cutting tools are milling and drilling operations. In *milling* the surface is generated by removing the material from the workpiece by feeding it into a rotating cutter.

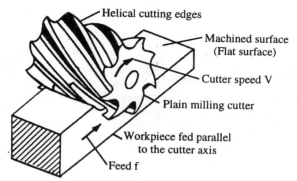

Fig. 8.18 Peripheral or plain milling.

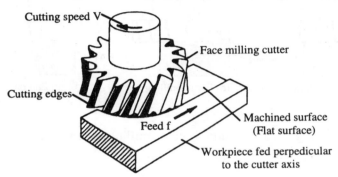

Fig. 8.19 Flat or face milling.

Milling operations can be broadly classified as:
- Peripheral or plain milling
- Face or end milling

In *peripheral milling* the axis of cutter is horizontal and the workpiece is fed parallel to the cutter axis and the surface is generated by cutting teeth located on the periphery of the cutter (Fig. 8.18). In *face milling* the cutter axis is perpendicular to the work surface and cutting is performed by teeth located on the periphery and face of the cutter (Fig. 8.19). Both flat and formed surfaces can be generated by these operations. Some of these are shown in Figure 8.20.

Milling operations are generally carried out under *conventional* or *up-milling* conditions, where the cutter velocity is opposite to the feed direction (Fig. 8.21). Sometimes *down-milling* or *climb-milling* is also used where the cutting and feed direction are the same.

In down-milling, the initial contact of the cutter is at the surface of the workpiece where hard surface or scale can damage the cutting edge during processing. Also the chip is at its thickest section at the surface and the resulting initial impact tends to pull the workpiece

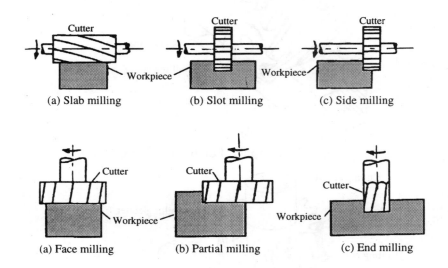

| (a) Slab milling | (b) Slot milling | (c) Side milling |
| (a) Face milling | (b) Partial milling | (c) End milling |

Fig. 8.20 Commonly used milling operations.

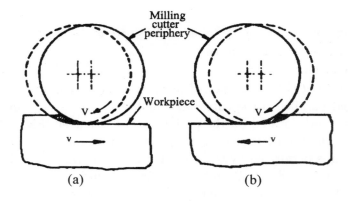

Fig. 8.21 (a) Up-milling and (b) down-milling.

into the cutter. The operation, therefore, must have a rigid set-up and any backlash in the drive mechanism must be eliminated. This set-up, however, holds the workpiece in place because of downward component of cutting forces thus permitting lower clamping forces. Down-milling also gives smoother cutting forces, and less feed marks because of plastic flow of material in the tangential direction at the end of each cut.

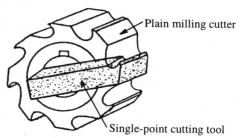

Fig. 8.22 Single-point cutting tool superimposed on a tooth of a plain milling cutter.

Each tooth of the milling cutter is very similar to a single - point cutting tool. This is clearly indicated in Figure 8.22 where a single-point cutting tool is shown superimposed on a tooth of a plain-peripheral milling cutter. The edges of teeth are parallel to its axis in plain milling cutters but are arranged helically in helical milling cutters. Helical cutting edges are equivalent to oblique cutting tools, while plain cutters are equivalent to an orthogonal cutting tool.

Figure 8.23 describes the geometry of a typical helical milling cutter and indicates various surfaces and angles. The radial rake angle (α_r) is the same as back rake angle and is equal to orthogonal rake angle since the principal cutting-edge angle $\gamma_p = 0$. The normal rake angle α_n of the tooth is obtained by taking the section perpendicular to the helical cutting edge as shown in the figure. The rake and flank angles on cutters are decided on the same consideration as those for single-point cutting tools. Typical values of radial rake and radial flank angles are given in Table 8.4.

Because of periodic nature of milling operation, the forces at the tool-work intersection also vary periodically. This affects the tool life and surface finish adversely. Effect of teeth spacing on resultant force fluctuation during plain milling with straight cutter is shown in Fig 8.24.

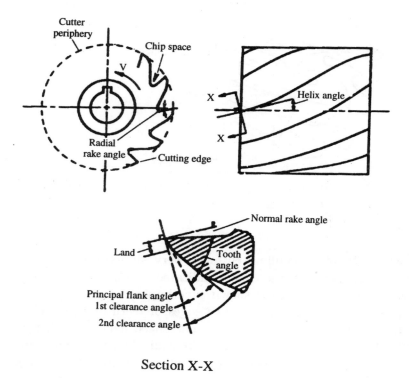

Section X-X

Fig. 8.23 Helical milling cutter.

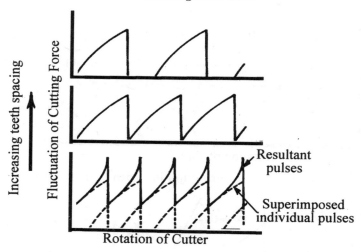

Fig. 8.24 Force fluctuation during plain milling with straight cutter.

Table 8.4 Typical peripheral milling cutter angles.

Tool material	Work material	Radial rake angle	Radial flank angle
HSS	Aluminium alloys	15°	8°
	Cast iron	12°	5°
	Mild steel	10°	6°
Cemented carbide	Aluminium alloys	10°	8°
	Cast iron	5°	6°
	Mild steel	0°	6°

The resultant pulses in the figure have been obtained through superimposition of individual pulses. It is obvious that force fluctuation can be reduced by increasing the number of cutting points but chip space requirement puts a limit on this. Considerable reduction in force fluctuation is achieved with helical cutter where initial tool-workpiece contact as well as disengagement are gradual. Also, more than one cutting teeth are always in contact with the workpiece during cutting. Figure 8.25 clearly shows the effect of these on force fluctuation.

Surface roughness in plain milling can be evaluated by superimposing the waviness that occurs during each revolution of cutter. This is shown in Figure 8.26 where the surface generated by each tooth is approximated by an arc of a circle whose diameter is equal to that of the cutter diameter (D). Using Figure 8.26, the feed per

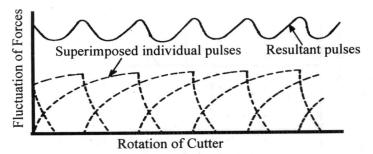

Fig. 8.25 Force fluctuation during milling with helical cutter.

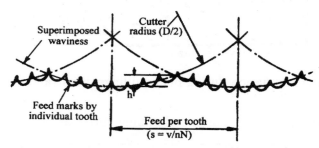

Fig. 8.26 Surface finish in plain milling.

tooth s can be obtained from

$$\left(\frac{s}{2}\right)^2 = \left(\frac{D}{2}\right)^2 - \left(\frac{D}{2} - h\right)^2 \qquad (8.18)$$

Also,

$$s = \frac{v}{nN} \qquad (8.19)$$

Therefore, mean peak-to-valley roughness

$$h = \frac{v^2}{4Dn^2N^2} \qquad (8.20)$$

Here v is the table speed, N is the cutter rpm and n is the number of teeth.

Drilling is one of the most common machining processes and is used for producing cylindrical holes in solid bodies. In this process the cutting or primary motion is provided by rotating the drill and the feed or secondary motion by pushing the drill in the axial direction. The drill has a high length-to-diameter ratio so that deeper holes may be produced.

In a common twist drill, cutting occurs on the chisel edge and the cutting edges. The drill is a multi-point cutting tool that has two cutting edges, similar to the cutting edges of single-point tools.

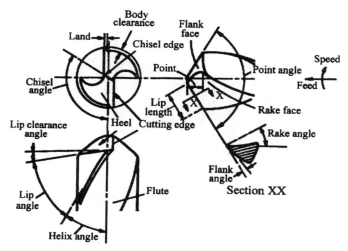

Fig. 8.27 Drill specification indicating various angles associated with a twist drill.

A section perpendicular to the cutting edge (Fig. 8.27) clearly shows the rake and flank angles. The rake angle, however, varies along the cutting edge and has largest value at the periphery of the drill. This angle is, therefore, defined in relation to its location from the drill centre. The drill-workpiece interaction produces two chips and these are guided upwards through the spiral grooves (flutes). The grooves also provide the passage for the flow of coolant to the cutting zone.

The main features of the drill point as depicted in Figure 8.27 are point angle, chisel angle, lip clearance angle and helix angle. Typical values of these angles are given in Table 8.5.

Table 8.5 Typical values of angles for HSS drills.

Work material	Chisel angle (deg)	Helix angle (deg)	Lip clearance angle (deg)	Point angle (deg)
Aluminium alloys	130	35	15	110
Gray cast iron	130	30	10	120
Mild steel	130	30	10	120
Tool steel	130	30	8	130

The flank angle of the drill must be larger than the lead angle of the path traced by the cutting edges so that rubbing is prevented. Excessive rubbing between the drill and the hole surface is prevented by decreasing the drill diameter over a substantial portion of its circumference leaving only the land to support the drill against the

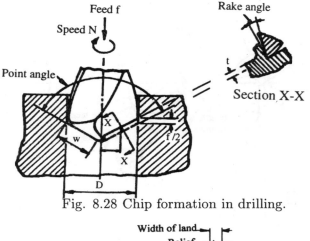

Fig. 8.28 Chip formation in drilling.

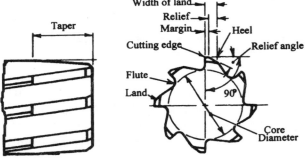

Fig. 8.29 Reamer geometry.

hole. The diameter of the drill D is also decreased along its length to further reduce rubbing and the corresponding heat generation. The point angle (β) serves the same purpose as the principal cutting-edge angle and provides gradual entry for the drill.

When the drill is fed downwards with feed f, each cutting edge removes a layer equal to $\frac{1}{2}f$ (Fig. 8.28) giving the values of undeformed chip-thickness t and chip width b as

$$t = \frac{f}{2}\sin\frac{\beta}{2} \quad \text{and} \quad b = \frac{D}{2\sin\frac{\beta}{2}} \tag{8.21}$$

Drilling is basically a roughing operation, therefore, surface finish is not of much concern. To obtain dimensionally a more accurate hole and improve the surface finish, reaming operation may be carried out.

Reamers are multi-point cutting tools with straight or helically fluted edges (Fig. 8.29) which remove only a small amount of material (less than 0.1mm) from the inside surface of drilled holes. The machine reaming operation is usually carried out at speed slower than the drilling speed but at higher feed rates. The cutting edges, typically 6 or 8, have rake, flank and helix angles as on twist drills. The number of cutting edges are always even and have diametrically opposite locations so that reamer diameter could be accurately measured. For even better dimensional accuracy and surface finish, internal grinding and honing operations are carried out on reamed holes.

8.2 Comparison of Machining Processes

The machining processes described in this chapter have been compared in terms of the range of surface finish and dimensional accuracy achievable (Table 8.6a) and the advantages and limitations of these processes (Table 8.6b).

Table 8.6(a) Surface finish and tolerance achievable.

Process	Surface finish AA (μm)	Dimensional accuracy (mm)
Turning	0.8-6.0	0.25-0.03
Milling	0.4-3.0	0.025-0.05
Shaping	1.5-12.5	0.025-0.125
Planing	1.5-12.5	0.025-0.125
Drilling	0.8-8.0	0.05-0.125
Reaming	0.4-3.0	0.025-0.05

8.3 Grinding and Finishing Operations

Grinding is the process of removing material by means of a rotating wheel, called the grinding wheel, which has a large number of hard abrasive particles held together by means of a suitable bonding material. When this wheel is rotated and the workpiece is fed into it (Fig. 8.30), the abrasive particles remove material from the workpiece in the form of chips. The process of material removal is very similar to that in peripheral milling discussed earlier, except that the cutting speed is much higher and the chips produced are much smaller. Unlike milling cutter, the geometry of cutting points on the wheel is not only random and varies from grain to grain but it also changes continuously during grinding due to wear.

8.3.1 The Grinding Wheel

Grinding wheels are made by mixing suitable quantities of abrasive particles and bonding material, pressing them to get the desired

Table 8.6(b) Comparison of machining processes.

Process	Advantages	Limitations
Turning	• All types of materials can be turned. • Most versatile machine capable of producing external and internal circular profiles and flat surfaces. • Low tooling cost. • Large components can be turned.	• Requires skilled labour. • Low production rate. • Close tolerances and fine finish cannot be achieved.
Boring	• All types of materials can be bored. • Variety of internal circular profiles can be obtained. • Low tooling cost. • Large components can be bored. • Provides better dimensional control and surface finish.	• Requires skilled labour. • Low production rate. • Suitable for internal profiles only. • Stiffness of boring bar is an important consideration.
Shaping	• Suitable for producing flat and contour profiles on small size workpieces. • Suitable for low production rate. • Low tooling and equipment cost.	• Requires skilled labour. • Large size workpieces cannot be used. • Only simple profiles can be obtained. • Close tolerance and fine finish cannot be obtained.

Planning
- Suitable for producing flat and contour profiles on large workpieces.
- Suitable for low production rate.
- Low tooling cost.
- Requires skilled labour.
- Only simple profiles can be obtained.
- Close tolerance and fine finish cannot be obtained.

Milling
- Variety of shapes including flats, slots and contours can be obtained.
- Versatile operation with wide variety of toolings and attachments.
- Suitable for low and medium production rate.
- Better dimensional control and surface finish.
- Requires skilled labour.
- Tooling relatively more expansion.

Drilling
- Inexpensive tooling and equipment.
- Most suitable for producing round holes of various sizes.
- High production rate.
- Machine can be used for reaming and tapping.
- Requires semi-skilled labour.
- Basically a rough machining operation.

shape, and baking it in a furnace. In order to get sufficient amount of pores or voids in-between the grain, a suitable amount of saw-dust is mixed with the abrasive particles before mixing with the bonding material. During baking saw dust burns off and voids are left behind in the wheel. These voids provide the space to accommodate the chips formed during grinding and their function is the same as that of chip space on a milling cutter.

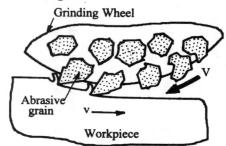

Fig. 8.30 Cutting actions in grinding.

The performance of a grinding wheel depends upon: (i) the type, size and distribution of abrasive grains, (ii) the type and amount of bonding material, and (iii) the volume of voids.

The two most commonly used abrasives are aluminium oxide (Al_2O_3) and silicon carbide (SiC). Aluminium oxide grains are generally used for grinding hard and tough materials like steels and ferrous alloys, while silicon carbide grains are preferred for hard and brittle materials like cast iron and glass, and for low strength non-ferrous materials like aluminium and brass. Diamond grain wheels are used for grinding of extremely hard materials like tungsten carbides and ceramics.

The size of abrasive particles used is expressed in terms of a sieve number (S) which indicates the number of openings (holes) per linear inch on the sieve. Sieve number S and the mean diameter of a abrasive particle g are related as $g(\text{mm}) = 68/S^{1.4}$. Thus, grain size 46 has a mean abrasive particle diameter g of about 320 μm.

The bonding materials commonly used are vitrified, resinoid, rubber, shellac and silicate. They provide the required strength to the wheel to withstand the stresses at grinding temperatures. Thus, the higher the amount of bonding material, the harder or stronger will be the wheel.

The volumetric composition of a grinding wheel can now be expressed as

$$(Vol)_{\text{abrasive}} + (Vol)_{\text{bond material}} + (Vol)_{\text{voids}} = 100\%$$

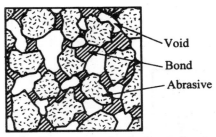

Fig. 8.31 Structure of grinding wheel.

In a typical grinding wheel (Fig. 8.31), the volume percentage of abrasive, bond material and voids are 50%, 10% and 40%. The characteristics of a grinding wheel can be changed by suitably altering these three constituents. The wheel can, therefore, be specified in terms of grain type, grain size, grade or hardness, structure and bond type.

The *grinding wheel specification* in alphanumeric system is indicated in Figure 8.32. This marking system for grinding wheels, a collection of letters and numbers, was recommended by International Standards Organization (ISO) and had been adopted by almost all the countries. Here grain type is denoted by a letter A for Al_2O_3 and C for SiC. A prefix to this letter is used to specify certain special characteristics. For example, a prefix A would mean a very friable aluminium oxide such as white Al_2O_3. The prefix could be a letter or a number depending upon the manufacturer's choice.

The *grain size* indicates the sieve number used for screening the grains. A higher sieve number would indicate finer grains. The grain sizes are broadly classified as coarse, medium, fine and very fine.

The *grade* or hardness of the wheel is designated by a letter with A representing the soft end and Z the hard end of the scale. This property of the wheel represents the ability of the bonding material to retain the grain and is measured in terms of the force required to dislodge the grain from the surface of wheel. A harder wheel, therefore, will have a higher percentage of bonding material and a smaller percentage of voids for a given wheel structure (Fig. 8.33a).

The *structure* of a wheel characterizes the mean void size and the distribution of grains. Thus, it represents the dispersion of grains. The wheel structure is designated by a number, 1 for a very dense or closely packed structure and 16 for a very open or loosely packed structure (Fig. 8.33b).

The bonding material used for mixing the grains in the wheel is indicated as bond type with letter B representing resinoid, E representing shellac and so on. Some manufacturers add a suffix in the

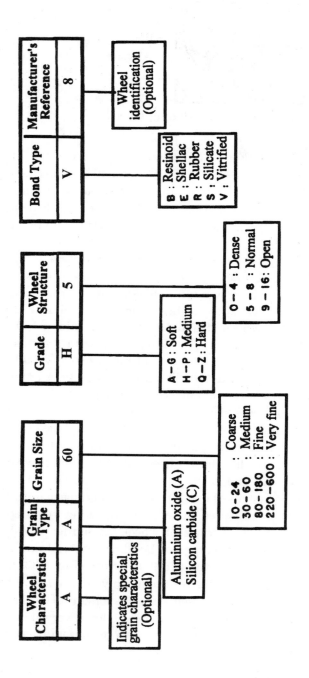

Fig. 8.32 Grinding wheel specification.

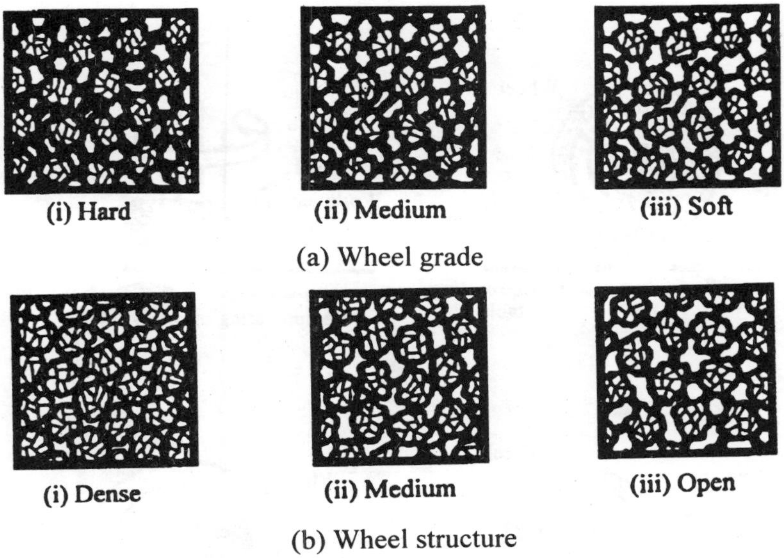

(i) Hard	(ii) Medium	(iii) Soft

(a) Wheel grade

(i) Dense	(ii) Medium	(iii) Open

(b) Wheel structure

Fig. 8.33 Variation in (a) wheel grade and (b) structure.

last column to indicate special characteristics of the bond material used.

Consider a wheel marked AA60-H5-V8. This indicates that the wheel has white aluminium oxide abrasive grains (AA) of medium grain size (60), medium grade (H), normal structure (5) with vitrified (V) as the bonding material. Number 8 at the end indicates that the wheel is suitable for fine grinding.

8.3.2 Grinding Operations

Grinding operations are carried out with a variety of wheel-work configurations and their selection for a particular application depends essentially on the shape and size of the workpiece (Figs. 8.34 and 8.35). The basic operations can, however, be classified as:
- Surface grinding
- Cylindrical grinding
- Internal grinding
- Centreless grinding

Surface grinding operations are used for obtaining flat surfaces. Here the relative motion of the wheel is along the surface of the workpiece. In horizontal surface grinding (Fig. 8.34a), the wheel is mounted on a horizontal spindle and grinding is carried out by reciprocating the table longitudinally and feeding laterally at the end of each stroke. For groove/slot grinding (plunge grinding) the

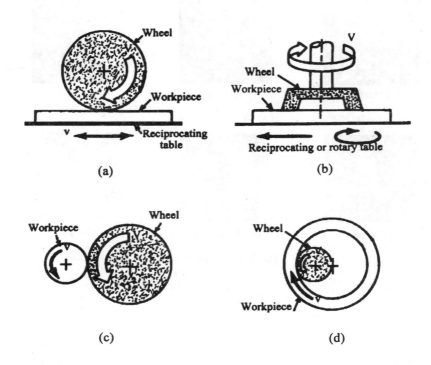

Fig. 8.34 Grinding processes: (a) & (b) Surface grinding (c) Cylindrical grinding and (d) Internal grinding.

wheel is fed radially into the workpiece after each stroke. Surface grinding is also carried out with wheels mounted on vertical spindles over reciprocating or rotary tables (Fig. 8.34b). This configuration is suitable for grinding large number of small pieces in one set-up.

Cylindrical grinding operations are carried out for obtaining external cylindrical surfaces (Fig. 8.34c). Both workpiece and grinding wheel are rotated and for obtaining a straight cylindrical surface the grinding wheel is reciprocated parallel to the axis of rotation of workpiece. Infeed is provided by feeding the wheel at right angle to the longitudinal axis. For form grinding the wheel of required form is fed radially into the workpiece.

Internal grinding operations are used for grinding the inside surface of a bore or large hole using a small grinding wheel (Fig. 8.34d). Here also, both wheel and workpiece are rotated and the wheel is arranged in such a manner that it can be reciprocated in and out of the workpiece. Infeed is provided by moving the wheel perpendicular to the axis of rotation. Formed wheels can be fed radially into the workpiece to get the desired profile.

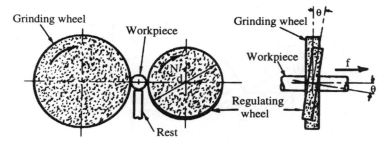

Fig. 8.35 Centreless grinding.

Centreless grinding operations are used for grinding cylindrical surfaces without supporting the workpiece at the ends. The process uses two wheels — the grinding wheel and the regulating wheel (Fig. 8.35). Grinding is carried out by the larger (grinding) wheel, while the smaller (regulating) wheel-mounted at an angle to the plane of grinding-controls the rotational and longitudinal (feed) motion of the workpiece. The grinding wheel rotates at regular grinding speed but the speed of regulating wheel is much smaller. The workpiece, held against the rest by the grinding forces, rotates at almost same speed as the regulating wheel.

The axial feed (f) obtained in centerless grinding operations is a function of diameter (d), rpm (N) and inclination (θ) of the regulating wheel. The axial feed can now be evaluated as

$$f = dN \sin \theta \qquad (8.22)$$

In the grinding operations described above, the speed of the grinding wheel is in the range of 25 to 50 m/s and that of the work in the range of 0.2 to 1 m/s. The infeed is typically in the range of 0.01 to 0.05 mm/pass. For fine finish, the wheel speed is kept at the higher end while the work speed and feed are maintained at the lower end.

Centreless grinding operations can provide surface finish in the range of 0.1 to 1.5 μm and the tolerance achievable is 0.005 to 0.03 mm.

8.3.3 Chip Formation

Grinding and other machining processes are basically the same, as both are chip forming processes. In both cases metal is plastically deformed in a narrow zone ahead of tool and the deformed metal

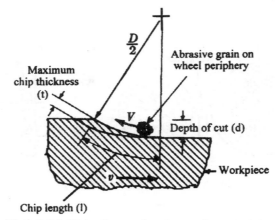

Fig. 8.36 Chip formation in surface grinding.

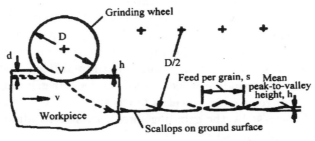

Fig. 8.37 Surface generated in horizontal surface grinding.

is removed in the form of chips. In grinding processes, the cutting teeth are individual abrasive grains on the interacting surface of the wheel (Fig. 8.30). Unlike milling, the abrasive grains are irregular in shape and are spaced randomly on the wheel periphery.

Consider the case of horizontal surface grinding (Fig. 8.36) where each grain removes a layer of metal like in peripheral milling. Since the grains are randomly placed, the feed per grains (s) will vary and the surface generated will appear as shown in Figure 8.37. The peak-to-valley height (h) also varies from spike-to-spike, but its average value (0.1 to 1.5 μm) is much smaller than that obtained in peripheral milling (0.4 to 6.5 μm).

8.3.4   Wheel Wear

Grinding wheel wears by three different mechanisms:
- Attritious wear
- Grain fracture
- Bond fracture

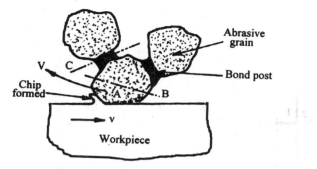

Fig. 8.38 Grinding wheel wear.

Attritious wear occurs on the grain-workpiece contact surface A (Fig. 8.38) and is gradual wearing of grain tip resulting in the formation of wear flat or wear land. This phenomenon is similar to formation of wear land on the flank face of single-point cutting tools. When the wear flats caused by attritious wear is excessive, the stresses on the grains increase to a sufficiently high value to cause grains to fracture and new cutting edges are produced (B). This wear mechanism is called *grain fracture*. When the grains are stronger than the bond posts, they get pulled out of the bond-post when sufficient force is applied at the grain tip. The grain-bond interface is generally quite strong and pulling out of grain from the bond post (C) is due to fracturing of bond post rather than separation at the interface. This wear mechanism is, therefore, called *bond-post fracture* or simply bond fracture. The typical sequence of events for wear of wheels should therefore comprise of dulling of grain tip due to attrition, followed by fracturing away of a portion of grain and finally fracturing of bond-post to release the remainder of the grain from the wheel.

When the wear flat formation is excessive, grains dull rapidly producing high temperature and excessive vibration and cutting becomes inefficient. The grains, therefore, must fracture at an optimum rate so that new cutting edges are always available for efficient cutting. Similarly, if the bond post is too strong to dislodge the dull grains, cutting will become inefficient. Too weak a bond post, will cause excessive wheel wear because grains will get dislodged very easily. Similarly, a grain with high attritious wear rate and low friability (ability to fracture) will also cause dulling of grains and inefficient grinding. The grinding wheel for a particular application should therefore be carefully selected so that the sequence of events for wheel wear indicated above is obtained and the wheel continues to perform efficiently for a long time.

When the metal chips produced during grinding fill the voids

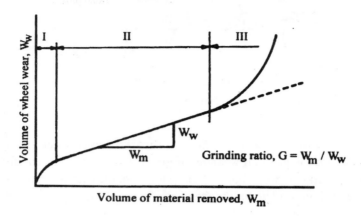

Figure 8.39 Wheel wear pattern.

or cavities on the wheel surface, the wheel becomes loaded. This phenomenon is called *wheel loading* or *loading* and leads to inefficient cutting. With increased loading, the cutting surface of the wheel becomes smooth and gets a polished or glazed appearance. This is called *glazing* of the wheel because of the shiny appearance of the wheel surface.

A wheel with dull grains and metal chips lodged in the cavities will not cut unless it is cleared and sharpened. Cutting ability of such a wheel is restored by *dressing* with a diamond point which is the process of removing the loaded layer and producing sharp new grains on the wheel surface. When the grinding wheels lose their geometry, the original shape is restored by *truing* (also a dressing operation) with a diamond tool.

The grinding wheel wear pattern also resembles the wear pattern of a single-point cutting tool (Fig. 7.16). The wheel wear - material removed curve for fine grinding (Fig. 8.39) shows three distinct regimes. Regime I indicates rapid wheel wear due to wearing of sharp grains having nominally zero surface area at the tip. Very soon the grains attain stable wear flats and stable grinding conditions with uniform wear rate is achieved. This marks the beginning of regime II and is represented by the linear portion of the curve. The limit of this phase represents the useful life of the wheel and is marked by sharp increase in grinding forces and vibrations. Regime III, therefore, signifies excessive loading and glazing of the wheel and the wheel must be dressed to restore its cutting ability before it enters this regime.

In rough grinding operations such as vertical surface grinding the linear portion of the curve extends almost infinitely as shown by the dotted line. In this and other rough grinding operations, larger grains, higher void volume and softer grade wheel ensure self-sharpening action through attritious wear-grain fracture - bond fracture sequence. This, however, is achieved at the cost of increased wear rate and inferior surface finish.

The performance of a grinding wheel is usually evaluated in term of the *grinding ratio* (G) which is defined as

$$G = \frac{\text{Volume of material removed}}{\text{Volume of wheel wear}}$$

The representative value of grinding ratio is, however, taken only in the stable grinding regime (Fig. 8.39). The slope of the linear portion of the curve, therefore, gives the value of G. For fine grinding operations such as horizontal surface grinding, the value of G is usually in the range of 10 to 60, while for rough grinding operations it is much less that 10.

8.3.5 Finishing Operations

For many applications, grinding cannot meet the accuracy and surface finish requirements. For such applications, workpieces are subjected to final finishing operations. Two such operations are honing and lapping.

Honing is a process primarily used for obtaining fine surface finish on internal cylindrical surfaces. The process uses a number of bonded abrasive sticks mounted on a mandrel which can expand radially against the work surface. This mandrel is rotated and reciprocated axially inside the bore to be finished (Fig. 8.40). The number of bonded strips may vary from two to eighteen depending upon the size of the bore, while the strip length is typically half the bore length.

When the bonded strips are pressed against the workpiece, a number of grains penetrate the work surface and the relative motion causes material removal in the form of chips - just like in grinding. The surface finish achieved depends upon the grain size, radial pressure and the speed used. Bonded strips having grain sizes 120-400 are commonly used and the pressure is usually in the range of 10-30 kg/cm^2. The speed, both rotary and reciprocating, is generally in

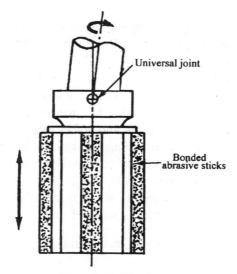

Fig. 8.40 Honing.

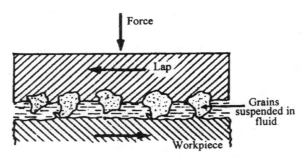

Fig. 8.41 Cutting action in lapping.

the range of 10-30 m/min. These conditions provide a surface finish in the range of 0.1 to 0.8 μm.

Lapping is also an abrasive process which provides accuracy and surface finish better than honing. In this process a layer of fine abrasive particles, usually suspended in a fluid, is held between the workpiece and the lap (Fig. 8.41). The lap material being softer than the workpiece (generally cloth, copper or cast iron) causes the abrasive grains to get embedded on to the lap surface when pressure is applied between the lap and the workpiece. These grains cut the work in the same way as in grinding when relative motion is provided between the workpiece and the lap. Because of variation in grain size from particle to particle, not all grains get embedded in to the lap and these loose grains roll and slide between the workpiece and the lap and cause some material removal. Embedded grains are, however, responsible for bulk of material removed and the abraded workpiece conforms to the shape of the lap.

Lapping may be done manually or on a power driven machine (Fig. 8.42). For uniform material removal, all points on the work surface must be subjected to the same velocity, distance travelled, pressure and abrasive encounters. This is best achieved by using a figure-eight type motion in hand lapping, and by allowing the work-holding rings to freely rotate during machine lapping.

Grain size, lapping speed and pressure are three most important parameters influencing accuracy and surface finish in lapping. Grain size in the range of 300 to 600 operating in the speed and pressure ranges of 100-250 m/min and 0.1 to 0.3 kg/cm^2, respectively provide accuracy of ± 0.0015 mm and surface finish in the range of 0.05 to 0.4 μm.

8.3.6 Comparison of Grinding and Finishing Processes

Table 8.7 compares the grinding and finishing operations described in this chapter.

8.4 New Machining Methods

Inspite of the rapid technological development in the machining processes, there are situations when the processes are not satisfactory or economical. These situations include machining of high-strength-temperature-resistant materials, complex internal and external shapes, very small diameter holes, slender or flexible workpieces and parts where residual stresses or temperature rise are unacceptable. In view of these limitations of conventional machining processes several new machining methods, often called unconventional machining processes, started appearing around 1950 and now a large variety of them are available.

These processes are summarized according to the type of energy, mechanism of material removal and medium of energy transfer in Table 8.8. The table lists only the commonly used processes, but there are many hybrid forms of these processes which have been developed for special applications.

Material removal rate in the new machining processes listed is very low, often less than 1% of the material removal rate achieved in conventional machining processes (Table 8.9). The new methods are, therefore, used only when the conditions warrant the extra expense.

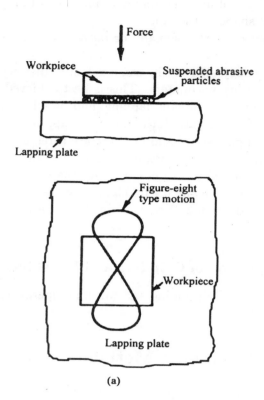

(a)

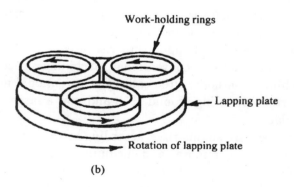

(b)

Fig. 8.42 (a) Hand lapping and (b) machine lapping.

Table 8.7 Comparison of grinding and finishing operations.

Process	Advantages	Limitations
Horizontal surface grinding	• Suitable for fine grinding of flat surfaces. • Close tolerance (± 0.0025 mm) and good surface finish (0.2 – 2.5 μm). • Medium labour skill.	• Low production rate. • Suitable for improving tolerance and surface finish on machined surfaces. • Thermal damage may occur due to high temperature during grinding.
Vertical surface grinding	• Suitable for rough grinding of flat surfaces. • High production rate. • Medium labour skill.	• Close tolerance cannot be obtained. • Suitable for stock removal only.
Cylindrical grinding	• Suitable for round shapes, stepped diameters, etc. • Tolerance and surface finish same as for horizontal surface grinding. • Medium labour skill.	• Low production rate. • Suitable for improving tolerance and surface finish on machined surfaces. • Thermal damage may occur due to high temperature during grinding.

Internal grinding
- Suitable for bores.
- Tolerance and surface finish same as for horizontal surface grinding.
- Medium labour skill.
- Low production rate.
- Suitable for improving tolerance and surface finish on machined surfaces.
- Thermal damage may occur due to high temperature during grinding.

Centreless grinding
- Suitable for long, round workpieces.
- High production rate.
- Low labour skill
- Tolerances and surface finish not as good as those obtained in cylindrical grinding.
- Not suitable for large diameter workpieces.

Honing
- Suitable for bores and holes.
- Very close tolerance (± 0.0015 mm) and extremely good surface finish ($0.01 - 0.35$ μ m).
- Low labour skill.
- No heat distortion.
- Very low production rate.
- Expensive operation.
- Limited amount of material can be removed.

Lapping
- Suitable for flat surfaces.
- Tolerance and surface finish same as that for honing.
- High production rate.
- Low labour skill.
- No heat distortion.
- Expensive operation.
- Limited amount of material can be removed.

Table 8.8   New machining methods.

Type of energy	Mechanism of material removal	Medium of energy transfer	Processes
Chemical	Corrosive action	Corrosive agent	Chemical machining
Electrochemical	Ion displacement	Electrolyte	Electrochemical machining Electrochemical grinding
Mechanical	Erosion	High velocity particle	Abrasive jet machining Ultrasonic machining
		High velocity fluid	Water jet machining
Thermal	Fusion and vapourization	Electric spark	Electric discharge machining
		Electron	Electron beam machining
		Ionized substance	Plasma arc machining Ion beam machining
		Radiation	Laser beam machining

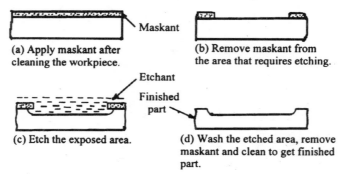

(a) Apply maskant after cleaning the workpiece.

(b) Remove maskant from the area that requires etching.

(c) Etch the exposed area.

(d) Wash the etched area, remove maskant and clean to get finished part.

Fig. 8.43 Basic steps in chemical machining.

Table 8.9 Comparison of material removal rate.

Processes	Material removal rate (mm^3/min)
Abrasive jet machining	0.8
Chemical machining	15
Electrochemical machining	15,000
Laser beam machining	0.1
Electric discharge machining	900
Ultrasonic machining	400
Turning	60,000

It is clear that the new techniques of machining are quite diverse in nature and have widely different characteristics and capabilities. In order to have some understanding of these processes, the main ones from each group will be described.

8.4.1 Chemical Machining (CHM)

This is the oldest unconventional machining process. In this process material is removed from selected areas of the workpiece through controlled chemical dissolution of material in contact with strong chemical reagents or etchants such as acids or alkaline solutions.

Chemical machining is widely used for the production of small, complex parts such as printed circuit boards and has, in fact, been the basic technology in the micro-electronics area.

The basic steps in chemical machining (Fig. 8.43) are:

- Clean the workpiece

- Mask the surfaces

- Remove masking from the areas that require etching

- Etch the exposed areas

- Wash etched areas to prevent further reactions

- Remove masking material, clean and inspect

- Perform additional finishing operations such as plating, if necessary.

When chemical machining is done using photo-sensitive resists as for fabricating printed circuit boards, the masking is obtained by coating a thin layer of photoresist emulsion. The master pattern of the finished part, obtained by reducing the enlarged drawing of the final part by photographic means, is then applied to the photoresist coated workpiece and exposed to light. Exposure to light hardens the selected areas which does not get washed off when the photoresist is developed. After exposure, the negative or the master pattern is removed and the workpiece is developed. This removes the coating from unexposed areas, exposing the areas to be acted upon by the etchant.

The characteristics of CHM are summarized in Table 8.10.

Table 8.10 Characteristics of CHM.

Material removal mechanism:	Corrosive action
Medium:	Corrosive agent
Common etchants:	Sodium hydroxide for aluminium, hydrochloric and nitric acids for steels
Maskants:	Tapes, paints, plastics and photoresist emulsion.
Process parameters:	Masking material (type and thickness), etchant (composition and concentration).
Applications:	Fabrication of printed circuit boards, engraving, weight reduction in machined, cast and formed sections.
Limitations:	Skilled operator is required, low production rate, low depth of material removal, etchant vapours are corrosive.

8.4.2 Electrochemical Machining (ECM)

Electrochemical machining utilizes the principle of metal removal by electro-chemical means and the rate of metal removal is governed by

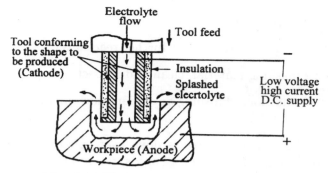

Fig. 8.44 Electrochemical machining.

Faraday's laws of electrolysis. The electrolyte cell, in this process is formed by the workpiece (anode) and the tool (cathode) in the midst of a flowing electrolyte (Fig. 8.44). When current is passed, anodic dissolution of workpiece occurs through the movement of ions. The workpiece is connected to the positive and the tool to the negative terminal because the objective is to remove metal from the workpiece.

To·understand how ECM is realized, let us consider Fe (workpiece) and Cu (tool) electrodes in aqueous solution of NaCl as the electrolyte. When the current is passed, the reaction at the anode is

$$Fe \rightarrow Fe^{++} + 2e \tag{8.23}$$

that is, the elctrode metal (Fe) dissolves releasing two electrons. At the cathode, the water gets these electrons and the reaction produces hydroxyl ions and releases hydrogen that is,

$$2H_2O + 2e \rightarrow 2(OH)^- + H_2 \uparrow \tag{8.24}$$

The positive ions of iron (Fe^{++}) moves towards the cathode and the negative hydroxyl ions (OH^-) move towards the anode. These ions combine as

$$Fe^{++} + 2(OH)^- \rightarrow Fe(OH)_2 \tag{8.25}$$

to form ferrous hydroxide, $Fe(OH)_2$, an insoluble precipitate, which is flushed out by the flowing electrolyte. Thus, metal is removed from the workpiece and no disposition occurs on the tool. This is the most important characteristics of ECM process. The choice of electrodes and the electrolyte should therefore be such that no deposition takes place at either electrode.

It is interesting to note that the process essentially uses the electrical energy and some water from the aqueous solution of salt

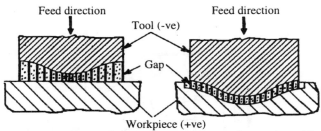

Feed direction   Feed direction

Tool (-ve)

Gap

Workpiece (+ve)

(Gap filled with dielectric fluid. Higher dissolution rate where gap is small.)

Fig. 8.45 Dissolution rate in ECM.

(NaCl). The electrolyte merely acts as a current carrier and no salt is consumed during the process.

Table 8.11 Characteristics of ECM.

Material removal mechanism:	Electrolysis
Medium:	Electrolyte (Sodium chloride), sodium nitrate, sodium sulphate and potassium chloride)
Tool materials:	Copper and brass
Workpiece materials:	Conducting metals and alloys
Process parameters:	Current, voltage, feed rate and electrolyte.
Applications:	Machining of complex cavities and curved shapes.
Limitations:	Cannot machine electrically non conducting materials, expensive equipment, very low material removal rate.

ECM is an inherently versatile process because of its capabilities to machine various kinds of metals and alloys and produce shapes and cavities which are very difficult to obtain using conventional machining processes. Consider a tool-workpiece-electrolyte set-up shown in Figure 8.45. Here the tool has the shape which is required to be produced on the workpiece. When current is passed, the dissolution of the workpiece (anode) occurs. The rate of dissolution is more where the current density is higher, or where the gap between the tool and

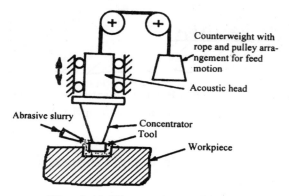

Fig. 8.46 Ultrasonic machining.

workpiece is less. As the tool is fed towards the workpiece, the work surface tends to take the shape of the tool and eventually the gap becomes uniform and the tool shape is reproduced on the workpiece.

The electrolyte is generally pumped at high pressure (130 to 2200 kPa) through the tool into the small gap (0.05 to 0.3 mm). DC supply is usually in the range of 5 to 25 volts giving current densities of 1.5 to 8 amp/mm². The metal removal rate achieved is very low, about 1500 mm²/min for each 1000 amp. the characteristics of ECM are summarized in Table 8.11.

8.4.3   Ultrasonic Machining (USM)

Ultrasonic machining is the process of material removal by repetitive impacts of high frequency abrasive particles against the workpiece. The process involves a tool vibrating at ultrasonic frequency (above 15 kHz) and a continuous flow of abrasive slurry in the small gap (0.2 to 0.5 mm) between the tool and the workpiece (Fig. 8.46). The vibrating tool causes impact of abrasive grains in the slurry against the work surface and the tool. The workpieces machined using this technique are generally hard and brittle and the impact of grains causes fracture at the worksurface and removal of material in the form of tiny particles. The flowing slurry removes these particles from the cutting zone. The tool material used is tough and ductile, to keep tool wear due to impacting abrasives at a very low value.

The acoustic head (Fig. 8.47) consists of a high frequency generator, a magnetostrictive transducer which converts mechanical motion

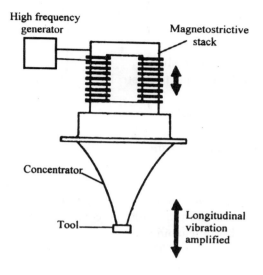

Fig. 8.47 The acoustic head with concentrator.

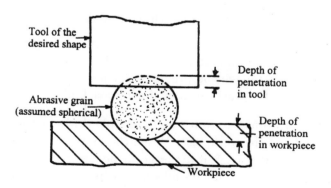

Fig. 8.48 Material removal in USM.

Table 8.12 Characteristics of USM.

Material removal mechanism:	Fracture of work material due to impact of grains.
Medium:	Abrasive slurry
Tool materials:	Brass and mild steel
Tool frequency:	15-30 KHz
Tool amplitude:	0.02 - 0.1 mm
Work materials:	Hard and brittle materials like semi-conductors, glass and ceramics.
Abrasive:	Aluminium oxide, silicon carbide and boron carbide.
Grain size:	Mess size 100-800.
Gap:	0.2 - 0.5 mm
Process parameters:	Frequency, amplitude, grain size, slurry concentration and feed force.
Applications:	Production of round or irregular holes and cavities and deburring
Limitations:	Suitable for machining of hard and brittle materials only, very low material removal rate, restricted to machining of small depth holes and cavities.

tion into high frequency vibration, and a concentrator to amplify the vibration and transmit it to the tool. The counterweight with rope and pulley arrangement provides the feed mechanism and is designed to apply the working force during machining.

Consider an abrasive grain (assumed spherical) in the gap between the tool and the workpiece. When the vibrating tool moves to its bottom position (Fig. 8.48), the grain penetrates the workpiece as well as the tool. This micro-indentation initiates fracture in the brittle work material leading to material removal in the form of tiny fracture particles. The abrasive particles outside the tool-workpiece interface zone remain inactive and do not contribute to material removal. The machined surface is, therefore, a replica of the tool form and by feeding the tool into the workpiece, holes and impressions can be produced.

Table 8.12 summarizes the characteristics of the process.

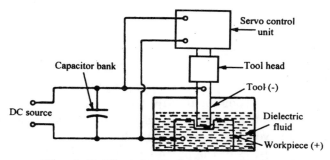

Fig. 8.49 Electric discharge machining.

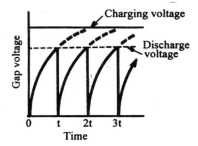

Fig. 8.50 Charging time of capacitor bank.

8.4.4 Electric Discharge Machining (EDM)

Electric discharge machining is the process of removing metal by controlled erosion through a series of electric sparks. The basic scheme is shown in Figure 8.49. When the electric current, stored in a capacitor bank, is discharged across a thin gap between the workpiece (anode) and the tool (cathode), the electric spark produces intense heat which melts and vapourizes the metal in the spark zone. The dielectric fluid confines the spark in the tool-work interface zone and also flushes out the metallic particles. The workpiece is connected to the positive terminal (anode) because it has been found that anode erodes faster than cathode when both electrodes are made of the same material.

Electric spark occurs where the gap between tool and workpiece surfaces is minimum. This spot, however, changes after each spark because of removal of metal and the spark travels all over the interface producing uniform metal removal rate. If the tool is fed downwards, maintaining the predetermined gap, the tool shape/profile will be reproduced on the workpiece.

The spark gap, generally 0.01 to 0.1 mm, is adjusted so that the gap voltage is around 70% of the supply voltage for charging the capacitor bank. Higher gap voltage although increases the discharge energy but it decreases the spark frequency due to increase in charging time of the capacitors (Fig. 8.50).

The servocontrol unit (Fig. 8.49) is provided to maintain the predetermined gap. It senses the gap voltage and compares it with the preset value and the difference in voltage is then used to control the movement of servomotor to adjust the gap.

The spark frequency commonly used is in the range of 50 to 500 kHz with supply voltage of 50 to 250 volts.

The characteristics of the process are summarized in Table 8.13.

Table 8.13 Characteristics of EDM.

Material removal mechanism:	Melting and vapourization
Medium:	Dielectric fluid (kerosene and paraffin oil)
Tool materials:	Copper, brass and graphite
Workpiece materials:	Conducting metals and alloys.
Process parameters:	Voltage, capacitance, spark gap and melting temperature of workpiece
Applications:	Complex shapes and cavities, non-circular holes and micro-holes
Limitations:	Limited to machining of conducting materials, low metal removal rate.

8.4.5 Laser Beam Machining (LBM)

Laser beam machining is the process of removing metal by focussing the laser beam on the work surface. Laser, an acronym of Light Amplification by Stimulated Emission of Radiation, is a highly coherent beam of electromagnetic radiation and can be focused to a very small diameter (0.05 mm) and produces a power density as high as 10^7 W/mm^2 in a short flash. This highly foccused, high density energy can melt and vapourize any material.

The principal lasers used for material removal are neodymium-yttrium aluminium garnet (Nd-YAG), neodymium-glass (Nd glass), ruby and carbon dioxide (CO_2) lasers. The most widely used laser for machining purposes are Nd-YAG and CO_2.

In order to understand the lasing phenomenon, consider the atoms of a medium at ground state (Fig. 8.51a). When energy from a light

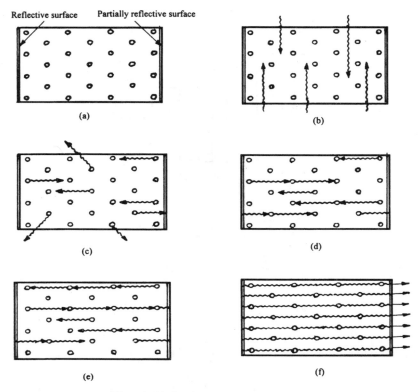

Fig. 8.51 Lasing phenomenon.

source falls on this medium, the atoms of the medium absorb radiation and go to a higher or excited state (Fig. 8.51b). This excited state is short lived and as they return to their ground state they emit energy in the form of photons (Fig. 8.51c). This automatic dropping back to the ground state and spontaneous release of photon energy is called spontaneous emission. The photons released in this manner are trapped between two mirrors which force them to move back and forth (Fig. 8.51d). Photons which do not travel parallel to the axis escape through the sides and do not contribute to the laser action. When the photons travelling parallel to the axis collide with another excited atom, that atom gets stimulated to emit a photon which is identical to the stimulating photon and moves in the same direction.

The photon emission achieved from an excited atom by an external field is called stimulated emission. These photons produce amplified, single frequency, coherent waves of light as they reflect back and forth between the mirrors (reflective surfaces) and trigger the emission of more identical photons (Fig. 8.51e). The photons there-

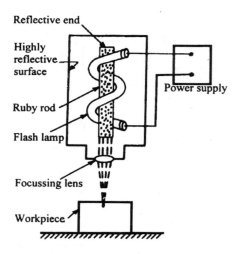

Fig. 8.52 Laser beam machining.

fore gather energy as they bounce back and forth between mirrors and some of these photons get sufficiently amplified to pass through the partially reflective surface to emerge as an intense laser beam of parallel rays (Fig. 8.51f). In other words, as the photon is reflected back and forth between the mirrors (reflective surfaces), it stimulates emission of light in waves which are in the same phase and the wave front formed produces an intense monochromatic coherent light beam. The location of the partially reflective surface predetermines the direction of laser beam. This parallel laser beam can be focussed on a small area to obtain sufficient energy to cause fusion and vapourization of materials.

The laser action, therefore, requires a lasing medium which provides a reservoir of active atoms which can be excited, an energy source to excite the medium, an optical resonator for building up the light wave, and an optical set-up to focus the beam. These are shown schematically in Figure 8.52 for a solid-state laser.

Lasers produce energy either in pulsed or continuous wave mode. In pulsed mode the laser emits short, intense burst of light energy, while in continuous wave mode the level of energy output is maintained over the entire duration of process cycle. Both Nd:YAG and CO_2 lasers can be operated in pulsed or continuous wave modes.

Laser drilling in pulsed mode occurs when a very short duration pulse (around 10^{-3} second) impinges on the workpiece surface and causes melting and vapourization of work material to produce small holes depending upon the power level, focused diameter and type of material. For laser cutting, the laser beam can be moved laterally (by fraction of a millimeter) to obtain a series of overlapping laser pulses. In continuous wave mode, the constant power mode moves in a continuous path to complete the cut.

Characteristics of LBM are given in Table 8.14.

Table 8.14 Characteristics of LBM.

Material removal mechanism:	Melting and vapourization
Medium:	Air
Tool :	High power focussed laser beam
Workpiece materials:	Any material
Process parameters:	Power intensity of laser beam, focused diameter of laser beam and melting temperature of workpiece material
Applications:	Drilling fine holes (upto 0.005 mm dia.), trimming, shape cutting and slitting
Limitations:	High power consumption, low efficiency, not suitable for reflective and high conductiviy materials, low material removal rate, limited to thin sheets/plates.

8.5 Comparison of New Machining Methods

The new machining methods described in this chapter have been compared in Table 8.15 in terms of material removal rate, dimensional accuracy, surface finish and power consumption.

Tables 8.16 and 8.17 compare the surface finish and tolerance achievable in various machining processes.

Table 8.15 Comparison of new machining methods.

Processes	Material removal rate (mm³/sec)	Dimensional accuracy (μm)	Surface finish (μm)	Power consumption (kWh)	Capital cost
Chemical machining	0.15-0.03	25-100	0.5-2.5	-	Medium
Electrochemical machining	200-300	15-100	0.1-2.5	100-150	Very high
Ultrasonic machining	5-10	7-15	0.2-2.5	2-3	Low
Electric discharge machining	10-20	15-50	0.2-2.5	2-4	Medium
Laser beam machining	0.001-0.002	10-100	0.5-1.5	0.003-0.005	Low/medium

Table 8.16 Surface finish achievable in various machining processes.

Process	Surface finish,μ m										
	25	12.5	6.3	3.2	1.6	0.8	0.4	0.2	0.1	0.05	0.025
Turning				▨▨▨▨							
Milling				▨▨▨▨							
Drilling			▨▨								
Shaping / planing		▨▨▨									
Grinding						▨▨▨▨					
Reaming				▨▨							
Honing							▨▨▨				
Lapping								▨▨▨			
Super finishing									▨▨		
EDM			▨▨								
ECM				▨▨▨▨							

Table 8.17 Tolerance achievable in various machining processes.

Process	Tolerance, mm x 10^3							
	250	125	50	25	12.5	5	2.5	1.25
Turning / Milling		▨▨▨▨						
Drilling		▨▨▨						
Grinding				▨▨▨▨				
Reaming				▨▨▨				
Lapping / Honing							▨▨▨	
EDM				▨▨▨▨				
ECM				▨▨				

Numerical Examples

Q.1 For a single point cutting tool, 8°, 8°, 5°, 5°, 8°, 30°, 1 mm (ASA), what are the values of angles i and α_n?

Solution:

Equation (8.1) gives

$$\tan i = \tan \alpha_b \cos \gamma_s - \tan \alpha_s \sin r_s$$

or $\quad \tan i = \tan 8° \cos 30° - \tan 8° \sin 30°$

or $\quad \tan i = 0.140 \times 0.866 - 0.140 \times 0.5 = 0.051 = 2.9°$

Equation (8.2) gives

$$\tan \alpha_n = \cos i (\tan \alpha_s \cos \gamma_s + \tan \alpha_b \sin r_s)$$

or $\quad \tan \alpha_n = \cos 29°(\tan 8° \cos 30° + \tan 8° \sin 30°)$

or $\quad \tan \alpha_n = 0.998(0.140 \times 0.866 + 0.140 \times 0.5)$

or $\quad \tan \alpha_n = 0.998 \times 0.191 = 0.191 = 10.8°$

Q.2 A single point turning tool has back rake angle α_b of 8° and side cutting-edge angle γ_s of 30°. What value of side rake angle α_s should be taken for achieving orthogonal cutting?

Solution:

Equation (8.1) gives

$$\tan i = \tan \alpha_b \cos \gamma_s - \tan \alpha_s \sin r_s$$

or $\quad \tan 8° \cos 30° - \tan \alpha_s \sin 30° = 0$

since $i = 0$ for orthogonal cutting.

$$\text{Therefore,} \quad \tan \alpha_s = \frac{\tan 8° \cos 30°}{\sin 30°}$$

$$\text{or} \quad \tan \alpha_s = \frac{0.140 \times 0.866}{0.5}$$

$$\text{or} \quad \tan \alpha_s = 0.242 = 13.6°$$

Q.3 Straight turning operation was carried out at the same feed using tools (1) 8-8-5-5-5-25-0 (ASA) and (2) 8-8-5-5-7-30-0 (ASA). Which tool will give a better surface finish?

Solution:

Tool 1 : $\gamma_e = 5°$; $\gamma_s = 25°$

Tool 2 : $\gamma_e = 7°$; $\gamma_s = 30°$

Peak-to-valley surface roughness

$$h = \frac{f}{\tan \gamma_s + \cot \gamma_e}$$

from eqn. 8.15. Substituting the values,

$$h_1 = \frac{f}{\tan 25° + \cot 5°} = 0.084f$$

$$h_z = \frac{f}{\tan 30° + \cot 7°} = 0.115f$$

This shows that tool 1 will give better surface finish since $h_1 < h_2$.

Q.4 A 150 mm long, 12 mm diameter rod is reduced to 11 mm diameter in a single pass straight turning. If the spindle speed is 400 rpm and feed rate is 200 mm/min, determine the material removal rate and cutting time.

Solution:

$$\text{Material removal rate } MRR = Vfd$$

where

$$v = \pi DN = \pi \times 12 \times 400 = 15072 \text{ mm/min}$$

$$f = \frac{200}{400} = 0.5 \text{ mm/rev}$$

$$d = \frac{12 - 11}{2} = 0.5 \text{ mm}$$

Therefore,

$$MRR = 15072 \times 0.5 \times 0.5 = 3768 \text{ mm}^3/\text{min}$$

Cutting time $= \frac{l}{fN}$

where $l = 150$ mm.

Therefore,

$$\text{Cutting time} = \frac{150}{0.5 \times 400} = 0.75 \text{ min}$$

Q.5 Determine the feed/tooth and the surface roughness during plain milling at a table speed of 250 mm/min and cutter speed of 100 rpm. The cutter diameter is 50 mm and has 10 straight teeth.

Solution:

Feed per tooth

$$s = \frac{v}{nN}$$

where

$$v = 250 \text{ mm/min}$$

$$n = 10$$

$$N = 100 \text{ rpm}$$

Therefore,

$$s = \frac{250}{10 \times 100} = 0.25 \text{mm/tooth}$$

Mean peak-to-valley roughness,

$$h = \frac{s^2}{4D} = \frac{v^2}{4Dn^2N^2}$$

$$= \frac{250 \times 250}{4 \times 50 \times 100 \times 10000}$$

$$= 3.125 \times 10^{-4} \text{ mm}$$

Q.6 In a centreless grinding operation with a 200 mm diameter regulating wheel rotating at 500 rpm, the feed rate obtained was such that a 3 m bar length was covered in 30 sec. What was the angle through which the regulating wheel was tilted?

Solution:

From equation 8.22, the axial feed during centreless grinding,

$$f = dN \sin \theta$$

where

$$
\begin{aligned}
d &= 200 \text{ mm} \\
N &= 500 \text{ rpm} \\
f &= \frac{3000 \times 60}{30} = 6000 \text{ mm/min}
\end{aligned}
$$

Therefore,

$$\sin \theta = \frac{6000}{200 \times 500} = 0.06$$

and

$$\theta = 1.05°$$

Review Questions

8.1 Which plane is normally considered for defining rake and clearance angles of a wedge-shaped tool?

8.2 Make a sketch of a single-point cutting tool specified by the following nomenclatures and indicate the angles on the diagrams.

(a) $7° - 5° - 8° - 9° - 11° - 13° - 1$ (ASA)

(b) $6° - 7° - 9° - 8° - 12° - 14° - 1$ (ORS)

8.3 What are the advantages of normal rake system of tool specification?

8.4 What is the significance of rake face inclination angle? What happens when: (a) the angle is 0° and (b) the angle is large?

8.5 Why negative rake angle is normally given to carbide tools?

8.6 Explain briefly why lower values of rake angles are used for harder work materials?

8.7 Why flank angles are provided to a cutting tool? What happens when flank angles are increased beyond the recommended value?

8.8 Higher values of flank angles are normally used for machining of softer work materials. Explain why?

8.9 What purpose do side cutting-edge angles serve on a single-point cutting tool?

8.10 On what considerations the range of end cutting-edge angles is decided?

8.11 Why is a single-point cutting tool provided with a nose radius?

8.12 What is the satisfactory range of nose radius in a single-point cutting tool? What happens if the higher value is exceeded?

8.13 Mention the motions to be provided to the tool and the workpiece for producing the following surfaces on a lathe: (a) Cylindrical, (b) Tapered and (c) Flat.

8.14 How is boring operation performed on a lathe?

8.15 How does shaping operation differs from the planing?

8.16 Why the return stroke is made faster than the forward stroke in a shaping machine? How this is achieved on a shaper?

8.17 Derive an equation to show that the surface finish in turning with a sharp tool mostly depends on the feed.

8.18 How peripheral milling differs from face milling?

8.19 Compare down milling with up milling and mention, which one is preferred in practice and why?

8.20 What are the characteristic features of helical milling cutters? How they are advantageous in operation in comparison to striaght milling cutters?

8.21 Explain why surface finish in general is better in milling than in turning.

8.22 Explain why the diameter of a drill is maximum at its land and then decreases along the length.

8.23 What is the purpose of point angle on a drill?

8.24 What is the purpose of reaming operation?

8.25 Why the number of cutting edges on a reamer is always even?

8.26 How does grinding process differ from the milling process?

8.27 What are the characteristic features of grinding process?

8.28 How are grinding wheels specified? How are grinding operations classified? Indicate the type of surface each of the classified grinding operations will produce.

8.29 Explain the working principle of the centreless grinding operation.

8.30 Describe the mechanism of grinding wheel wear?

8.31 What is wheel loading? How is the cutting ability of a loaded wheel restored?

8.32 What is wheel dressing? How does it differ from truing?

8.33 How the performance of a grinding wheel can be evaluated.

8.34 What is the purpose of honing?

8.35 Indicate the parameters that influence accuracy and surface finish in lapping.

8.36 Summarize the reasons for the development of new machining methods.

8.37 For what types of job, the chemical machining process is used? What is the material removal mechanism of this process?

8.38 Explain the principle of material removal in electrochemical machining process.

8.39 What is the role of electrolyte in ECM?

8.40 Explain the mechanism of material removal in USM and also explain the mechanism of material removal in electro discharge machining process.

8.41 Why is the workpiece made an anode is EDM?

8.42 What is the use of servocontrol unit in EDM? What will happen if the servo control fails to function?

8.43 Why mechanical properties of workpiece materials are not important for most new machining methods?

Chapter 9

Fundamentals of Machine Tools

9.1 Introduction

The process of machining is affected by relative motion between the tool and the workpiece. Depending upon the nature of this relative motion various shapes can be produced. A *machine tool* is a contrivance that has a combination of mechanisms which that has enable the tool and the workpiece to operate in a pre-conceived manner so that a component of desired shape, size and finish can be produced.

A machine tool can be described as an input-output system (Fig. 9.1) in which the inputs in the form of energy and control information regarding shape, size and surface finish are fed. On manually-operated machines, the control information is provided by the operator. The machine tool then gives the desired output in the form of components of required shape, size and finish. The surplus material removed from the workpiece is also an ouput which has to be disposed as a waste. Other undesirable outputs are defective components, vibration and noise.

A machine tool, in view of the requirements, must have certain

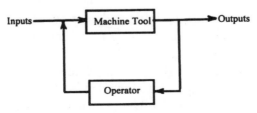

Fig. 9.1 Machine tool system.

basic features. These are:
- Accuracy
- Capacity
- Reliability and maintainability
- Ease of operation

Accuracy: Within the limit of tolerance, the machine tool should be able to provide the required dimensional accuracy and surface finish. This basically depends upon the rigidity of the elements of the machine.

Capacity: The machine tool should have the capacity to produce the required number of components per unit time.

Reliability and Maintainability: The probability of failure of machine tool should be low. Also the machine tool should be easy to service.

Ease of operation: Through use of appropriate devices and controls, within the constraints of cost, the operating features should be such that loading/unloading, tool setting and in-process measurements. could be carried out easily.

Machine tools can be broadly classified as:
- General purpose machine tools
- Production machine tools
- Special purpose machine tools

The *general purpose machine tools* are manually operated and have limited automation. These machines perform metal cutting within their range of operations. Lathe, milling, drilling, shaping, planing, grinding and similar machines come under this category.

The *production machines* are specially designed machine tools for achieving higher production rates. On these machines a number of tools operate simultaneously, or a number of operations are performed automatically and successively on the workpiece in order to reduce the production time per piece. Turret lathes, multiple-head drilling machines and screw cutting machines are examples of this type of machine tools.

The *special purpose machines* are specially designed machine tools for mass producing a particular component. These could be camshaft grinder, piston turning lathe and gear generators.

The level of automation increases as we move from general purpose to special purpose machines. On earlier machines, automation was mostly achieved through use of mechanical devices. On second generation machines automation included integrated flexible electric controls such as timers and relays which could be quickly set-up for production of different parts. The present generation machines use programmable electronic controls where set-up time for different part configurations are minimal. These and other similar machines are covered in Chapter 11.

9.2 Basic Machine Tools

The basic machine tools are: lathe, milling, drilling, shaping and planing machines. Some of these are shown in Fig. 9.2 and their basic features are indicated in the block diagrams (Fig. 9.3). These and other machine tools have five basic elements:

- Primary drive
- Secondary drive
- Guideways
- Structure
- Control system

9.2.1 Primary Drive

The primary drive provides the cutting motion or the cutting speed. The most commonly used primary motions are rotation and straight-line reciprocation. Rotary motion may be transmitted either to the workpiece as on lathes (Fig. 9.3a) or to the tool as on milling and drilling machines (Fig. 9.3b and c). A straight-line reciprocating motion is employed on shapers and planers. On shapers this motion is transmitted to the tool, and to the work on planers. These motions are depicted in Fig. 9.3(d).

The commonly used primary drives are:

- Stepped-pulley drive
- Stepped-pulley drive with back gearing
- Gear drive
- Friction-type drive
- Crank-rocker mechanism
- Electrical drive

In *stepped pulley drive* (Fig. 9.4) both power and motion are transmitted from input to output spindle by friction between belt and pulley. The number of speed steps obtained depends upon the number of steps provided on the pulley.

The transmission ratio i for belt drive is defined as the speed ratio of driving and driven pulley, that is,

$$i = \frac{\text{rpm of driving pulley}}{\text{rpm of driven pulley}} = \frac{\text{diameter of driven pulley}}{\text{diameter of driving pulley}} \quad (9.1)$$

(a)

(b)

Fig. 9.2 General purpose machine tools (a) lathe and (b) milling machines. (Courtesy HMT Ltd., Bangalore)

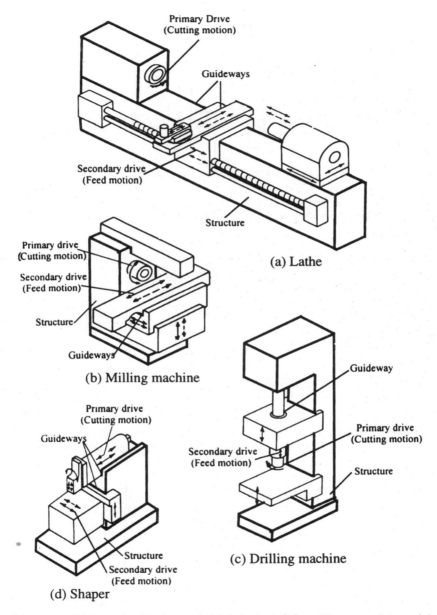

Fig. 9.3 Schematic diagrams of (a) lathe, (b) milling machine, (c) drilling machine and (d) shaper.

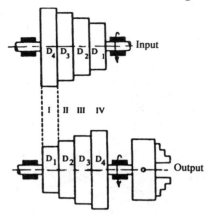

Fig. 9.4 Stepped pulley drive.

Thus, for the four-stepped pulley shown, the speed steps are

$$N_1 = N\frac{D_4}{D_1} = \frac{N}{i_1}$$

$$N_2 = N\frac{D_3}{D_2} = \frac{N}{i_2}$$

$$N_3 = N\frac{D_2}{D_3} = \frac{N}{i_3}$$

$$N_4 = N\frac{D_1}{D_4} = \frac{N}{i_4}$$

(9.2)

depending upon the belt position. N is the input rpm.

In *stepped-pulley drive with back gearing*, the number of speed steps get doubled because back gearing is added to the stepped pulley arrangement (Fig. 9.5). With back gearing disengaged (Fig. 9.5a), the speed steps N_1 to N_4 are obtained. When gears are engaged, the transmission ratio i is obtained as

$$i = \frac{\text{rpm of driving gear}}{\text{rpm of driven gear}} = \frac{\text{No. of teeth on driven gear}}{\text{No. of teeth on driving gear}} \quad (9.3)$$

Here the stepped pulley is attached to gear Z_1 but is free on the main spindle, while gear Z_4 is keyed to the main shaft. When back gearing is disengaged, the power to the main spindle is transmitted through bolt C. Pushing bolt C connects gear Z_4 to the stepped pulley (Fig. 9.5a). When back gearing is engaged, bolt C is pulled out which disconnects Z_4 from the stepped pulley and the power is transmitted via gears Z_2 and Z_3 (Fig. 9.5b). The transmission ratio with back gearing is obtained as

$$i_{bg} = \frac{Z_2}{Z_1} \cdot \frac{Z_4}{Z_3} \quad (9.4)$$

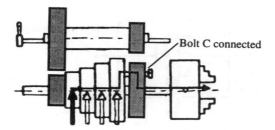

(a) Back gearing disengaged to get the first four speeds

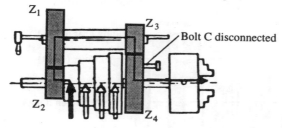

(b) Back gearing engaged to get the next four speed steps.

Fig. 9.5 Stepped pulley with back gearing.

and the four new speed steps are

$$N_5 = \frac{N_1}{i_{bg}}$$

$$N_6 = \frac{N_2}{i_{bg}}$$

$$N_7 = \frac{N_3}{i_{bg}}$$

$$(9.5)$$

$$N_8 = \frac{N_4}{i_{bg}}$$

The stepped-pulley drive with back gearing is simple and inexpensive, but speed changing is time consuming and also a bit dangerous. Most modern machines use *gear drives* where speed change is effected by shifting gears. A simple three-speed gear box is shown in Fig. 9.6. By sliding the stepped gear on the driving shaft and meshing it with the other gears attached to the driven shaft, three different speeds are obtained.

Machine tool operation, however, requires several speed steps. In order to achieve this the main drive usually has several two-or three-stepped gears connected with each other and assembled in a casing filled with lubricating oil to reduce wear. One such gear box to obtain nine speeds is shown in Fig. 9.7. Each pair of gear block has a fixed block of gears and a sliding block of gears mounted on

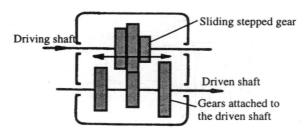

Fig. 9.6 Three-speed gear box.

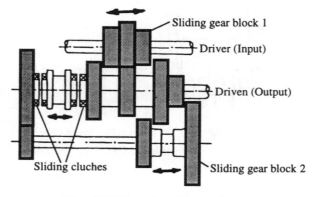

Fig. 9.7 Nine-speed gear box.

a separate shaft. Only one pair of gears mesh at a time and the spacing between the fixed gears is such that meshing of a pair of gears starts only after the previous pair is completely disengaged. Gears are engaged only when they are stationary or rotating at a very low speed. For this purpose clutches are used. Sliding clutches shown in Fig. 9.7 are keyed to the respective shafts whereas the gears are free until engaged by a clutch. The power transmission in friction clutches is through friction between two clutch plates.

A simple *friction drive* is shown in Fig. 9.8. Here two pairs of conical pulleys are used; one pair is fixed on the driving shaft and the other on the driven shaft. The cone pulleys are symmetrically adjusted by a lever system. Depending upon the diameter ratio of the driven and driving pulleys, the output speed can be increased or decreased.

To obtain reciprocating motion such as on shapers, *crank- rocker mechanism* (Fig. 9.9) is commonly used. Here the rotary motion is converted into a straight line motion of the ram by a rocker arm. The rotary motion given to bull gear (h) by an electric motor causes the pivoted rocker arm (i) to swing to and fro. As the crank (k) rotates, the sliding block (l) slides in the guideway of the rocker arm and gives

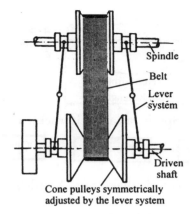

Fig. 9.8 Friction drive.

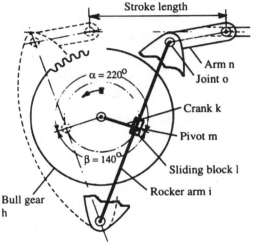

Fig. 9.9 Crank rocker mechanism.

swinging motion which is transmitted to the arm (n) through joint o. The ram stroke (Fig. 9.9) is varied by adjusting the position of pivot m on the crank. For maximum stroke length, the pivot is located at the farthest distance from the gear centre. Angle α through which the pivot rotates during the forward stroke is much greater than the angle of rotation (β) during the return stroke. The return stroke, therefore, takes lesser time which is useful because no work is done during the return stroke. Angle α is typically set at 240° and β at 120°. At these values the return stroke will take half the time taken by the forward stroke. As the stroke length is reduced, the difference between angle α and β also decreases.

The cutting and return speeds (v_c and v_r) of the ram can be

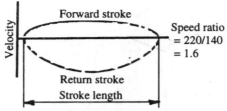

Fig. 9.10 Speed variation in rocker-arm drive.

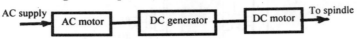

Fig. 9.11 Schematic diagram of Ward-Leonard drive.

obtained from stroke length and time for the stroke. Thus,

$$v_c = \frac{\text{Stroke length }(l)}{\text{Time for forward/cutting stroke }(t_c)} \quad (9.6)$$

and

$$v_r = \frac{\text{Stroke length }(l)}{\text{Time for return stroke }(t_r)} \quad (9.7)$$

In rocker-arm drives, the speeds are not uniform (Fig. 9.10). It starts from zero, reaches a maximum value and finally returns to zero at the end of stroke. The speed changes when the stroke length is altered (without changing the motor speed), since the distance covered changes for the same length of time. This kind of drive is suitable for small jobs only, since somewhat constant cutting speed is obtained only in a smaller portion near the centre of the stroke.

The stroke length l can be obtained as

$$l = \frac{2sr}{e} \quad (9.8)$$

where s is the length of rocker arm, r is the crank radius and e is the offset distance between crank centre and rocker arm pivot.

Usually electrical motor serves as the drive for providing various motions on machine tools through gear boxes. One *electrical drive*, generally known as *Ward-Leonard drive*, is extensively used on planing machines. The unit consists of a DC motor-generator set which can provide variable rectilinear speed to the planing machine table. In this set-up (Fig. 9.11) an AC motor drives a generator which produces DC voltage. The voltage level depends on the excitation strength and its polarity in the excitation direction. This DC voltage is supplied to a DC motor whose speed depends on the input voltage and the direction of rotation on its polarity. Thus the speed

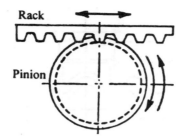

Fig. 9.12 Rack and pinion drive.

on planing machine table is controlled by the input voltage to the driving DC motor and the change of polarity at the end of forward or cutting stroke causes the table traverse to reverse.

The rotary motion of motor is converted into translatory motion by means of a rack and pinion assembly (Fig. 9.12). The motor drives the pinion which causes the rack (attached to the planing machine table) to travel a distance equal to the distance covered by the rotating pinion. Thus the travel distance L by the rack can be obtained from the relationship

$$L = zpN \qquad (9.9)$$

where z is the number of teeth, p is the pitch and N is the rpm of the pinion. Larger diameter pinions in which more teeth are simultaneously in mesh with the rack are prefered because quiter and smoother motion is obtained.

9.2.2 Secondary Drive

Secondary motions on most common machine tools are obtained by converting rotary motions into translations. The following three drives are comonly used:

- Rack and pinion drive
- Screw and nut drive
- Hydraulic drive

The most commonly used secondary drive is the *rack and pinion drive* described in the previous section.

In the *screw and nut drive*, the rotation of a screw (fixed in the axial direction) causes the nut (held against rotation) to move along the screw as shown in Fig. 9.13. The nut is usually made in two parts so that the clearance between threads on the screw and the nut could be controlled by loosening or tightening the nut on to the screw. By

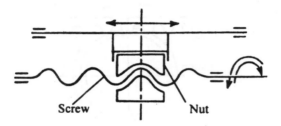

Fig. 9.13 Screw and nut drive.

suitably adjusting this clearance the backlash could be minimised. Variable speed is provided to the screw by driving it through a gear box.

The travel distance L depends upon the rpm of screw N, the pitch p and the number of starts s on its threads, that is,

$$L = spN \qquad (9.10)$$

A single-thread screw has only one continuous thread, as on most commercially available screws, and $s = 1$. A double-thread screw has two threads $(s = 2)$, a triple-thread screw has three threads $(s = 3)$ and so on. This type of drive is extensively used on machine tools primarily because of their smoothness, accuracy and low transmission ratio.

Several machine tools have hydraulic drives primarily because they provide smooth motion and reversal of speed is without shock. Such drives are expensive and are used on machines such as surface grinding machines because they contribute to good surface finish and close tolerance. Hydraulic drives are mainly used for obtaining rectilinear motions although rotary motions can also be obtained.

Hydraulic drive is achieved by a hydraulic pump and cylinder arrangement. A simple set-up for obtaining reciprocating motion using a fixed delivery pump is shown in Fig. 9.14. The fluid from an electrically driven pump is injected into the cylinder to displace the piston. The output of the pump is controlled by means of a solenoid operated valve. The motion of piston is transmitted to the machine table and at the end of stroke the link strikes the limit switch which operates the solenoid valve and reverses the oil flow direction. The reciprocating motion is thus achieved through limit switches which can be appropriately located to limit the table traverse on either side.

Table 9.1 summarizes the type of drives provided on commonly used general purpose machine tools.

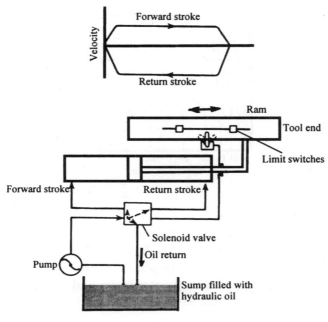

Fig. 9.14 Hydraulic drive.

Table 9.1 Drives for some commonly used machine tools

Drive	Machine tool
Stepped-pulley drive	Lathe, drilling machine
Stepped pulley with back gearing	Lathe
Gear drive	Lathe, drilling and milling machines
Crank-rocker mechanism	Shaper
Ward-Leonard drive	Planing machine
Rack and pinion drive	Lathe, drilling, milling and planing machines
Screw and nut drive	Lathe, milling machine
Hydraulic drive	Surface grinding machine

9.2.3 Selection of Speeds and Feeds

Machining operations should be carried out at optimum cutting conditions which depend upon the tool-work combination, and the required dimensional accuracy and surface finish. The cutting speeds and feeds for various requirements can be obtained from experiments or from handbooks.

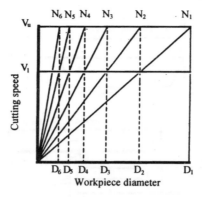

Fig. 9.15 Cutting speed vs. workpiece diameter for various rpm.

The maximum and minimum cutting speeds, V_{max} and V_{min}, on machine tools are usually decided on the basis of tool-work combinations. If D_{max} and D_{min} are the largest and the smallest diameters that can be processed on a lathe, the maximum and minimum spindle speeds (rpm) can be obtained as

$$N_{max} = \frac{V_{max}}{\pi D_{min}}; N_{min} = \frac{V_{min}}{\pi D_{max}} \qquad (9.11)$$

The ratio N_{max}/N_{min} is usually called the range ratio R. The values of R commonly used are given in Table 9.2.

Similarly, the maximum feed rate f_{max} corresponds to the recommended value for rough machining and the minimum value of feed f_{min} is for finishing cut.

Table 9.2 Commonly used values of R.

Machine tool	Range ratio
General purpose lathe	40-60
Shaper/Planer	30-50
Milling machine	30-50
Drilling machine	20-30
Grinding machine	1-10

Consider again the turning operation. If the cutting speed V is plotted against the workpiece diameter D, a straight line relationship is obtained for each spindle speed (Fig. 9.15). Suppose the recommended cutting speed for a given tool-work combination is V_c with permissible upper and lower limits as V_u and V_l. This would mean that the cutting speed for any workpiece diameter in the prescribed range D_{max} to D_{min} must be within the permissible speed variation

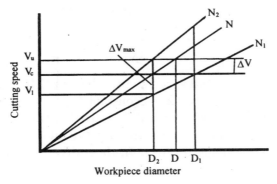

Fig. 9.16 Speed loss in G.P.

range. Spindle speed $N_1 = N_{max}$ can, therefore, be selected to get V_c within the permissible range at maximum diameter $D_1(= D_{max})$. At N_1 rpm all diameters in the range D_2 to D_1 can be turned. The next spindle speed N_2 can now be selected to cover the diameter range D_2 to D_3. The process of selection of spindle speed is continued until the minimum diameter $D_6(= D_{min})$ is covered.

Referring to Fig. 9.15, the ratio $\frac{V_u}{V_l}(= r)$ is obtained as

$$r = \frac{\pi D_2 N_2}{\pi D_2 N_1} = \frac{\pi D_3 N_3}{\pi D_3 N_2} = \frac{\pi D_4 N_4}{\pi D_4 N_3} = \frac{\pi D_5 N_5}{\pi D_5 N_4} = \frac{\pi D_6 N_6}{\pi D_6 N_5} \quad (9.12)$$

or

$$N_2 = rN_1; \quad N_3 = rN_2; \quad N_4 = rN_3; \quad N_5 = rN_4; \quad N_6 = rN_5 \quad (9.13)$$

Thus the speed steps are

$$N_1, rN_1, r^2 N_1, r^3 N_1, r^4 N_1, r^5 N_1$$

which follow a geometric progression (G.P.) with step ratio of r.

It is clear from Fig. 9.15 that for covering the workpiece diameter range in minimum number of speed steps, the spindle speeds should be arranged in G.P. It has also been shown that for optimum machining cost the speed steps should be in G.P.

Suppose a work diameter D which lies between D_1 and D_2 has to be machined (Fig. 9.16), then spindle speed N_1 has to be used instead of the required spindle speed, say N. The speed loss ΔV in using N_1 instead of N, which is not available, is

$$\Delta V = \frac{N - N_1}{N} \quad (9.14)$$

and the maximum speed loss ΔV_{max} is

$$\Delta V_{max} = \frac{N_2 - N_1}{N_2} = 1 - \frac{1}{r} \qquad (9.15)$$

which is a constant at all speed steps. Thus, in G.P. layout of speed steps the maximum speed loss is constant for all speed steps.

In stepless drives such as Ward-Leonard drive and hydraulic drive the output speed can be set at any desired value within the maximum and minimum speed range. In these drives the speed is easily controllable and are usually infinitely variable type.

9.2.4 Guideways

The main purpose of providing guideways on machine tools is to ensure that the elements carrying the tool or the workpiece move along the predetermined path. This imposes certain basic requirements on machine tool guideways. The important ones are:

- High accuracy
- Durability
- Low friction
- High stiffness and rigidity

The above requirements are necessary for maintaining the alignment of guides under operating conditions. The dimensional accuracy and surface finish on the guideways must be sufficiently high for achieving the desired accuracy level from the machine. The durability requirements ensure that the initial accuracy is retained for sufficiently long time. Low friction requirement helps in maintaining the accuracy level through reduced wear. Stiffness and rigidity requirements provide protection against static load, and pulsating and inertial forces.

The nature of friction between guideways and the operating element may be sliding or rolling friction. The guideways with sliding friction at the interface are often called *slideways*, while those with rolling friction are known as *anti-friction ways*. Anti-friction ways are expensive and its use is generally restricted in precision machine tools, or where the traverse distance is small. All general purpose machine tools use slideway, that is, guideways with sliding friction.

The slideway profiles most commonly used on machine tools are:

- Flat type
- Vee type
- Dovetail type
- Cylindrical type
- Combination type

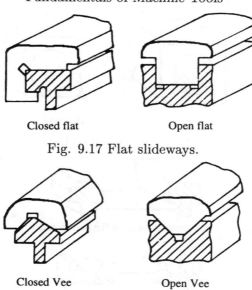

Closed flat   Open flat

Fig. 9.17 Flat slideways.

Closed Vee   Open Vee

Fig. 9.18 V-slideways.

Flat slideways (Fig. 9.17) can be easily manufactured but are very poor in retaining lubricant and also tend to accumulate dirt and chips. They, however, offer a large bearing area and can transmit heavy loads.

V-slideways (Fig. 9.18) are more difficult to manufacture but are self-adjusting type since the clearances automatically get adjusted under the weight of the moving element. In inverted V-type, the chip and dirt accumulation is not a problem but lubrication is difficult. They also do not check the overturning tendency of sliding elements.

This type of slideways may have symmetrical and asymmetrical Vee-profiles. Asymmetrical V-slideways are generally used with longer face of Vee perpendicular to the direction of resultant force for increasing the load bearing capacity and reducing the overturning tendency.

Dovetail slideways (Fig. 9.19) are relatively more difficult to man-

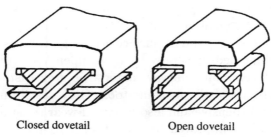

Closed dovetail   Open dovetail

Fig. 9.19 Dovetail slideways.

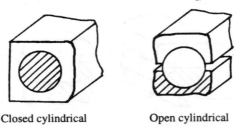

Closed cylindrical   Open cylindrical

Fig. 9.20 Cylindrical slideways.

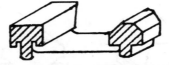

(a) Combination closed flat and closed V.

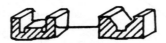

(b) Combination open flat and open V.

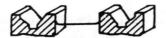

(c) Combination open V and open V.

Fig. 9.21 Combination type slideways.

ufacture but have large load carrying capacity and also check over-turning tendency. They are suitable for guiding parts for both horizontal and vertical movements. These slideways are extensively used on machine tools (milling machine tables, saddles and knees).

Cylindrical slideways (Fig. 9.20) are very simple to manufacture and offer restraint-free guidance if high accuracy (close tolerances) is achieved. They are generally used on machine tool elements requiring infrequent movement such as a lathe tail-stock and overarm of milling machine.

In order to achieve restraint-free movements and large bearing capacity, *combination-type slideways* are commonly used on machine tools. A combination of Vee and flat is often used on general-purpose lathe beds (Fig. 9.21a) and on surface grindingmachines (Fig. 9.21b). Planing machine beds generally have two open Vees (Fig. 9.21c).

The most common slideway material is grey cast iron when it is an integral part of the machine tool. Grey cast iron is preferred because it is inexpensive and also has good wear resistance. Its wear resistance is often improved by induction hardening of the mating surface. Often low carbon steel slideways manufactured separately and duly hardened by carburisation are screwed on to the machine tool beds. These slideways have much higher load carrying capacity and wear resistance.

9.2.5 Structure

Bases, beds, columns, carriages, tables and housings are called the structure of machine tools and they constitute 70 to 90% of the weight of machine tools. The structure is designed to have high degree of accuracy so that the relative positions of various parts mounted on it are accurately maintained. The structure should also provide safe operation and maintenance of machine tool. Two features of machine tools that are fundamental to fulfilment of the above requirements are:

- Material for machine tool structures.
- Static and dynamic stiffness of structure.

Traditionally, various elements of structure have been made of grey cast iron, primarily because of the low cost advantage. Cast iron also has high compressive strength, good damping capacity, and better lubricating properties due to the presence of free graphite. Cast iron is also easy to machine and has excellent castability. It is, however, heavy which increases the transportation and handling costs.

Light weight structures have been made by welding steel sections, but because of increased fabrication cost and loss of damping capacity these have not become popular. For general purpose machine tool structures, grey cast iron is almost universally used.

The performance of machine tools is significantly influenced by the static and dynamic stiffness of its structure. The static stiffness or rigidity is defined by the degree of deformation undergone by a machine element when subjected to an external load. The static stiffness K for a tensile load can be defined as

$$K = \frac{aE}{l} \qquad (9.16)$$

where a is the cross-sectional area of the section, l its original length and E is the modulus of elasticity. Similarly, stiffness in torsion K_T of a shaft of length l is given by

$$K_T = \frac{GJ}{l} \qquad (9.17)$$

where G is the modulus of rigidity and J its polar moment of inertia.

During machining, the machine tool structure is subjected to tension, compression, bending as well as torsion. If the structure does not possess high rigidity, elastic deformation of machine tool elements will cause inaccuracy during machining. Lack of rigidity due to elastic deformation of joints causes excessive vibration which is another source of inaccuracy.

Static stiffness is generally controlled through appropriate choice of cross-section for the machine tool elements. The four commonly used cross-sections are shown in Table 9.3 which also compares their bending and torsional stiffness for equal cross- sectional area. It is clear that box-section is best suited, both in terms of strength and stiffness if an overall assessment is made. The strength of box-section can be further increased by adding ribs, particularly when the section requires openings on one or more sides for mounting of other elements. In fact, wherever possible various elements which have to be mounted on the bed of machine tools are connected in such a way that a closed box-section frame is obtained.

During machining, machine tools are subjected to dynamic loads associated with tool-work interaction, and movements of machine elements. These may be due to initial impact of the tool, nature of cutting (intermittent cutting like in milling) and unbalanced mass. These factors together with the demand for higher cutting speeds require high dynamic stiffness on machine tools so that vibration effects are kept to a minimum.

Table 9.3 Static stiffness of commonly used sections (All sections have equal cross-sectional area.)

Section	Bending load		Torsional load	
	Relative stress	Relative deflection	Relative stress	Relative twist angle
Rectangular	1	1	1	1
Tubular	1.1	1.2	43	8.8
I	1.8	1.8	4.5	1.9
Box	1.4	1.6	38.5	31.5

Dynamic rigidity or stiffness is defined as the ratio of amplitude of vibratory force to the vibratory displacements at a given frequency. Thus it is a measure of the resistance of structure, when subjected to vibrations.

The static and dynamic stiffness are related as

$$\frac{K_d}{K} = A \tag{9.18}$$

where A is the magnification or amplification factor defined as the ratio of dynamic and static displacements when the dynamic force is equivalent to the static force. The magnification factor depends on the ratio of the excitation frequency and the natural frequency of the element, and on the damping characteristics of the material. The lowest dynamic rigidity or stiffness of any system is at its natural frequency. The machine tool structure should, therefore, be designed to have it natural frequency much above the cutting frequency.

The natural frequency f_n of an element can be estimated when

$$f_n = \sqrt{\frac{K}{m}} \tag{9.19}$$

where K is the static stiffness and m is the mass of element. Therfore, for high natural frequency, the static stiffness of machine tool structure should be large and the mass as small as possible. This can be achieved through use of materials which have high strength-to-weight ratio. Table 9.4 compares the tensile strength-to-weight ratio of grey cast iron and steels. Clearly cast iron structure will have lower natural frequency compared to steel structures. The steel structures are, therefore, preferred on machine tools which have to operate at high cutting speed, thus requiring high natural frequency.

Table 9.4 Unit strength of cast iron and steels.

| Material | Relative Unit Strength | |
	Tension	Bending
Grey cast iron	1	1
Low carbon steel	1.8	0.9
Medium carbon steel	2.6	1.2
Alloy steel	4.8	1.7

9.2.6 Control System

All machine tools require control system for their operation. Control system is a feed-back device which permits the operations to be performed in the desired sequence. On a manually controlled system, the machine tool operator receives information from digital displays, pointers and graduated dials installed on the machine, or by directly observing the operation. The operator then processes the information in his mind and controls the process by operating appropriate controls which may be in the form of hand wheels, levers, pedals and switches. Manual control devices are usually classified as hand or pedal controlled. These devices:

(i) control the position of tool and workpiece,

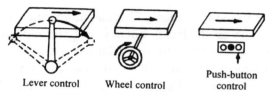

Fig. 9.22 Manual controls of machine tools.

(ii) control the speed, feed and depth of cut,

(iii) provide for changing over from one set of operating conditions to another, and

(iv) control for safety of machine and the operator.

Most manual controls are through lever, wheel and push-button operations. For ease of operating various makes of machine tools, the International Standards Organisation (ISO) has prescribed a set of guidelines for the operation of these devices. A few simple examples are illustrated in Fig. 9.22. Table 9.5 indicates the direction of operation for levers and hand-wheels for various controls on lathe.

Most general purpose machine tools have manual control but there is ever-increasing trend in machine tool technology to introduce greater degree of automaticity. Several mechanical and electrical devices have now been installed. These include limit switches for automatic control of travel distance, dog-controlled speed reversal device, travel control by dropping worm, interlocking devices for parallel shafts and shafts at right angles, single-lever speed change device, indexing and locking devices and many others.

The control devices of machine tools are designed to suit the physical, physiological and mental capabilitites of the operator. For this purpose the data collected through ergonomic studies are extensively used. *Ergonomics* derived from Greek words *ergos* and *nomos* meaning work laws, deals with man-machine interaction aspects and helps in the collection and evaluation of data on body size, limits of body movements, physical strength for pushing, pulling and lifting and turning. These factors vary extensively from person to person. Even in a single family it is impossible to design a machine which will suit every individual. Representative data, however, can be used as a guideline so that a substantial number of users get satisfied.

Table 9.5 Operation of levers and hand wheels on lathe.

Movement	Device	Direction
Carriage movement to-wards head stock	Hand wheel	Anti-clockwise
Cross-slide movement away from the operator	Hand wheel	Clockwise
Forward movement of tool slide	Crank	Clockwise
Outside movement of tail stock quill	Hard wheel	Clockwise
Half nut movement to-wards lead screw	Lever	Downwards

Numerical Examples

Q.1 The minimum and maximum speeds on a general purpose lathe are 30 and 960 rpm, respectively. If the machine has 6 speed steps, determine the speed?

Solution:

Assuming the speed steps to be in G.P., the steps are

$$N_{min}, \ rN_{min}, \ r^2N_{min}, \ r^3N_{min}, \ r^4N_{min}, \ r^5N_{min} \text{ or } N_{max}$$

where

$$N_{min} = 30 \text{ and } N_{max} = r^5N_{min} = 960$$

Therefore,

$$r = \sqrt[5]{\frac{960}{30}} = 2$$

and the speeds are 30, 60, 120, 240, 480, 960 rpm.

Q.2 If the speed steps on a machine tool are 30, 42, 60, 84, 118, 166 rpm, show that the maximum speed loss is constant at all speeds.

Solution:

Maximum speed loss,

$$\left[\Delta V_{max}\right]_1 = \frac{N_2 - N_1}{N_2}$$

$$\left[\Delta V_{max}\right]_2 = \frac{N_3 - N_2}{N_3}$$

$$\left[\Delta V_{max}\right]_3 = \frac{N_4 - N_3}{N_4}$$

$$\left[\Delta V_{max}\right]_4 = \frac{N_5 - N_4}{N_5}$$

$$\left[\Delta V_{max}\right]_5 = \frac{N_6 - N_5}{N_6}$$

Since,

$$r = \frac{42}{30} = \frac{60}{42} = \frac{84}{60} = \frac{118}{84} = \frac{166}{118} \approx 1.4$$

the speed steps are in GP. Therefore,

$$\left[\Delta V_{max}\right]_1 = \left[\Delta V_{max}\right]_2 = \left[\Delta V_{max}\right]_3 = \left[\Delta V_{max}\right]_4$$

$$= \left[\Delta V_{max}\right]_5 = 1 - \frac{1}{r} = 0.286$$

Q.3 In the stepped pulley drive shown in Figure 9.4, the input shaft is driven by a motor at 180 rpm. The first two transmission ratios i_1 and i_2 are 0.59 and 0.84, respectively. Find the speed steps in the drive.

Solution:

$$N_1 = \frac{N}{i_1} = \frac{180}{0.59} = 305.1 \text{ rpm}$$

$$N_2 = \frac{N}{i_2} = \frac{180}{0.84} = 214.3 \text{ rpm}$$

$$N_3 = \frac{N}{i_3} = N\, i_2 = 151.2 \text{ rpm}$$

$$N_4 = \frac{N}{i_4} = N\, i_1 = 106.2 \text{ rpm}$$

Q.4 The rocker arm drive of a shaping machine having 200 m long rocker arm and 5 cm crank radius, has been given an offset of 20 mm. If the cutting velocity is 10 m/min, determine the time for forward stroke?

Solution:

Stroke length,

$$l = \frac{2 \times s \times r}{e}$$

$$= \frac{2 \times 200 \times 50}{20} = 1 \text{ m}$$

$$\text{Time for forward stroke} = \frac{\text{Stroke length}}{\text{Cutting Velocity}}$$

$$= \frac{1}{10} = 0.1 \text{ min or 6 sec}$$

Review Questions

9.1 What is a machine tool? List its basic elements.

9.2 What is the purpose of primary drive? List the primary drives commonly used on machine tools?

9.3 Why a back-gearing arrangement is sometimes added to a stepped pulley drive?

9.4 If a back-gearing arrangement is added to a four-stepped pulley drive, how many speed steps are obtained?

9.5 What is the purpose of a gear box? What purpose does a clutch serve?

9.6 In a 9-speed gear box, how many sliding blocks of gears have to be used? How many gears each of these sliding blocks should have?

9.7 Draw a schematic diagram of a friction drive and show how the output speed can be varied.

9.8 How the speed of a rocker-arm drive can be changed without changing the motor speed? Why the speeds are not uniform in this type of drive?

9.9 How the quick-return ratio gets affected when the rocker-arm length is decreased?

9.10 What are the major advantages of a hydraulic drive? Why they are extensively used as secondary drives on machine tools?

9.11 Why machine tool speeds are generally arranged in geometric progression (G.P.)?

9.12 What purpose do guideways serve on a machine tool? What are the basic requirements of machine tool guideways?

9.13 What are the most commonly used machine tool slideway profiles? Mention the main advantages and disadvantages for each of them.

9.14 Why box-section is best suited for machine tool structure?

9.15 Why should the natural frequency of machine tool structure be much above the cutting frequency?

Chapter 10

Welding and Allied Processes

10.1 Introduction

Welding is a material addition operation used for making permanent, continuous metallic bonds between polycrystalline workpieces. The components are permanently joined by localised coalescence at the mating surfaces through the application of temperature and pressure. Coalescence implies the growing together into one body of the material being welded. For coalescence to occur, the surfaces to be welded must come into such intimate contact that the activities between atoms result in the formations of common metallic crystals.

When two atoms are brought sufficiently close to each other, an attractive force develops between them. For this interacting attractive force to exist, the interatomic distance must be less than a few atomic spacing, that is, the atoms must be less than a few angstroms apart. This attractive force increases rapidly with decrease in the in-

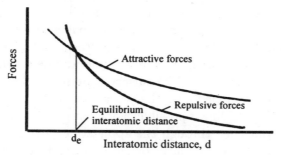

Fig. 10.1 Force variation with interatomic distance.

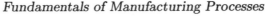
Surface layer with peaks (asperities) and valleys

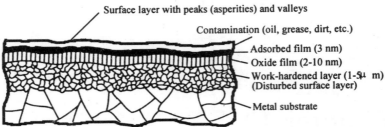

Contamination (oil, grease, dirt, etc.)

Adsorbed film (3 nm)
Oxide film (2-10 nm)
Work-hardened layer (1-5μ m)
(Disturbed surface layer)

Metal substrate

Fig. 10.2 Cross-section of a metallic surface.

teratomic distance (Fig. 10.1). The atoms, however, do not collapse because of the manifestation of a repulsive force with decreasing interatomic distance. The interaction between these attractive and repulsive forces gives equilibrium condition at distance d_e, known as the equilibrium interatomic distance. At d_e both attractive and repulsive forces are of the same magnitude but the slope of repulsive force is greater than that of the attractive force. The equilibrium achieved is therefore a stable one.

It is possible to bring two metallic surfaces so close to each other that nothing but grain boundaries separate them. Under these circumstances the two bodies will adhere to each other with a large attractive force resulting in permanent bonding. The process of achieving permanent bonding in this manner has come to be known as welding.

The formation of ideal metallurgical bonds requires:

- The metals to have single crystals with ideal structure and orientation and without any impurities.

- The contacting surfaces to be flat, smooth and free from oxides, absorbed gases and other contaminants.

It is impossible to obtain such ideal conditions in practice. Engineering materials are polycrystalline and cannot meet the first requirement. Close examination of a metallic surface indicates that it consists of layers of work-hardened material, oxides, absorbed gases and other contaminants (Fig. 10.2). Beside these the surface layer is never flat and smooth and has always some waviness with superimposed roughness in the form of surface asperities. Several techniques have been developed over the years to overcome the second requirement so that welding is possible. For example, flat and smooth surfaces can be obtained through the application of pressure or by melting the surface layer. Similarly, oxides, absorbed gases and other contaminants can be removed by squeezing the contaminated surface layers out of the interface zone through heating or application of pressure. Thus application of pressure and heat can bring metallic surfaces in close proximity for welding purposes. The range varies from high temperature and no pressure to high pressure and no heating.

Welding and allied processes can be classified into the following three broad categories:

- Solid-state welding processes.
- Liquid-state welding processes.
- Solid/liquid-state bonding processes.

10.2   Solid-state Welding Processes

In *solid-state welding processes* the surfaces to be joined are brought into close proximity by:

- Heating the surfaces without causing melting and applying normal pressure.

- Providing relative motion between the two surfaces and applying light normal pressure.

- Applying high pressure without heating.

In these processes the materials remain in solid state and welding is achieved through the application of heat and pressure, or high pressure only.

Forge welding is the oldest method of welding in this category. In this process the surfaces to be joined together are heated till they are red hot and then forced together by hammering. It is a crude method of welding and the quality of welding depends upon the skill of the welder. A modern version of welding in this category is manufacture of butt-welded pipes. In this process, the skulp heated upto the required welding temperature is pulled through a die (Fig. 10.3) which forces the two edges of the heated skulp to come in contact under pressure and get welded.

In *friction welding process* the two surfaces to be welded are rotated relative to each other under light normal pressure (Fig. 10.4). When the interface temperature increases due to frictional rubbing and when it reaches the required welding temperature, sufficient normal pressure is applied and maintained until the two pieces get welded.

In *explosive welding process* welding is achieved through very high contact pressure developed by detonating a thin layer of explosive

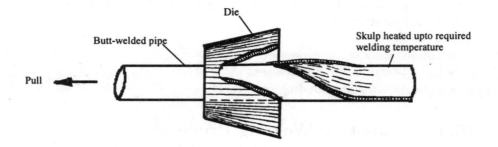

Fig. 10.3 Butt-welded pipe.

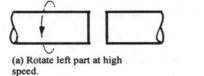

(a) Rotate left part at high speed.

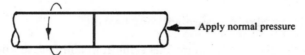

(b) Bring right part in contact and apply axial force.

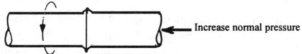

(c) Flash begins to form when axial force is increased.

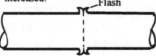

(d) Stop rotating left part when flash is formed.

Fig. 10.4 Friction welding.

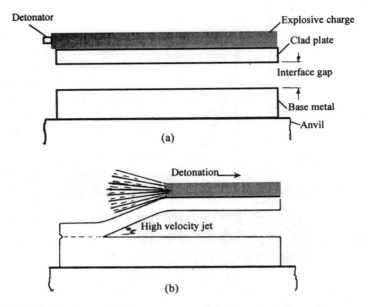

Fig. 10.5 Explosive welding process: (a) constant interface gap set-up and (b) high-velocity jet emanating from the striking point and flowing into the space between the plates.

placed over one of the pieces to be joined (Fig. 10.5). The detonation imparts high kinetic energy to the piece which on striking the other piece causes plastic deformation and squeezes the contaminated surface layers out of the interface resulting in a high quality welded joint.

10.3   Liquid-state Welding Processes

In liquid-state welding processes, interatomic bonding is essentially obtained by melting the metallic pieces around the joint. Filler metals, which are extra metals added to the joint area during welding, are invariably used because a small gap is usually provided between the pieces to be joined. When filler metal is added, the process appears to be somewhat similar to the casting process. Heat provided melts both the parent as well as filler metals and the melt is confined to joint area where it rapidly cools to form the welded joint. Liquid-state welding processes are also known as *fusion welding processes* since the metals in the joint area are simply melted without any application of pressure.

There are two inherent problems with this type of welding processes. The first one is the effect of localized heating and rapid

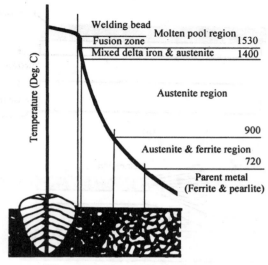

Fig. 10.6 Heat-affected zone.

cooling on the microstructure and properties of the parent metals. The other is the effect of residual stresses developed in the parent metals due to restrained expansion or contraction on the impact and fatigue life of weldment.

Consider welding of two mild steel pieces (C 0.06-0.08%). During welding the molten pool will be at temperature above the melting temperature, that is, 1530°C. The regions near the weld will be at a comparatively much lower temperature giving a steep-temperature gradient from the molten pool to the parent metal. Crystal structure of all types can, therefore, be found in the vicinity of welded joint depending upon the temperature reached. The changes in microstructure is further affected by the rate of cooling. Thus the rate of heat input, the rate of cooling, and the temperature reached in the zone affect the microstructure and properties of the metal in the welded zone.

The region of the base metal adjacent to the weld zone where temperature rise has caused changes in microstructure is generally called the *heat-affected zone* (HAZ). Figure 10.6 shows a typical variation in temperature in the heat-affected zone during welding of mild steel. The heat-affected zone reveals the following:

- The molten pool region at a temperature above the melting temperature, that is 1530°C.

- The mixed delta iron and austenite region with temperature around 1400°C.

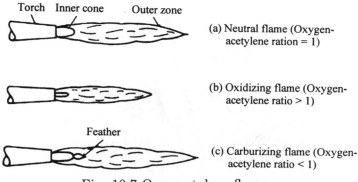

Fig. 10.7 Oxy-acetylene flame.

- The austenite region with temperature above 900°C but below 1400°C.

- The austenite and ferrite region with temperature in the range of 720 to 900°C.

- The parent metal of ferrite and pearlite with temperature below 720°C.

In addition, the welded joint may absorb oxygen or nitrogen. Oxidation causes reduction in impact and fatigue strength of welded joint. Formation of iron nitride makes the weld brittle. When the cooling is quick, the weld becomes tough and strong but brittle because of the presence of martensite. With slow cooling, ferrite and pearlite formed give lower strength and hardness, but increased ductility and impact strength. Thus, the choice of welding method and rate of cooling is considered on the basis of desired properties of welded joint. The properties of the finished weld obviously depend on the structures that remain on cooling.

The heat sources that have been used in this type of welding processes are:
- Chemical flame
- Electric arc
- Electrical resistance heating
- Exothermic chemical reaction

In *gas welding* the heat source is the oxy-acetylene flame-a flame produced by the combustion of acetylene and oxygen. Here the primary combustion occurring in the inner zone (Fig. 10.7) gives

$$C_2H_2 + O_2 \rightarrow 2CO + H_2 + Heat$$

and the second reaction in the outer zone gives

$$2CO + H_2 + 1.5O_2 \rightarrow 2CO_2 + H_2O + Heat$$

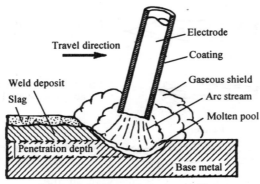

Fig. 10.8 Electric arc welding.

The maximum temperature at the tip of inner cone, because of these reactions, reaches upto 3500°C. Most gas welding is performed by keeping this inner zone tip just above the metal to be welded so that maximum temperature is available for welding. The outer zone which is at much lower temperature serves to preheat the welding area and provides shielding against oxidation.

Three types of flame that can be obtained by varying the ratio of oxygen and acetylene are:

• Neutral flame
• Oxidizing flame
• Carburizing flame

A *neutral flame* is obtained when the mixture ratio (ratio of oxygen and acetylene) is 1 and all reactions are carried to completed. Most gas welding operations are carried out by this type of flame. An *oxidizing flame* is obtained when oxygen in the mixture is in excess, that is, the mixture ratio is more than 1. This type of flame is not suitable for welding steels since the excess oxygen present reacts with carbon in steel and is generally used for welding of copper and copper alloys. When the mixture ratio is less than 1, that is, when the ratio of oxygen is reduced, a *carburizing flame* is obtained. In this type of flame acetylene decomposes into carbon and hydrogen and the flame temperature gets reduced. Joining operations such as brazing and soldering which require lower temperature generally use this type of flame.

In gas welding operations, filler metals are used to supply additional materials to the weld zone. *Flux* is often used to clean the surfaces and to retard oxidation by providing inert gas shield around the welding area. It also helps in removing oxide and other impurities. Borax is the most commonly used flux, but sometimes other substances are added to improve its effectiveness.

In *electric arc welding* a sustained arc provides the heat required for melting the parent as well as filler material (Fig. 10.8). In this process, the workpiece and the electrode are connected to the two terminals of the power source. The arc is started by momentarily touching the electrode on to the workpiece and then withdrawing it to a short distance (a few millimetres) from the workpiece. When the electrode and workpiece are in contact, current flows and when they are separated an arc is generated and the current continues to flow. The arc is generated by electrons liberated from cathode and moving towards anode. The arc changes the electrical energy into heat and light. About 70% of the heat is liberated at anode by the striking electrons which raises the anode temperature to a very high value (5,000-30,000°C). This heat melts the base metal as well as the tip of electrode in the area surrounding the arc. A weld is formed when the mixture of molten base and electrode metal solidifies in the weld area. Since 70% of the heat is developed at the anode, the workpiece when connected to the +ve pole will melt may be 50% faster than if connected to the −ve pole. This is why the workpiece is usually made positive and electrode as negative, and *straight polarity* is said to be in use. When the work and electrode connections are reversed, *reverse polarity* is said to be employed.

Both direct and alternating currents can be used for arc welding operations but DC is generally preferred. When the welder strikes an arc, both arc length and arc voltage are zero because of short circuit. As the welding rod is pulled away from the workpiece, the length of arc increases and the voltage required to sustain this arc increases and the current decreases. If the arc length is continued to increase, the voltage will continue to rise but beyond a point the arc will cease to exit because the machine is unable to supply the desired voltage. At this point an open circuit voltage (OCV) exists and the current falls off to zero value. The open circuit voltage is generally kept in the range of 40 to 90 volts but when the arc is operating the voltage range is 20 to 40 volts. The current range may be from 150 to 1000 amp, depending upon the application.

During manual arc welding it is difficult to maintain a constant arc length and inadvertent changes in arc length are inevitable. The machine, however, is designed to provide relatively constant current despite changes in voltage with variations in arc length. The voltage-ampere relationship on such machines is shown in Fig. 10.9 which clearly indicates that OCV must be significantly higher than the operating voltage so that current variation with changes in arc length is not significant.

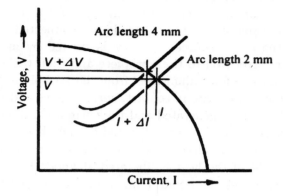

Fig. 10.9 Voltage-ampere relationship in manual arc welding.

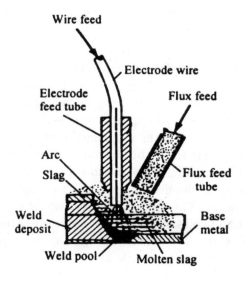

Fig. 10.10 Submerged arc welding.

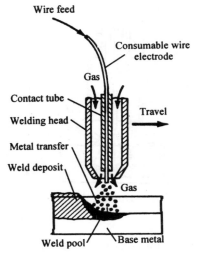

Fig. 10.11 Gas metal-arc welding.

The electrodes used can be either non-consumable or consumable. Consumable electrodes usually have a coating on its outer surface which on melting release gases like hydrogen or carbon dioxide to form a protective covering around the molten pool. The electrode coating also reacts to form slag which is a liquid, lighter than the molten metal. The slag, therefore, rises to the surface and on solidification forms a protective covering over the hot metal. This also slows down the rate of cooling of the weld. The slag layer can be easily removed by light chipping. Electric arc welding with this type of electrodes have come to be known as *shielded metal-arc welding*. More than 50% of industrial arc welding is done using this process. The process has one inherent disadvantage. Since the coatings are always brittle, only straight electrodes can be used. This limits the application of the process to manual operation.

For continuous arc welding operations, the consumable electrode is bare wire in the form of a coil and the flux is fed into the welding zone, or the weld area is covered by an inert gas. In *submerged-arc welding* the bare wire electrode is shielded by granular flux supplied from a hopper (Fig. 10.10), while in gas *metal-arc welding* shielding of the weld area is provided by an inert gas such as argon, helium and carbon dioxide. (Fig. 10.11).

Non-consumable arc welding processes use tungsten electrodes and shielding is provided by injecting an inert or semi-inert gas around the weld area. One such process, the *gas tungsten arc welding* (GTAW), also called *tungsten inert-gas* or *TIG welding* utilises tungsten alloy electrode in argon or helium gas shield (Fig. 10.12).

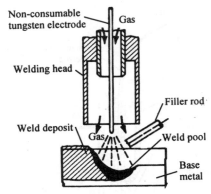

Fig. 10.12 Non-consumable arc welding.

The tungsten electrode is not consumed because of inert atmosphere. Filler metal if required is supplied by a separate rod or wire.

Resistance welding utilizes the heat generated at the metallic junction when two pieces are pressed together and high current is passed through the interface (Fig. 10.13). In these processes the applied voltage is usually less than 10 V, while the current (usually AC) can be as high as 100,000 A. The heat input H is evaluated from $H = I^2Rt$, where I is the current, R is electrical resistance and t is the time duration of current flow. Since, maximum temperature is desired at the metallic junction where weld is to be made, the resistances at all other places should be kept to a very low value in comparison to the interface resistance. The heat generated at the interface causes melting to occur. Melting is not always necessary for coalescence if sufficient pressure is applied through the electrodes. Outside the welding zone the temperature is kept low by cooling the electrodes with water. The heat distribution at the interface is also shown in Fig. 10.13.

In *resistance spot welding*, the most commonly used resistance welding process, two opposing solid cylindrical electrodes are pressed against the lap joint of two metallic sheets to be welded. Electric resistance heating with current in the range of 3,000 to 40,000 A depending on the requirement causes a weld nugget of size varying from 6 to 10 mm diameter to be formed at the metallic interface.

The spot welding cycle is depicted in Fig. 10.14. After inserting the plates to be spot welded between the electrodes, the electrodes are brought together and pressure is applied. The current is now switched on for a duration lasting 0.1 to 0.5 seconds. The applied pressure is maintained, even after switching off the current, until the weld solidifies.

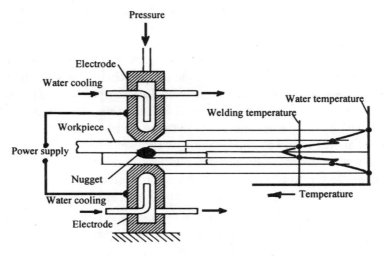

Fig. 10.13 Resistance welding.

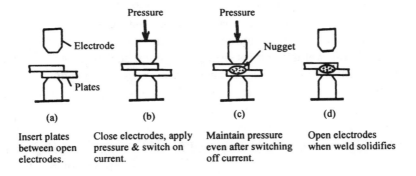

Fig. 10.14 Resistance spot welding cycle.

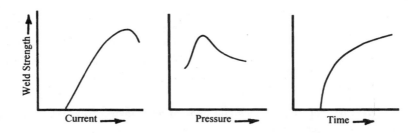

Fig. 10.15 Effects of current, pressure and time on weld strength in resistance spot welding.

Good quality welds are obtained through proper application of current, pressure and timing. The effects of these variables on weld strength are shown in Fig. 10.15. Variation of welding current indicates that beyond a certain value the weld strength decreases because the plates become soft and electrode indentation causes the metal at the interface to squeeze out of the weld. Initially the weld strength increases with increase in current until welding temperature is reached. Similarly, at low pressures, the resistance and heat are high and the melted metal tends to squeeze out of the weld. At higher pressure, the resistance decreases and heat is less and smaller weld formed provides lower weld strength. Thus, for a given set of conditions, optimum electrode current and electrode pressure are indicated.

Time duration of current flow must be longer than the minimum required for coalescence. The strength of the weld increases when the time duration is increased beyond the minimum value, but at a decreasing rate. The time duration of current flow should not be increased beyond a certain value, because the heat then has a chance to spread and harm the workpiece and electrodes.

The optimum values of current and pressure, and the duration time for current are interrelated and depend to a large extent on the material being welded and its size. For heavier sections, both current and its duration are increased because more heat is needed. Under ideal conditions, the temperature should be low at the electrodes and must rise sharply to a value little above the welding temperature at the interface of the workpiece.

A laser beam, similar to one used for machining (see Chapter 8), can also be used for welding. A laser beam is capable of producing a power density as high as 10^7 W/cm^2. In *laser beam welding* this high-intensity beam acts as the heat source and when focussed it penetrates into the metal and provides a thin column of vapourised metal with a liquid pool surrounding it. As the laser beam traverses, the liquid metal pool fills up the vapourised metal channel to produce a weld with a depth-to-width ratio greater than 4:1. This makes the process most suitable for welding narrow and deep joints. Laser welds as small as 0.025 mm are easily produced with minimum distortion. This makes the process extremely useful for electronic industry.

Thermit welding utilizes the heat of exothermal reaction for welding. Welding is achieved by filling the joint with molten metal that is obtained by reducing its oxide by aluminium. The commonly used material for welding steel and cast iron is a mixture of iron oxide and aluminium. The reaction is initiated by mixing finely divided iron oxide and aluminium, typically in the ratio of 3 to 1 by weight, and

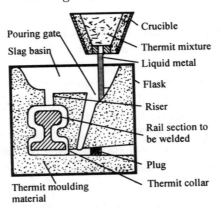

Fig. 10.16 Thermit welding.

igniting it by a magnesium fuse which has an ignition temperature of around 1200°C. The resulting reaction,

$$3Fe_3O_4 + 8Al \rightarrow 9Fe + 4Al_2O_3 + Heat$$

raises the temperature to around 3000°C in less than a minute. This superheats the molten iron which flows into the joint and provides both heat and filler material for welding. Since thermit welding involves flow of molten metal into the joint, a wax pattern of the desired weld is made around the joint and a sand mould with runners and risers is rammed around the welding zone (Fig. 10.16). Before pouring the molten metal, a torch is inserted to melt the wax pattern and heat the pieces to be joined. The superheated metal fuses appreciably with the heated parent metal which on solidification and cooling gives a strong and homogeneous weld. The welded piece is taken out by breaking the sand mould.

Thermit welding is a very old process but it is still used for on-site welding of thick sections such as cables, rails and large castings.

10.4   Solid/Liquid-state Bonding

Low temperature joining methods are used when the metal to be joined cannot withstand high temperature, or intricate sections are to be joined, or dissimilar metals are to be joined, or weldability of metal is poor. These low temperature joining methods are essentially solid/liquid state bonding processes where the gap between the metal pieces to be joined is filled with molten filler metal after heating the base metal. Thus, bonding is not due to melting of parent metal as in electric arc or gas welding because the base metal is merely heated and not melted. Even the filler metal is a low melting point material whose melting point is much lower than that of the metal pieces to be joined.

In *solid/liquid-state bonding processes* the filler metal is drawn into the gap between the metal pieces to be joined by capillary action (entering of fluid into tightly fitted surfaces) and the bond formation is initiated when the molten filler metal comes under intimate contact with the solid surface as in solid-state welding processes. The nature of bond formed, however, is much more complex in solid/liquid-state bonding processes because there is invariably some degree of inter-solubility between the filler and the base metal. The interdiffusion at the base metal surface and the resulting alloy has a strength which is very close to that of the base metal. Therefore, for good joint strength the liquid filler metal must flow into the gap between the metal pieces to be joined and cover the entire surface area without gaps or blow holes. The following usually ensure good bonding:

- Clean base metal surfaces to be joined.

- Maintain optimum gap between pieces to be joined.

- Heat the joining area to a temperature above the melting temperature of the filler material.

- Use fluxes for welding of base metal surfaces.

Figure 10.17 shows that for maximum joint strength there exists a maximum gap thickness. When the gap thickness is large, the joint strength approaches that of the filler material and below the optimum gap, the entire joint is not filled due to resistance to capillary flow and joint strength decreases. The gap maintained is generally in the range of 0.03 to 0.75 mm depending upon the type of filler metal used.

Brazing and soldering are two common solid/liquid-state bonding processes. These are different from welding as bonding here requires capillary action and that some degree of alloying action between the filler and base metal always occurs. Also the composition of filler material is significantly different and its strength and melting point are substantially lower than that of the base metal.

In *brazing* the joint is made by heating the base metal red hot and filling the gap with molten filler metal whose melting temperature is above 450°C but below the melting temperature of base metal. The filler metals, generally used for brazing are copper alloys. Copper-zinc and copper-silver alloys are the most commonly used filler ma-

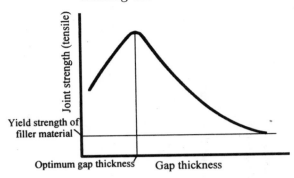

Fig. 10.17 Variation of joint strength with gap thickness in solid/liquid bonding processes.

terials since they form alloys with iron that has a strength very close to iron itself. Brazing is usually carried out with a gas flame.

Soldering is very similar to brazing except that the filler material is usually a lead-tin based alloy which has much lower strength and melting temperature (around 250°C). Also, less alloying action between the base and filler metals gives lower joint strength. Soldering is usually carried out with electric resistance heating since much lower temperatures are involved.

10.5 Comparison of Welding and Allied Processes

In Table 10.1, the advantages and limitations of various welding processes are compared.

Numerical Examples

Q.1 What would be the change in welding current (I) when arc length (l) changes from 4 mm to 5 mm? Given

Arc voltage (V) and arc length (l) characterisitcs: $V = 20 + 4l$

Volt-ampere characteristics: $I^2 = -400(V - 100)$

Solution:

When $l = 4$ mm,

$$V = 20 + 4 \times 4 = 36 \text{ volts}$$

Therefore,

$$I^2 = -400(36 - 100)$$

Table 10.1 Comparison of welding and allied processes.

Processes	Advantages	Limitations
Forge welding	• Semi-skilled operation • Inexpensive equipment	• Labour intensive process (Low production rate) • Poor joint strength • Weld quality dependent on operator's skill • Can be used only where hammering is possible.
Friction welding	• Good weld strength • Narrow heat affected zone • High production rate • Can weld dissimilar metals	• High equipment cost • Can be used only when some rotational symmetry exists.
Explosive welding	• Inexpensive equipment • Can weld dissimilar metals • Can weld large size plates • Good for plate cladding • High joint strength	• High set-up time • Trained operators are required • Inherently dangerous process
Gas welding	• Portable low cost equipment • Good weld quality • Suitable for repair work and low quantity production	• Skilled operator required • Manual operation hence low production rate • Difficult to prevent contamination • Large heat affected zone

Electric arc welding

- Very versatile process
- Portable and relatively inexpensive equipment
- Weld quality depends upon operator's skill in manual operations
- Large heat affected zone
- Not suitable for thin sections

Resistance spot welding

- Very economical process
- High production rate
- High skill not required
- Most suitable for welding sheet metals
- Dissimilar metals can be welded
- Small heat affected area
- High Equipment cost
- Suitable for thin sheets only

Laser beam welding

- Good weld quality
- High depth-to-width ratio of weld
- Dissimilar metals can be welding
- Suitable for thin sections
- Welding can be done in inaccessible locations
- Minimum distortion
- High production rate
- High equipment cost
- Highly skilled operation
- Eye protection required
- Suitable for welding narrow and deep joints

Thermit welding

- Low set-up cost
- Can be used anywhere
- Not a highly skilled operation
- Most suitable for welding of thick sections

- High set-up and cycle time
- Only thick sections can be welded

Brazing

- Good joint strength
- Not much skill is required
- Dissimilar metals can be joined
- Suitable for joining intricate and light weight shapes
- Very little distortion
- Low equipment cost

- Joint strength not as high as in gas or arc welding
- Not suitable for thick sections
- Joints not suitable for high temperature applications
- Joint colour may not match with base metal

Soldering

- No distortions
- Suitable for making leak proof joints
- Low equipment cost

- Low joint strength
- Joints suitable for low temperature applications

and

$$I = 160 \text{ A}$$

When

$$l = 5 \text{ mm}$$

$$V = 20 + 4 \times 5 = 40 \text{ volts}$$

and

$$I^2 = -400(40 - 100)$$

Therefore,

$$I \approx 155 \text{ A}$$

and change in welding current = 160 - 155 = 5 A

Q.2 For resistance spot welding of two aluminium plates, each 2mm thick, a current of 5000 A was passed for 0.15 s. The total resistance was estimated to be $75\mu\Omega$ and the nugget diameter and thickness was measured to be 5 mm and 2.5 mm, respectively. What would be the proportion of heat energy utilized for welding if the melting energy per unit volume for aluminium is taken as 2.9 J/mm^3.

Solution:

Heat generated

$$\begin{aligned} H &= I^2Rt \\ &= (5000)^2 \times 75 \times 10^{-6} \times 0.15 \\ &= 281.25 \text{ W-sec or J} \end{aligned}$$

$$\text{Volume of weld nugget} = \frac{\pi D^2 H}{4} = \frac{\pi \times 5^2 \times 2.5}{4} = 49.1 \text{ mm}^3$$

Heat required for melting = $2.9 \times 49.1 = 142.4$ J

Proportion of heat utilized for welding

$$= \frac{142.4}{281.25} = 0.506 \text{ or } 50.6\%$$

Review Questions

10.1 Under what conditions ideal metallurgical bonds are formed?

10.2 Why engineering materials cannot meet the requirements for formation of ideal metallurgical bond?

10.3 What is the fundamental feature that distinguishes solid-state welding from liquid-state welding?

10.4 What is the source of heat in friction welding?

10.5 How welding is achieved in explosive welding?

10.6 What are two inherent problems associated with liquid-state welding?

10.7 Describe the two stages of combustion in gas welding? What is the location of maximum temperature in oxy-acetylene flame?

10.8 What functions are served by the outer zone of the oxy-acetylene flame?

10.9 What types of flames can be produced by varying the ratio of oxygen and acetylene?

10.10 Explain the basic principle of electric arc welding. What is the main role of electrode coating in shielded metal-arc welding?

10.11 What current characterisitcs are necessary for manual-arc welding?

10.12 Describe the sequence of steps in resistance spot welding.

10.13 Discuss the effects of cuurent, pressure and timing is resistance welding. What are the consequences of too little or too great pressure during resistance welding?

10.14 What is the source of heat in thermit welding?

10.15 Explain the principle of brazing. Discuss the effects of gap thickness in brazing.

Chapter 11

Recent Developments in Manufacturing

11.1 Introduction

From the simple beginning when an artisan provided all the necessary physical and mental inputs to design, produce and deliver a product, manufacturing has grown to become a 'system' where a number of inter-related activities such as design, planning, production and marketing. interact in a dynamic manner. This evolution has come through developments at various stages. Broadly, the present day concept of 'manufacturing system' has evolved through five distinct stages. These are:

- Manual Manufacturing
- Mechanization
- Hard Automation
- Soft Automation
- Integrated Manufacturing

11.2 Manual Manufacturing & Mechanization

In manual manufacturing the tool of integration was the human mind. The artisan himself integrated the various elements of manufacturing. A village blacksmith, for example, who would have all the information to design, fabricate and deliver say an agricultural tool. Here the quality of the product almost entirely depended on the skill of the artisan. Also, the rate of production was very low and repeatability was not high, that is, the quality of product varied from piece to piece.

The next stage of development brought in mechanization through application of small machines and mechanisms. Mechanization not only reduced the dependence on human skills but it also resulted in improved product quality and higher production rates. The scale of production was, however, limited by the available power. The development of the steam engine made power available in large quantities and facilitated growth of production. This marked the beginning of first industrial revolution with mechanical power supplementing the physical power of workers.

11.3   Hard Automation

Towards the middle of 19th century, several simple and repetitive tasks performed by operators were taken over by machines. Development in this area was further aided by the introduction of electric power at the beginning of 20th century. Machines could now be individually driven with electric motors controlled by electric circuits. This encouraged development of machines with fair degree of sophistication. The introduction of mass production concept to increase productivity and lower the cost of production, brought automation in manufacturing industries. This automation was primarily 'automatic mechanization' and, in fact, the word was derived from the combination of these two words. A large variety of special purpose machines were now available for producing huge quantities of a particular item. During those days (till mid 20th century), the product variety was small and demand for individual items was large. This encouraged hard automation as it is called now, where automation was achieved through specially designed hardware. For example, the information about the shape and size of workpiece can be stored in the geometries of cam profiles and through movement of these cams controlled movements can be given to the tool to obtain the desired workpiece. In these kinds of arrangements, changing from one job to another would involve substantial changes in hardware—tooling, fixtures, cams, etc. This change over is not only expensive but also time consuming. Often the entire set-up has to be discarded because its adaptation for the new product is not possible.

11.4   Soft Automation

Figure 11.1 shows how the demand for a product varies with time. Earlier the demand for a particular product used to be fairly steady for sufficiently long time (many years) and use of hard automation (special purpose machines) was justified for manufacturing such products. With growing competition and availability of a variety of similar product, the product life started decreasing (Fig. 11.1).

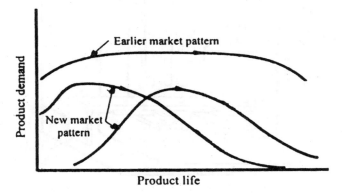

Fig. 11.1 Market pattern.

To survive in a competitive market, the manufacturing units had to produce good quality and reliable product at a low cost. In order to cope up with a dynamic market involving short lived products, the manufacturing units had to keep on changing the production rate and also improve the product. The manufacturers now started shifting from hard automation to soft automation or flexible automation.

11.4.1 NC/CNC/DNC

The first major step in this direction was the development of numerical control (NC) for machine tools. Once the concept of computer emerged in the late 1940s, it became possible to store and retrieve information with the help of numbers. On NC machines the necessary information for producing a particular component is provided with the help of numbers, letters and symbols in a form known as an NC programme. Switching over from one job to another now involved preparation of the NC programme with practically no modification of the hardware. The machine now became 'flexible' since change over from one job to another could be achieved in a short time with very little expenses. NC not only overcame the limitations of human operators, but it made it possible to automatically generate complex machine motions and produce a variety of parts with accuracy far beyond human capability. Use of such flexible machines later came to be known as soft automation or flexible automation.

A *NC machine tool system* (Fig. 11.2) has two basic components:

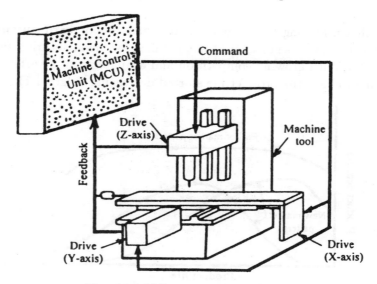

Fig. 11.2 NC machine tool system.

(a) the machine control unit (MCU) and
(b) the machine tool itself.

MCU has two basic units:

(a) the data processing unit and
(b) the controller unit.

The data processing unit processes the NC programme from the tape and passes the information regarding position of each axis, direction of motion, feed rate, etc. to the controller unit which then activates the movements and finally signals completion of operation. In other words, the data processing unit interprets and feeds the geometric and kinematic data to the controller unit which then governs the physical system on the basis of input data to complete the job.

The NC programmes were earlier written on punched paper which was later replaced by magnetic plastic tape. The main problem associated with these tapes was that even minor changes in the programme was difficult to incorporate. This led to the development of *direct numerical control* which simply eliminated tape as the medium for programming instructions. In direct numerical control machines tools (Fig. 11.3), the programme is stored in the host computer and fed directly to the machine tools through the data transmission linkages. DNC, first introduced in late 1960s, had several machine tools directly controlled by a host computer (central main frame computer). This was necessary because computers during those days were large and expensive. This meant that when the host computer

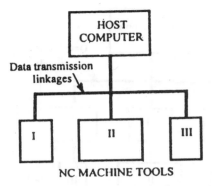

Fig. 11.3 Direct numerical control.

Fig. 11.4 A CNC turning centre. (Courtesy HMT Ltd., Banglore)

was down, all machine tools became idle.

With the development of smaller, less expensive computers, it became practical to provide a small computer for each machine tool. This concept came to be known as *computer numerical control* (CNC). With CNC each machine tool has a micro-computer which allowed for input and storage of programmes at each individual machine tool. This system allowed programmes to be developed off-line and down-loaded to individual machine tools. Increased flexibility and greater accuracy in CNC systems makes them popular.

The only problem associated with the CNC system (Fig. 11.4) was data management. Often the same programme had to be loaded on a number of machines with no communication between associated microprocessors. This problem of data management led to the development of distributed numerical control, also called DNC. In

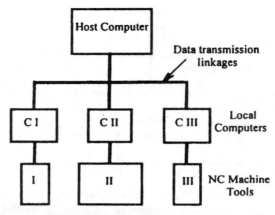

Fig. 11.5 Distributed numerical control.

distributed numerical control (Fig. 11.5) both host as well as local computers are available to individual machine tools. It stores the programmes in the host computer for better management and allows them to be downloaded to local computers. It also allows interaction at machine level through local computers. This way the distributed numerical control combines the best aspects of direct numerical control and computer numerical control.

One of the main reasons for using NC (including CNC and DNC) is to reduce the total machining time through savings in non-productive time such as handling time, set-up time and tool changing time, but can do very little to reduce the in-process time. *Adaptive control* (AC) was developed in late 1960's to reduce the in-process time. While NC guides the tool position and its path during machining, adaptive control determines the proper speed and feed during machining as a function of depth of cut, part geometry, work material, etc. AC senses temperature, pressure, force, torque, vibration, deflection, etc. generated in the cutting zone and feeds the information to the machine control unit where speed, feed, etc. are corrected to achieve the optimum machining conditions (Fig. 11.6).

11.4.2 Industrial Robots

Studies have shown that in shop fabrication operations, for almost 95% of the total production time the parts are either moved from one place to another or just waiting for the next operation (Fig. 11.7). Of the remaining 5% of the time they spend on the machine, only about 25% of the time is spent on actual cutting operation while the remaining 75% is lost on loading/unloading, tool positioning, ganging, etc. Therefore for increased productivity the method of

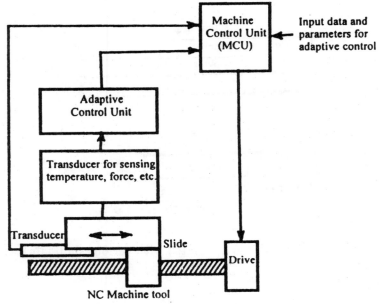

Fig. 11.6 Adaptive control system.

material movement/material handling had to be improved and there were enough incentives to mechanize and automate these.

Along with developments in computers, micro-electronics and sensor technology, another technology that appeared was 'industrial robotics'. These *industrial robots* are essentially automatic electro-mechanical/electro-hydraulic devices which can be programmed again and again to carry out specific manipulative functions.

Industrial robots may vary widely but they are basically made up of the following components: a manipulator, a control unit and a power supply, (Fig. 11.8). The manipulator is an assembly of axes capable of providing motion in various directions as shown. The various axes of motion are powered by electric or hydraulic motors and have feed-back devices which sense and measure the position. The information is sent to the control unit which sequences and co-ordinates the motion of various axes of the robot and provides interlocking communication with external devices and machines. The power supply unit provides the energy (electric, hydraulic or pneumatic) to move and regulate the drive mechanisms of the robot.

With the development of industrial robots, it became possible to realize true automation in manufacturing. Human work force for tending machines and inspection stations could now be replaced by industrial robots.

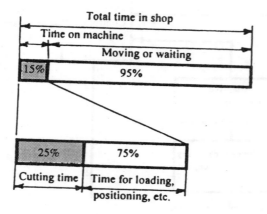

Fig. 11.7 Percentage of time associated with various shop fabrication activities.

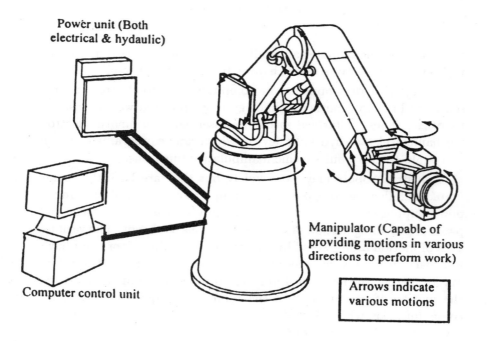

Fig. 11.8 Industrial robot system. (After Lindberg 1990)

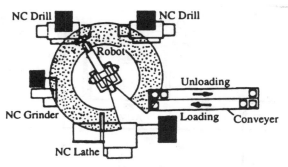

Fig. 11.9 Flexible manufacturing cell. (After Lindberg 1990)

Fig. 11.10 A flexible manufacturing cell for turning. (Courtesy HMT Ltd., Bangalore)

11.4.3   FMC/FMS

One of the most important developments in distributed numerical control (DNC) was the introduction of *flexible manufacturing cell* (FMC) and *flexible manufacturing system* (FMS). The flexible manufacturing cell generally has more than one CNC machine which are served by flexible material-handling devices such as an industrial robot. For machining operations, the FMC may consist of machines like CNC lathes, milling machines, drilling machines, grinders, etc. and may even have automatic inspection stations. The job of the operator now reduces to loading the racks for the robot to pick up the parts, clamping the parts on to the machines, removing the finished parts, changing the tools and cutters, etc. (Fig. 11.9). FMC is generally designed for a fixed process, and the parts flow sequentially between operations. A FMC consisting of a gantry robot system integrated with a CNC turning centre is shown in Fig. 11.10.

Use of FMC not only provides greater flexibility, but also reduces

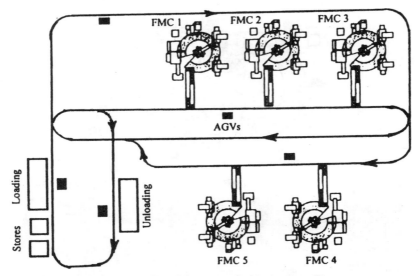

Fig. 11.11 Flexible manufacturing system.

cycle time of the parts produced and the in-process inventory of parts. Further, because of elimination of human error the product quality improves.

When all the flexible manufacturing cells of a plant are inter-linked, a flexible manufacturing system (FMS) is created. In fact, FMCs are small FMSs. Therefore for creating a FMS, several FMCs are first installed and then interlinked (Fig. 11.11).

The major components of a FMS are:

- Machine tools
- Control system
- Handling system
- Operators

A flexible manufacturing system uses various kinds of CNC ma-chines, depending on the requirements. The control system guides the operations on various machines to produce the required parts. It also regulates the flow of workpieces and monitors their location within the system through the material handling systems. In princi-ple, it is possible to build a fully automated factory where all tasks (processing, material handling, tool changing, inspection, etc.) are accomplished without any assistance from the operators. This, how-ever, has not yet been achieved and the human operators still play critical roles.

Flexibility is an important characteristic of a modern manufactur-ing system. Flexibility means that the system is versatile and adapt-

Fig. 11.12 A flexible manufacturing system using automated guided vehicles.

able. Flexible manufacturing systems are versatile because they can produce a variety of parts and are adaptable since the system can be quickly modified to produce a completely different set of parts. FMS consists of several CNC machines which are served by computer controlled material handling devices and has tool changing capability. A FMS can be easily reconfigured to produce a wide variety of parts because of computer control and tool changing capability. Because of this capability, such manufacturing systems have come to be known as flexible manufacturing systems. Figure 11.12 shows a flexible manufacturing system (FMS) with automated guided vehicles (AGVs) as handling device.

Figure 11.13 shows the relationship between production flexibility and production capacity. It clearly shows that at high production volume, the ability to produce a wide variety of parts diminishes. When the production quantity is small (*job shop production*) general-purpose machine tools are used. On these machines different parts can be produced with minimum changes in production operations and tooling. These machines, however, require skilled operators and give low production rate, hence the cost per piece is high (Fig. 11.14). When the production quantity required is high (*mass production*), special-purpose machines are used. With high level of automation on these machines the equipment cost is high but the labour cost is considerably reduced. This reduces the cost per piece when the quantity produced is large. These machines, however, lack flexibility

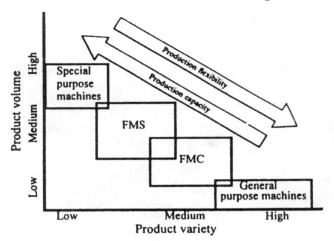

Fig. 11.13 Relationship between production flexibility and production capacity.

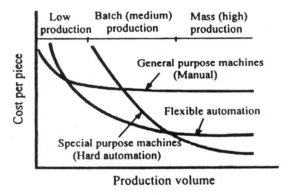

Fig. 11.14 Relationship between production volume and cost per price

because they are designed for a specific product. In between the general-purpose and special-purpose machines are FMC and FMS for medium and batch production and medium part variety.

As shown earlier, the life time of a product in the present day competitive environment is very short. In order to cope with the market requirement involving short-lived products, a company has to produce new products more often. For surviving in such a competitive market, cost effective production in small or medium batch sizes is essential. Flexible automation in the form of FMC and FMS not only makes small and medium batch production cost effective but the computer control adopted in these systems makes it possible to integrate the various activities of a manufacturing company.

11.4.4 Computer-aided design/ Computer-aided manufacturing (CAD/CAM)

The use of computers for design activities started in early 1960s but its use was primarily confined to drafting. Subsequently, with enhancement in computer capabilities, the use of computers was extended to analysis and design activities and this came to be known as *computer-aided-design* (CAD). It was now possible to define the part shape, analyse the stresses and strains, check the mechanical and functional aspects and produce the engineering drawings.

The use of computers in manufacturing started before CAD got developed as a tool but its application was primarily for NC part programming. This got known as *computer-aided-manufacturing* (CAM) and was totally delinked from CAD, that is, both CAD and CAM were entirely separate activities.

The need for integration between CAD and CAM soon became evident. CAD now involves modelling, analysis, review and documentation, the four broad aspects of design. A geometric model of the required product is developed that describes the product mathematically or analytically. The digital data obtained from the model is converted into a graphic image of the part which could be edited or modified by the designer. After the geometric features are established, the design is subjected to engineering analysis that may include analyzing stresses, strains, vibrations, temperature distribution, etc. The next step is design review which includes checking the accuracy of all aspects of design. At this stage the part is precisely dimensioned and tolerances are indicated as required for manufacturing. Interference checking ensures trouble-free assembly of parts and that the moving members are operating as intended. The final stage is documentation where the drawings needed to document the design is produced using the database created during the design process. Documentation software permits development of sectional views, scaling of drawings, transformations, etc.to present various views.

Computer-aided manufacturing (CAM) can be defined as the use of computer system to plan, manage and control all manufacturing operations including part programming, process planning, scheduling, material requirements planning, tool design and quality assurance and control. Here part programming refers to the control programmes prepared for CNC machines, process planning refers to preparation of operation sequence required to process a particular product, scheduling refers to determination of production schedule required to meet the production requirements, material requirements

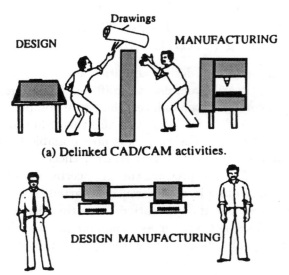

(a) Delinked CAD/CAM activities.

DESIGN MANUFACTURING

Fig. 11.15 CAD/CAM integration. (After Goetsch, 1988)

planning determines when to procure raw materials and components
and in what quantity, tool design refers to design of tools, dies, fixtures, etc. to be used for production, and quality assurance and
control ensure that the product conforms to the standards relating
to materials, dimensions, tolerances, appearance, performance, reliability, etc. that have been specified by the designer.

Initially CAD and CAM evolved as separate activities, totally
delinked from each other (Fig. 11.15). The design department completed the drawings and other related documents and passed them
to the manufacturing department to produce the product. This
lack of communication between design and manufacturing depart-
ments often resulted in loss of production. Integration of CAD
and CAM, generally referred to as computer-aided-design/computer-
aided-manufacturing (CAD/CAM), was thought of essentially to remove the barrier that had traditionally existed between design and
manufacturing activities. With CAD/CAM, the information flowing
in both directions ensures that the parts and assemblies are designed
with capabilities and limitations of manufacturing processes and materials in mind. The real interface between design and manufacturing in CAD/CAM system is the database which both share right
from the start of design activity. The manufacturing department
can, therefore, start part programming, process planning, material
requirements planning, tool design, etc. while the design department is creating the database and documenting the designs (Fig.
11.16). In CAD/CAM systems, the common database contains an-

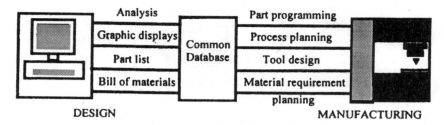

Fig. 11.16 CAD/CAM system

alytical models, graphic displays, the parts list, bills of materials, dimensions and tolerances, and other relevent information needed to manufacture the product.

11.5 Rapid Prototyping

In order to reduce the development time, quick and inexpensive fabrication of prototype is essential. This has been made possible by generative manufacturing or rapid prototyping processes. In rapid prototyping (RP) a solid object with prescribed dimensions and finish can be directly produced from the geometric model data of the part generated in a CAD system. The first step in RP processing is, therefore, geometric or solid modelling of the part on a CAD system to provide complete and unambiguous mathematical representation of the part geometry. The CAD model is then sliced into closely space horizontal layers as shown in Fig. 11.17(a). These layers are subsequently used for fabricating the physical model.

Several rapid prototyping techniques have been developed during the last decade and these can be broadly classified as: (i) liquid-based, (ii) solid-based, and (iii) powder-based rapid prototyping processes. Popular RP processes under these categories are: (i) stereolithography and solid ground curing, (ii) laminated object manufacturing and fused deposition modelling, and (iii) selective laser sintering and three-dimensional printing. Currently the most widely used RP process is stereolithography. The process is shown schematically in Fig. 11.17(b). Stereolithography creates acrylic or epoxy parts by curing a liquid photopolymer by an ultraviolet laser beam. Parts are built on an elevated platform that incrementally lowers the part into the generating vat by the distance equal to the layer thickness. An NC drive system controls the movement of the platform. To build a layer the UV laser beam is guided onto the top surface of liquid with the help of servo-controlled galvanometer mirrors. The computer control of reflecting mirrors ensures that the beam traces the

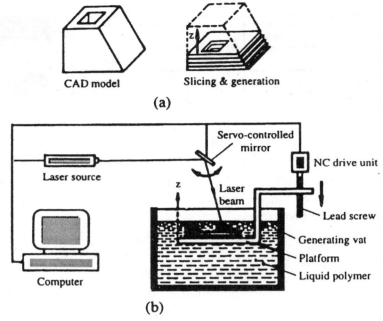

(a)

(b)

Fig. 11.17 Rapid prototyping: (a) basic principle and (b) schematic arrangement for stereolithography. (After Ghosh, 1997).

required path on the surface to generate the cross-section. After the first layer (typically a few tenths of a mm) is cured, the platform is lowered and the laser beam scans the next cross-section. The cycle is repeated till the top most layer is generated to complete the part. The generated part is now removed from the vat for ultrasonic cleaning for removing excess material, and alcohol bath to remove any unused polymer.

11.6 Integrated Manufacturing

Modern manufacturing encompasses all activities starting from need for a product to its design and development, procurement of raw materials, production, marketing and service support. These activities are depicted in Fig. 11.18.

The modern view of manufacturing that started with the integration of CAD/CAM is to link together all element of manufacturing depicted in this figure. This integration can provide complete and instanteneous sharing of information among all elements of the system. This new approach to manufacturing was conceived in early eighties (1980s) and was called *computer-integrated-manufacturing* (CIM). So computer-integrated manufacturing can be defined as the total inte-

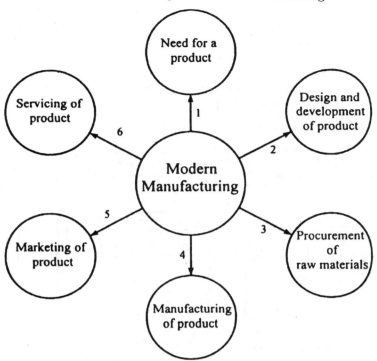

Fig. 11.18 CIM-integration of all elements of manufacturing.

gration of all aspects of design, planning, production, marketing and management through use of computer into a single, smoothly operating system as shown in Figs. 11.19 and Fig. 11.20. CIM is, therefore, not a new manufacturing technology, it is a new approach to manufacturing. It is not an assemblage of equipment and computers, it is a methodology.

CIM got developed primarily in response to market demand for more product variety, better quality, and lower prices. Earlier attempts towards integration primarily attempted to lower the direct labour cost through use of new equipment and processes. In early 1990s, the emphasis shifted to other elements of the system, since the direct labour cost in most cases was a small fraction (10-15%) of the total manufacturing cost.

CIM attempts to create an operational environment that existed when manufacturing was a craft and the craftsman represented total integration. He was the company. He conceptualized the product, designed the project, financed it, made the product and market it. He was one man operation and his brain did what CIM tries to get through use of computers. With growth of manufacturing business through mechanization and later with automation, compartmental-

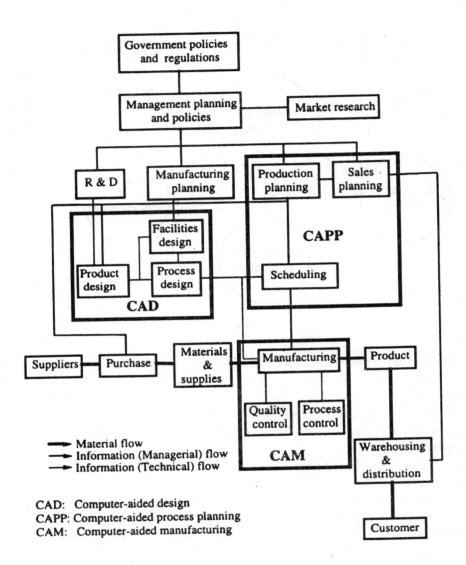

Fig. 11.19 A general structure of CIM.

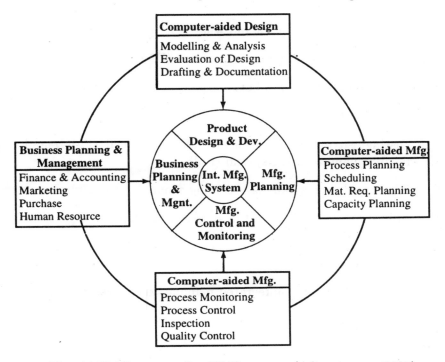

Fig. 11.20 Elements of a CIMS system (After grover, 1987).

ization started with design, production, marketing and management becoming specialized functions. Now CIM, through increased computarization, is trying to bring total integration back into manufacturing operations.

CIM is expensive and can be prohibitively expensive for small and medium-size companies, but with the developments is microelectronics the cost is declining rapidly. CIM plants with high level of integration in which computers and flexible automation produce the goods with very little human intervention do exist today. But plants with total integration and fully automated operations, a factory of future, is still a few decades away.

Review Questions

11.1 Distinguish between hard and soft automation?

11.2 How does mechanization differs from automation?

11.3 List some advantages of NC and CNC systems over manual machine tools.

11.4 What is adaptive control and what is its purpose?

11.5 What is distributed numerical control (DNC)?

11.6 What is an industrial robot?

11.7 What is a CAD/CAM system?

11.8 Distinguish between flexible manufacturing cell (FMC) and flexible manufacturing system (FMS)?

11.9 Why rapid prototyping is becoming a popular technique?

11.10 Indicate the steps involved in stereolithography.

11.11 Explain the relationship between production flexibility and production capacity?

11.12 What is a computer-integrated manufacturing system?

Bibliography

1. Agarwal, B. K., *Introduction to Engineering Materials*, Tata McGraw-Hill, New Delhi, 1988.

2. Alexander, J.M. Brewer, R.C. and Rowe, G.W., *Manufacturing Technology*, Ellis Horwood, Chichester (England), 1987.

3. Amstead B.H., Ostwald, P.F. and Begeman, M.L., *Manufacturing Processes*, John Wiley, Singapore, 1987.

4. Armarego, E.J.A. and Brown, R.H., *The Machining of Metals*, Prentice-Hall, Englewood Cliff (USA), 1969.

5. Ashby, M.F. and Jones, D. R. H., *Engineering Materials: An Introduction to their Properties and Applications*, Vol.1, Pergamon, New York, 1980.

6. ASME Handbook: *Metals Engineering Processes*, Vol. 4, McGraw Hill, New York, 1965.

7. Bhattacharyya, A., *Metal cutting - Theory and Practice*, New Central Book Agency, Kolkata, 1984.

8. Boothroyd, G., *Fundamentals of Metal Machining and Machine Tools*, McGraw-Hill, Tokyo, 1975.

9. Bralla, J.G., *Handbook of Product Design for Manufacturing*, McGraw Hill, New York, 1986.

10. Brent S.A., *Plastics Materials and Processing*, Prentice Hall, New Jesley, 2000.

11. Cook, N.H., *Manufacturing Analysis*, Addition-Wesley, Reading (Mass.), 1966.

12. Davies, A.C., *The Science and Practice of Welding*, Cambridge University Press, New York, 1993.

13. DeGarmo, E.P., Black, J.T. and Kohser, R.A., *Materials and Processes in Manufacturing*, Prentice-Hall, Englewood Cliff (USA), 1991.

14. Dieter, G., *Engineering Design: A Materials and Processing Approach*, McGraw Hill, New York, 1983.

15. Dieter, G.E., *Mechanical Metallurgy*, McGraw-Hill, New York, 1986.

16. Doyle, L.E., Keyser, C.E., Leach, J.L., Schrader, G.F. and Singer, M.S., *Manufacturing Processes and Materials for Engineers*, Prentice-Hall, Englewood Cliff (USA), 1985.

17. Flinn, R.A., *Fundamentals of Metal Casting*, Addison -Wesley, Reading (USA), 1963.

18. Fried, J.R., *Polymer Science and Technology*, Prentice-Hall (India), New Delhi, 1995.

19. Garrison, E., *A History of Engineering and Technology*, CRC Press, Boca Raton (USA), 1991.

20. German, R.M., *Powder Metallurgy Science, Metal Powder Industries Federation*, Princeton (USA), 1984.

21. Ghosh, A. and Mallik, A.K., *Manufacturing Science*, Affiliated East-West, New Delhi, 1985.

22. Ghosh, A., *Rapid Prototyping*, Affiliated East-West, New Delhi, 1997.

23. Girling, H., *All About Machine Tools*, Wiley Eastern, New Delhi, 1961.

24. Goetsch, D.L., *Fundamentals of CIM Technology*, Delmar (USA), 1988.

25. Grover, M.P., *Automation, Production Systems and Computer Integrated Manufacturing*, Prentice-Hall, Englewood Cliff (USA), 1987.

26. Grover, M.P., *Fundamentals of Modern Manufacturing (Materials, Processes and Systems)*, Prentice-Hall, Englewood Cliff (USA), 1996.

27. Heine, R.W., Loper, C.R. and Rosenthal, C., *Principles of Metal Casting*, Tata McGraw Hill, New Delhi, 1976.

28. Jain, P.L., *Principles of Foundry Technology*, Tata McGraw Hill, New Delhi, 1979.

29. John, V.B., *Introduction to Engineering Materials*, Macmillan, New York, 1983.

30. Johnson, W. and Mellor, P.B., *Engineering Plasticity*, Van Nostrand, London, 1973.

31. Juneja, B.L. and Sekhon, G.S., *Fundamentals of Metal Cutting and Machine Tools*, Wiley Eastern, New Delhi, 1987.

32. Kalpakjian, S., *Manufacturing Engineering and Technology*, Addison -Wesley, Reading (USA), 1993.

33. Kalpakjian, S.,*Manufacturing Processes for Engineering Materials*, Addison-Wesley, Reading (USA), 1991.

34. Koenigsberger, F.,*Design Principles of Metal Cutting Machine Tools*, Pergamon Press, Oxford, 1964.

35. Lal, G.K.,*Introduction to Machining Science*, New Age International, New Delhi, 1996.

36. Lancaster, J. F.,*Metallurgy of Welding*, Chapman and Hall, London, 1993.

37. Lenel, F.V.,*Powder Metallurgy: Principles and Applications*, Metal Powder Industries Federation, Princeton (USA), 1980.

38. Lewis, K.B,*The Grinding Wheel*, GWI, Cleveland (USA), 1959.

39. Lindbeck, J.R., Williams, M. and Wygrant, R.,*Manufacturing Technology*, Prentice-Hall, Englewood Cliff (USA), 1990.

40. Lindberg, R.A., *Processes and Materials for Manufacturing*, Prentice-Hall, Englewood Cliff (USA), 1990.

41. Malkin, S., *Grinding Technology — Theory and Applications of Machining with Abrasives*, Ellis Horwood, Chichester (England), 1989.

42. Mehta, N.K., *Machine Tool Design*, Tata McGraw-Hill, New Delhi, 1984.

43. *Metals Handbook: Welding, Brazing and Soldering*, Vol. 6, ASM, USA, 1983.

44. *Metals Handbook: Powder Metallurgy*, Vol. 7, ASM, USA, 1984.

45. Miller, E (Ed.), *Plastics Products Design Handbook: Materials and Components*, Part A, Marcel Dekker, New York, 1981.

46. Miller, E.(Ed.), *Plastic Products Design Handbook: Processes and Design for Processes*, Part B, Marcel Dekker, New York, 1983.

47. Mishra, P.K.,*Non-conventional Machining*, Narosa, New Delhi, 1997.

48. Mitchell, F.H.,*CIM Systems: An Introduction to Computer-integrated Manufacturing*, Prentice-Hall, Englewood Cliff (USA), 1991.

49. Mukherjee, P.C.,*Fundamental of Metal Casting Technology*, Oxford and IBH, New Delhi, 1988.

50. Mullick, B.K. and Bhattacharya, A., *Technology of Machining Systems*, New Central Book Agency, Kolkata, 1990.

51. Niebel, B.W., Draper, A.B. and Wysk, R.A., *Modern Manufacturing Process Engineering*, McGraw-Hill, New York, 1989.

52. Ostwald, P.F. and Munoz, J., *Manufacturing Processes and Systems*, John Wiley, Singapore, 1998.

53. Pandey, P.C and Singh, C.K., *Production Engineering Sciences*, Standard Publishers, New Delhi, 1992.

54. Pandey, P.C. and Shan, H.S., *Modern Machining Processes*, Tata McGraw-Hill, New Delhi, 1980.

55. Parmar, R.S., *Welding Processes and Technology*, Khanna Publications, Delhi, 1992.

56. Pollack, H.W., *Manufacturing and Machine Tool Operations*, Prentice-Hall (India), New Delhi, 1968.

57. Rajan, T.V., Sharma, C.P. and Sharma, A., *Heat Treatment: Principle and Techniques*, Prentice-Hall (India), New Delhi, 1992.

58. Rao P.N., *Manufacturing Technology*, Tata McGraw-Hill, New Delhi, 1998.

59. Rees, H., *Mold Engineering*, Hanser, Munich, 2000.

60. Rolt, L.T.C.,*A Short History of Machine Tools*, MIT Press, Cambridge, 1965.

61. Rowe, G.W., *Principles of Industrial Metal Working Processes*, Arnold, London, 1979.

62. Schey, J.A., *Introduction to Manufacturing Processes*, McGraw-Hill, New York, 1987.

63. Sen, G.C. and Bhattacharyya, A., *Principles of Machine Tools*, New Central Book Agency, Kolkata, 1967.

64. Sharma R.C.,*Principles of Heat Treatment of Steels*, New Age International, New Delhi, 1998.

65. Shaw, M.C.,*Metal Cutting Principles*, Clarendon Press, Oxford, 1984.

66. Shaw, M.C.,*Principles of Abrasive Processing*, Clarendon Press, Oxford, 1996.

67. Steels W., *A History of Machine Tools*, Clarendon Press, Oxford, 1969.

68. Taylor, H.F. Fleming, M.C. and Wolff, J., *Foundry Engineering*, John Wiley, New York, 1959.

69. Titov, N.D. and Stepanov, Y.A.,*Foundry Practice*, Mir Publishers, Moscow, 1981.

70. *Tool and Manufacturing Engineers Handbook: Machining*, Vol. 1, SME, Dearborn (USA), 1983.

71. *Tool and Manufacturing Engineers Handbook: Forming*, Vol. 2, SME, Dearborn (USA), 1984.

72. Upadhyaya, G.S.,*Powder Metallurgy Technology*, Cambridge University Press, New York, 1997.

73. Vajpayee, S. Kant,*Principles of Computer-integrated Manufacturing*, Prentice-Hall, Englewood Cliff (USA), 1995.

74. *Welding Handbook: Welding Technology*, Vol. 1, American Welding Society, Maimi (USA), 1991.

75. *Welding Handbook: Welding Processes*, Vol. 2, American Welding Society, Maimi (USA), 1991.

Index